THE SOCIAL FOUNDATIONS OF GLOBAL FINANCE

Finance Matters

Series Editor: Kathryn C. Lavelle

This series of books provides advanced introductions to the processes, relationships and institutions that make up the global financial system. Suitable for upper-level undergraduate and taught graduate courses in financial economics and the political economy of finance and banking, the series explores all aspects of the workings of the financial markets within the context of the broader global economy.

Published

Banking on the State: The Political Economy of Public Savings Banks
Mark K. Cassell

British Business Banking: The Failure of Finance Provision for SMEs
Michael Lloyd

Credit Rating Agencies
Giulia Mennillo

The European Central Bank
Michael Heine and Hansjörg Herr

Quantitative Easing: The Great Central Bank Experiment
Jonathan Ashworth

Regulating Banks: The Politics of Instability
Andrew Whitworth

The Social Foundations of Global Finance
Edited by Chris Clarke and Ben Clift

Sovereign Wealth Funds: Between the State and Markets
Adam D. Dixon, Patrick J. Schena and Javier Capapé

Terrorist Financing
William Vlcek

THE SOCIAL FOUNDATIONS OF GLOBAL FINANCE

The Political Economy of Timothy J. Sinclair

EDITED BY

CHRIS CLARKE AND BEN CLIFT

agenda
publishing

An electronic version of the book is freely available, thanks to the support of libraries working with Knowledge Unlatched (KU). KU is a collaborative initiative designed to make high quality books Open Access for the public good. The Open Access ISBN for this book is 978-1-78821-809-2. More information about the initiative and links to the Open Access version can be found at www.knowledgeunlatched.org.

First published in 2025 by Agenda Publishing

Agenda Publishing Limited
PO Box 185
Newcastle upon Tyne
NE20 2DH
www.agendapub.com

ISBN 978-1-78821-808-5

British Library Cataloguing-in-Publication Data
A catalogue record for this book is available from the British Library

Typeset by Newgen Publishing UK
Printed and bound in the UK by 4edge

EU GPSR authorised representative:
Logos Europe, 9 rue Nicolas Poussin, 17000 La Rochelle, France
contact@logoseurope.eu

CONTENTS

CONTRIBUTORS

Chris Clarke is Reader in Political Economy in the Department of Politics and International Studies at the University of Warwick. His research interests lie in the political economy of money and finance including global finance and the everyday, platform lending, fintech, and ethics and economic governance. Previously he was a Leverhulme Trust Early Career Fellow and an Economic and Social Research Council Visiting Fellow at Brown University.

Ben Clift is Professor of Political Economy at the University of Warwick where he has taught since 2003. Before Warwick he held posts at Brunel and Sheffield Universities. He received his PhD from Sheffield University (2000). His research and teaching interests lie at the interface of comparative and international political economy. He recently held a Leverhulme Major Research Fellowship exploring the politics of technocratic economic governance.

Norbert Gaillard is an economist and independent consultant. He completed his PhD at Sciences Po Paris and Princeton University in 2008. His main areas of expertise are sovereign risk and country risk. He has served as a consultant to various international institutions, financial firms and think tanks. He has published seven books and more than 30 research articles and book chapters since 2010.

Randall Germain is Professor of Political Science at Carleton University, Canada. His teaching and research examine the political economy of global finance, issues and themes associated with economic and financial governance, and theoretical debates within the field of international political economy (IPE). His current research explores how the idea of history has informed disciplinary debates in IPE.

Fumihito Gotoh is a Lecturer in the School of East Asian Studies at the University of Sheffield. His research interests lie in international political economy (IPE), globalization and resistance, and comparative capitalisms (particularly between

Anglo-American countries), and the politics of finance. He completed his PhD at the University of Warwick in 2018. He previously pursued a career in international finance.

Aida A. Hozic is an Associate Professor of International Relations and Associate Chair of the Department of Political Science at the University of Florida. Her research is situated at the intersection of political economy, cultural studies and international security. Her current research projects focus on crime and state in southeastern Europe, visual representations of race in international politics and the diffusion of global arts markets in the twenty-first century.

Kathryn C. Lavelle is Ellen and Dixon Long Professor of World Affairs at Case Western Reserve University. She is a past president of the International Political Economy Section of the International Studies Association. Her research explores global governance, multilateralism and US foreign policy. Her work on international organizations specifically concerns the role of the United Nations, International Monetary Fund and World Bank in coordinating financial relations across developed and developing countries.

Richard ("Rick") Michalek is the senior partner of RJM Consulting, which offers services to privately held hedge funds as well as government agencies involved with supervising and monitoring rating agencies. Rick has a JD/MBA from Columbia University and held positions as an attorney with the international law firm Skadden Arps, as a legal consultant in the New Zealand law firm Chapman Tripp, and as a senior credit officer at Moody's, the global rating agency.

Johannes Petry is a Senior Researcher at Goethe University Frankfurt and the Principal Investigator of the DFG-funded "StateCapFinance" research project that analyses national variety in the configurations of states, markets and finance within the global financial system. As a political economist researching the politics of global finance, his research agenda investigates post-crisis transformations of the global financial system and their impact on global norms, institutions and governance. He received his PhD from the University of Warwick.

Magnus Ryner is Professor of International Political Economy at King's College London. Before King's he held posts at Brunel and Birmingham Universities. His research embraces a holistic approach in the spirit of classical pre-disciplinary as well as post-disciplinary political economy, analysing the European Monetary Union, the eurozone crisis and neoliberalism. He studied political science and economics at Trent University, Peterborough, Canada, before completing his PhD (1996) at York University in Toronto.

Timothy J. Sinclair was Associate Professor of International Political Economy at the University of Warwick. He was a leading scholar of the global political economy of money and finance. His work challenged the idea that financial markets are the domain of technocrats and economists, highlighting the social foundations of finance. Following a career at the New Zealand Treasury, he studied for a PhD at York University, Toronto, with Robert W. Cox and Stephen Gill. He developed and sustained an "eclectic" research approach. Tim joined the Department of Politics and International Studies at the University of Warwick in 1995.

Mathew Watson is Professor of Political Economy in the Department of Politics and International Studies at the University of Warwick. His research interests are concentrated at the intersection of the broad areas of political economy and the history of economic thought. Before Warwick he was a lecturer at Birmingham University (1999–2007). Between October 2013 and February 2019 he was an Economic and Social Research Council Professorial Fellow engaged on the project, "Rethinking the Market".

Dan Wood is a PhD candidate at the University of Warwick and a senior postgraduate teaching assistant. His research interests focus on international political economy (IPE), specifically the politics of global finance. His doctoral research explores the political economy of passive investment, and the politics embedded in strategies and power of institutions such as asset managers and index providers involved in passive investment processes.

FOREWORD

Kathryn C. Lavelle

Timothy J. Sinclair was a giant in the field of the political economy of finance. This statement is far from an exaggeration. His work on credit rating agencies opened new paths for research into an array of topics related to the subject, and he connected it to its sociological foundations in new and innovative ways. As any biography of Tim would note, he began his career at the New Zealand Treasury and later studied for his doctorate at York University in Toronto, Canada where he worked with Robert W. Cox and Stephen Gill. Later teaching at the University of Warwick in the UK, he broadened their approaches to include that of his colleague Susan Strange. Thus, his approach to the field was heterodox, and grew even more so as his career progressed. In later years, he became fascinated with emerging work in economic sociology that goes beyond the supposed rationalism of human conduct in order to consider the impact of informal norms, networks and power on economic behaviour (see, e.g. Fligstein 2001).

The chapters in this volume speak not only to Tim's academic brilliance and contributions to international political economy (IPE), but to his role in so many lives as a colleague, collaborator, mentor and friend. The stated theoretical goal of the collection is to elucidate how Tim's work on the role of credit rating agencies in the world economy helped to advance a distinctive social foundations approach to study. The chapters assemble the work of a group of scholars who re-examine Tim's work in order to deepen that approach in many dimensions in order to provide an inclusive perspective on the way the global financial system works. The upshot is that this wide-ranging look at Tim's work also opens important new avenues for research such as the connection between credit rating agencies and nationalism, the global operation of the public-private hybrid realm of financial infrastructures, the distinction between synchronic and diachronic forms of understanding in relation to how others have understood social structures, the notion of legitimacy across audiences for bond indexing and reconsidering the place of Marxist thought in the contemporary political economy of finance. As Randall Germain's contribution sums it up: Sinclair's research offers the social sciences a dialogue among three core features of social life: institutions, intersubjectivity and disruptive change.

Yet Tim did not simply make contributions to theory. Given his early work experience in the "real" work of financial governance, he never lost sight of the ultimate connection between what he studied and the political and economic reality of ordinary peoples' lives. Tim's work actively demonstrated that the use of insights from a social foundations approach could inform policy deliberations and offer a degree of predictive capability outside the narrow confines of rationalist social science. In one early example, he co-authored a 2003 piece with Michael R. King who was then a PhD student at the London School of Economics and had worked in investment banking himself for seven years prior to graduate study (King & Sinclair 2003). Thus, both authors were acutely aware of the nuances of financial regulation and its connection to market stability. The paper reviewed a proposal before the Basel Committee on Banking Supervision to reform the capital adequacy framework as it existed then by incorporating banks' own internal ratings and external bond ratings from the rating agencies. The authors set forth a set of negative implications from the use of private rating agencies as a substitute for state-based regulations, given the incentives that had emerged within the ratings industry. The piece predicted negative social and economic consequences. Later analyses of the 2008 crises have pointed to the Basel Accord's use of external institutions as a key factor in aggravating the events (e.g. Tarullo 2008; Becker & Linder 2020).

Following the 2008 subprime crisis, Tim's and Lena Rethel's *The Problem with Banks*, employed the distinction between the use of a synchronic outlook and neglect of diachronic issues that prevents banks from acting in the public interest, even when they are so important to public welfare (Rethel & Sinclair 2012). *The Problem with Banks* did not just review the proposals for banking reform and raise criticism, it also considered alternative ways of regulating and shaping banks. Written in an accessible manner, the book is a rare investigation into banks and their regulation that provides food for thought to the present day.

Many of these strands of Tim's life and work were apparent when I met him at the International Studies Association after finishing my own PhD in 1996. Tim graciously stepped in for a colleague who could not make it as discussant for a panel I had organized. We struck up a friendship that was initially based on our mutual experiences working in the field of banking and frustration with what I perceived to be an overly quantitative approach in the American system. While we both saw strengths in much of the new scholarship coming out at the time, we were also critical of some of the academic excesses and had a common sense that the field was in danger of losing touch with what actually goes on in the worlds of finance and government. Nonetheless, we shared an appreciation for the heuristic aspects of the interpretivist IPE of the day, and both appreciated predictive capabilities when they could be demonstrated.

In the years that followed, we had numerous discussions of our own understanding of what has been called the "transatlantic divide" in IPE (see Cohen 2009; Weaver 2009). In light of Tim's life experience and education in several countries and my own background in banking and finance as well as foundational work in African politics, we did not find the dichotomy useful and looked for ways to collaborate that would offer theoretical insight without having to take a side (Lavelle 1999, 2000, 2001). Moreover, despite the sophistication of Tim's theoretical contributions to IPE, he remained concerned with its connection to the broader community of scholarship across disciplines and educated professionals. He approached me to work with him on the book series *Finance Matters* so that we could offer work from many disciplines and from the United States, Europe, and elsewhere that would be useful in bringing the social context of finance to those otherwise not exposed to it, both with respect to academic focus and international appeal.

In the years that followed, we were able to accomplish these goals with volumes that opened the worlds of the German banking system, the European Central Bank, the practice of quantitative easing, British business banking and other topics to new audiences and academic disciplines. Tim remained an active enthusiast for new topics and new approaches to many longstanding global problems. Having lived a life cut far too short, he was an outstanding colleague, collaborator, mentor, husband, father and friend. Reaching across the aisle, his impact was felt far beyond the confines of any one field. Yet that is not to say that his wide contribution was not deep. This volume returns to Tim's theoretical origins and opens it to new dimensions in exactly the sort of way that would excite and energize him to continue on what was a remarkable academic journey.

References

Becker, M. & S. Linder 2020. "How the Basel Accord's dependence on external institutions aggravated the 2008 Financial Crisis". LSE Blog Team, 24 February. https://blogs.lse.ac.uk/europpblog/2020/02/24/how-the-basel-accords-dependence-on-external-institutions-aggravated-the-2008-financial-crisis/.

Cohen, B. 2009. "The transatlantic divide: why are American and British IPE so different?" *Review of International Political Economy* 142 (2): 197–219.

Fligstein, N. 2001. *The Architecture of Markets: An Economic Sociology of Twenty-First Century Capitalist Societies.* Princeton, NJ: Princeton University Press.

King, M. & T. J. Sinclair 2003. "Private actors and public policy: a requiem for the new Basel Capital Accord". *International Political Science Review* 24 (3): 345–62.

Lavelle, K. C. 1999. "International financial institutions and emerging capital markets in Africa". *Review of International Political Economy* 6 (2): 200–24.

Lavelle, K. C. 2000. "The international finance corporation and the emerging markets funds industry". *Third World Quarterly* 21 (2): 193–214.

Lavelle, K. C. 2001. "Architecture of equity markets: the Abidjan regional bourse". *International Organization* 55 (3): 717–42.
Rethel, L. & T. J. Sinclair 2012. *The Problem with Banks.* New York: Zed Books.
Tarullo, D. 2008. *Banking on Basel: The Future of International Financial Regulation.* Washington, DC: Peterson Institute for International Economics.
Weaver, C. 2009. "Reflections on the American school: an IPE of our making". *Review of International Political Economy* 16 (1): 1–5.

1

INTRODUCTION: TIMOTHY SINCLAIR'S SOCIAL FOUNDATIONS APPROACH TO GLOBAL FINANCE

Chris Clarke and Ben Clift

Introduction

The goal of this book is to explore Timothy Sinclair's key contributions to scholarship and his pioneering approach to international political economy (IPE) analysis. The chapters explore the multifaceted ways in which Sinclair's *oeuvre* provides IPE scholars with the tools to understand the role of credit rating agencies (CRAs) in the world economy. More fundamentally, the chapters delineate how Sinclair's scholarship was built on a distinctive "social foundations" of global finance perspective, one which has much wider applicability beyond the realms of credit rating.

This volume thus seeks to deepen our understanding of the politics of global finance, taking inspiration from Sinclair's social foundations approach (SFA) to global finance. The book grew out of commemorative events, some held at the University of Warwick, which took place after Sinclair's untimely death, celebrating his life and work and his contributions to our understanding of international politics. A number of conceptual themes at the heart of Sinclair's approach weave through the chapters of this book. We selected the themes that best showcase Sinclair's key contributions to understanding world order, IPE and the politics of global finance. Our decisions were guided by a concern to reflect things that, as Matthew Watson puts it, "Tim felt really needed to be said". There were a number of aspects of Sinclair's research agenda and intellectual make-up that made him something of a trailblazer for fresh ways of thinking about the IPE of global finance.

This volume unites a diverse array of scholars inspired by Sinclair's pioneering work, and their chapters critically engage, apply and expand his SFA to global finance in a range of directions. The book reflects an eclectic commitment, in terms of scholarly traditions, influences and approaches, which was an important element of Sinclair's identity as an IPE scholar. As editors, we wanted to bring together scholars at different career stages, working in different national academic cultures, indeed belonging to different generations of IPE, all of whom have been profoundly influenced by Sinclair's approach. As the chapters reveal in their distinctive ways, the SFA provides crucial starting points to develop a fuller understanding of the *politics* of global finance. It offers many fresh insights into the important power relations, knowledge practices and authority dynamics that operate within and through the institutions and processes at the heart of global finance.

There are a number of dimensions of Sinclair's approach to IPE and global finance that we elucidate along the way. First, the chapters examine and position the SFA theoretically and put it into conversation with other IPE scholarship on the political economy of finance. Second, chapters trace a variety of theoretical lineages and intellectual influences on Sinclair's work discussing how they shaped and informed his SFA and delineating their relevance for understanding the politics of global finance today. Third, in substantive analytical terms, many chapters showcase the latest research on rating agencies and rating practices by those taking inspiration from Sinclair's path-breaking work. Fourth, animated by Sinclair's investigation of consequential "micro-practices" of CRAs in the realms of global finance, some chapters follow a similar methodological path. They drill down into other "micro-practices" and specific institutions, revealing fresh insights into global finance and its politics, and possible futures for global finance. A final recurring dimension reflects Sinclair's focus on the politics of knowledge and the social construction of epistemic authority.

The contributions in their different ways speak to and mobilize the rich intellectual resources Sinclair and his SFA provided. This introduction organizes the contributions thematically. An important aim we have for this book is to explore the antecedents to and influences on Sinclair's *oeuvre*. In Randall Germain's chapter, in particular, we get a sense of how Sinclair was standing on the shoulders of giants. In addition to a short list of significant intellectual influences, notably Robert Cox, Susan Strange and Stephen Gill, a much wider array of minor influences drawn from a relatively broad and eclectic church is evident in Sinclair's work. This breadth and variety of sources of inspiration was a noteworthy facet of Sinclair as a scholar, and it is important to reflect that in these pages.

Sinclair's research agenda was animated, as Germain and others note, in part by the need to analyse globalization processes in new ways. Sinclair's works revisit understandings of power relations within the global political economy. Notably, he shone light on the increasingly crucial and configuring role of private authority within global finance. A desire to escape traditional International Relations (IR) thinking in terms of the primacy of state sovereignty was important here. One intellectual motivation that underpins Sinclair's work was throwing off some of the state-centric shackles of traditional IR, whose strictures he found – perhaps channelling Strange here – both overly constraining and ultimately unconvincing. There was not sufficient place, within mainstream state-centric IR analysis, for considering *private* authority. Furthermore, for Sinclair, this private authority needed to be analysed by focusing on its intimate attachment to the role of knowledge – understood as a social phenomenon – in the world economy. As a number of the chapters underline, Sinclair was an original thinker who opened up new avenues on how IPE could and should engage with knowledge, ideas and private authority in the context of increasingly significant and pervasive processes of disintermediation in financial markets.

Escaping the strictures of traditional IR thinking also found expression, for Sinclair, in a multi-levelled investigative approach which, as Johannes Petry notes in his chapter, was adept at "weaving together the micro, meso, and macro levels of analysis". This, too, was partly about escaping IR's disciplinary confines in analysing globalization, and searching for new ways to think about power, authority and the social realm. Flowing from this was a methodological instinct, and an analytical move, to engage in a bottom-up account of global finance. This led to a career of looking at particular hitherto under-studied institutions, and the "micro-practices" through which they enacted global finance. Sinclair demonstrated how a traditional focus on sovereign states presented at best a partial picture, missing how private authority wielded by CRAs was reshaping global finance. This "politics of rating", as Sinclair's work showcased, pervaded and shaped world order (Sinclair 2005: 20; 1994b).

Sinclair's attention to these "micro-practices", and to neglected institutions wielding significant power and authority, was guided by a desire to look at how key actors "make sense" of their world, and to see this as a crucial site of politics. This focus on the social construction of knowledge, on cognitive frameworks, and epistemic politics and power was in some ways a key constructivist move. It was, as his books underscored, in the system-wide repercussions and implications of CRA authority and their mental schemata that their true significance in shaping the global political economy was demonstrated. These were path-breaking insights for those IPE scholars who would come to focus more and more on epistemic power, what James calls the "epistemic turn" in IPE (2024). Sinclair was a key early mover in this direction, forging a path that many followed. Epistemic authority, for Sinclair and his SFA, was crucial for private authority – it enabled institutions to make authoritative judgements and meant that their audience perceived these judgements as legitimate.

Interrogating the role of private authority within global finance and the social construction of epistemic authority seen as operating at different levels are Sinclair's key contributions to IPE. These informed his exploration of the institutional complexities of global financial markets. His work assessed the implications of these intersubjective ideational processes for constructing economic rectitude, for the study of global finance and for world order. These formed the building blocks of a distinctive SFA perspective Sinclair developed. These elements, as the chapters in this book illustrate, offer fresh perspectives on the way global finance and its politics work.

The social foundations approach: the politics of global finance and the ideational realm

One of the central underpinnings of the SFA, and indeed of the broader contribution that Sinclair made, was the recognition that finance is not a mechanical process, and it cannot be decoded with mathematical precision. Finance, and financial markets, are social and political constructs – not naturally occurring phenomena. This insight opened up the contingency and deliberation over how to think about global finance, both on the part of scholars and of practitioners. SFA rejects the mainstream economics and finance view that "markets reflect fundamental economic forces, which are not subject to human manipulation" (Sinclair 2005: 5). This was crucial for making sense of the *politics* of global finance. Part of Sinclair's critique of excessively structuralist accounts of finance, as Matthew Watson's chapter explores, was that they lose sight of the key agential dynamics and foibles, and human frailties of the actual practitioners, working for CRAs, who – in their deliberations and decisions about investments and creditworthiness – make finance happen.

One fundamental heterodox insight underpinning and animating the SFA is that finance and financial markets have an in-built tendency towards instability and crisis. For Sinclair, as for Keynes, Polanyi and Marx, crises are endogenous to financial markets – not exogenous phenomena. The fundamental point is that "financial markets are more social – and less spontaneous, individual" than is commonly taken for granted (Sinclair 2005: 5). As Aida Hozic's chapter notes, for Sinclair (2010d), Keynes' tabloid beauty contest metaphor encapsulated the endogeneity of financial crises to the capitalist system. Crucial here is how to mould the average opinion of what the average opinion might be about a particular asset. This shows how market valuation is a social phenomenon shaped by confidence and reputation, one prone to herd behaviours. Within this endogenous understanding of crisis, Hozic underlines how, for Sinclair, "understanding and interpretation of crises by experts is a key factor of their reproduction". This all reinforces the value, in making sense of global finance, of unorthodox conceptions of markets and of heterodox views on actor behaviour that abandon rationalist assumptions. As Watson notes, financial market models used by CRAs presumed "perfect market equilibration" and these models were key to the agencies' epistemic authority. Yet these models have at best limited real-world traction because "actual market prices" are driven and shaped by "exaggerated mood swings" (Rethel & Sinclair 2012; Sinclair 2021: 79).

Sinclair's approach, Petry notes, is "thoroughly political all the way down". Sinclair was always underlining to his students the importance of focusing on the politics of global finance and of the rating process. From an SFA perspective, it is a mistake to think of finance as a technical, still-less-natural system as much economistic thinking about finance tends to. The financial models central to CRA workings are, as Watson underlines, also human systems whose day-to-day use requires human judgement. The people behind the models bringing them to life are the key to grasping CRAs (and, indeed, fiscal councils – see Clift 2023). Furthermore, important shortcomings of those mathematical financial market models are linked to how they are blind to human intuition and herd behaviour. In these and other ways, the SFA brings with it an invitation to critical analysis to explore finance as a political realm.

With the SFA's attentiveness to intersubjective dynamics, and notions of repute and intellectual authority, there is an epistemic politics at work, of rival knowledge claims and struggles to establish and maintain intellectual authority, in the way Sinclair approaches CRAs and global finance. Sinclair's concept of "embedded knowledge networks" highlighted the political economic significance of particular worldviews and understandings of appropriate market relations entailed and contained in the work of financial market institutions and practitioners. CRAs and ratings orthodoxy involves US-inspired views on the appropriate relations between states and markets, and the way that financial capitalism should be ordered. This becomes further entrenched and reproduced in and through the ratings process. Ratings agencies and their judgements are simultaneously "viewed as endogenous rather than exogenous" to financial markets (Sinclair 2005: 15). Yet CRAs operate as market actors as well as market intermediaries. Their legitimacy as expert assessors of creditworthiness, Watson notes, is as both "judges" and "consultants" – despite the tensions between those roles. These are some of the ways that the *politics* of global finance manifest themselves.

Sinclair's *oeuvre* draws our attention to what Petry calls "the politics of powerful market ordering devices" shining a light on the way that "mundane practices shaped global financial flows and reconfigured power constellations". Chris Clarke's chapter explores these power relations within the co-constitutive relationship between financial markets and technological development through the rise of "fintech". Focusing on the private authority that fintech actors enjoy shows how "financial markets, practices and regulation" are reshaped through new kinds and forms of "judgement practices", as "financial firms becoming ever more digitalized in their operation", they unleash processes of reintermediation and centralization. This generates, as Clarke notes, shifting patterns of inclusion, exclusion and wealth ownership in global finance. Datafication advances under centralizing "platform capitalism" as enormously powerful yet largely unaccountable big tech firms integrate payment systems into their platforms to harness the monetization possibilities of the transactional payment data generated.

Always attuned to "the global politics of ratings", Sinclair's work explores the shifting location of power within global politics and global finance. The changing power configurations in finance were driven in part by increasing disintermediation, as Hozic's chapter demonstrates. Disintermediation increased the significance and scope of what Hozic terms "multiple actors second-guessing each other and their moves on the market". This fuelled the rising epistemic authority of CRAs as key providers of market confidence, via their judgements about creditworthiness.

Thus, crucial within this new disintermediated financial order was increasingly significant power exercised by private market authorities. One facet of this ideational power within the new global finance, analysed by Watson's chapter, is "how financial models are constructed" presuming smoothly equilibrating price movements. These CRA models "promise specific visualization techniques" for making sense of financial markets, presuming them to have efficient characteristics. As Petry explores in this volume, this focus on private authority and epistemic power exercised by financial institutions was both novel and groundbreaking for IPE. Petry underlines the importance of Sinclair's path-breaking insights into the power and authority of private market actors, what Petry terms their "mediating power within the global financial system". These were insights that, Petry argues, subsequent scholars would do well to draw on. It opens up new avenues, for example, exploring financial infrastructures.

CRAs' ratings provide a "rule of thumb" (Sinclair 2005: 2) that facilitate investment decision-making. Key for an SFA approach is understanding financial institutions in terms of "what people observe and collectively agree" those institutions are doing (Sinclair 2021: 81). The credence they are afforded is a crucial source of their power. Yet, as Watson points out, CRAs' workings entail a problematic conflation of the model world and the real world. Models as "abstract mathematical artefacts" depicting and operating under idealized circumstances are assumed to "plug epistemic gaps" and have direct lessons and implications for the real world of global finance. However, this view of the epistemic status of CRA judgements does not take account of the unlikelihood of "idealized conditions of the model" being replicated in the real world.

These shortcomings of the knowledge created by CRAs notwithstanding, ratings are highly consequential, as Petry puts it, "because other actors view them as important". Intersubjectivity shaped how Sinclair thought about finance, centring attention on the relational aspects of finance, creditworthiness and so forth. Germain considers how this intersubjectivity "defines institutional agency" in Sinclair's work. These social and intersubjective dynamics at the heart of the SFA were some of the main reasons why Sinclair was frustrated by mathematical approaches that mistakenly treat financial markets like machines (the car engine was an analogy that he often turned to).

The weight that judgements by these private authorities carry manages to cut through the complexities of finance, with CRAs "passing judgement" in ways that played "a crucial role in constructing the markets" (Sinclair 2005: 15). CRAs are crucially important primarily because of how others view them rather than because of what they do. Just how important they are to the functioning of disintermediated global financial markets is one of the more arresting arguments from Sinclair's *oeuvre.* Indeed, ratings became the "key benchmarks in the cognitive life" of financial markets and as such an integral "part of the internal organization of the market" (Sinclair 2005: 52). As reputational intermediaries, Sinclair argued CRAs are "essential to the functioning of the [global financial] system" (Sinclair 2012b: 142). This constitutive role that ratings play in financial markets explains their epistemic power and the sources of their authority. These groundbreaking insights charted new territory in constructivist IPE as it engaged with global finance.

We have already noted the importance of politics and power to the way Sinclair thought about global finance. Power is exercised, in Sinclair's approach to finance, in and through these ideational forms and intersubjective dynamics. As noted by Petry, the mental frameworks used in ratings are one important "feature of the structural power of the agencies" (Sinclair 2021: 6). These mental frameworks inform and shape how they make sense of the act of credit rating. Watson outlines multiple forms of moral, epistemic and human fallibility surrounding the use of mathematical models by CRAs, delineating how hypothetical mathematical modelling generated misplaced confidence. This was a conspicuous feature of the CRAs' role in causing the Great Financial Crisis as Sinclair explored so tellingly in his final book *To the Brink of Destruction.*

The mental frameworks used by CRAs, whether they accurately depict the financial realm or not, contain distinctive conceptions of both government and market failure. They entail particular understandings of appropriate state–market relations, and these are some of the reasons why CRAs and their mental frameworks matter politically. The SRA approach foregrounded how these intersubjectivities have political consequences – such as ratings orthodoxy being anchored to a conception of the self-regulating market. As Fumihito Gotoh, Norbert Gaillard and Rick Michalek note, it is *within* those mental frameworks that we find key shifts that have reshaped global finance and the CRAs' role within it. One of the more consequential changes is how the agencies morphed from "conservative financial gatekeepers" to international "short-term profit maximizers disseminating short-termist universalism" in ways that would fuel the global financial crisis (GFC). Similarly, Watson notes how CRAs "increasingly tried to face in two directions at once", continuing to pass judgement on financial products, "but only after having pocketed substantial consultancy fees for having advised on the initial securitization process". This saw the CRAs, as Clarke puts it, "reneging on their commitment (or pretence) to impartiality".

This centrality of intersubjectivity that Sinclair refined over the years has been taken forward by those who have followed in his footsteps. Dan Wood's work on financial indexes draws on Sinclair's insights into "constitutive rules" as "intersubjective understandings" and how they "represent the social foundations of markets" in that they create "specific collective rules that produce specified forms of behaviour" (Sinclair 2009). Hozic identifies the centrality of key "mutually agreed fictions" within the "deepening of disintermediation of (economic) knowledge – and re-politicization of expert knowledge". Hozic further underlines how Sinclair's approach provides the tools for ongoing analysis of expertise and private authority in global finance as dynamic and contingent epistemic practices. The SFA sheds fresh light on how private and epistemic authority are reproduced and renegotiated over time.

These are some of the ways the SFA offers pathways into analysing the politics of global finance, and ideational and intersubjective dynamics shaping the role of private authority within global capitalism. Sinclair's approach to global finance was built on and enriched by a variety of intellectual influences. Indeed, as we explore in the next section, this spirit of eclecticism, taking forward the insights of other great scholars, was one of the animating features of Sinclair's approach to IPE.

Intellectual influences and their relevance to the politics of global finance

As well as providing indications of how his work can be built on, this book explores how Sinclair was himself standing on the shoulders of giants, inspired by working with some of the field's leading lights in what Germain calls "the critical tradition in IPE", not only Cox and Gill as PhD advisers, but also the *oeuvre* of Strange. Sinclair worked initially within a critical political economy tradition shaped by Cox, with whom he collaborated closely. Yet his insights and approach were not limited to that tradition.

One feature of the chapters in this book is that many of them locate Sinclair's SFA within some lineages of broader political economy intellectual traditions. This helps draw out his key points of departure and explore how these influences can help us to understand global finance today. There is also attention to how the SFA offers intellectual resources that other strands of contemporary political economy scholarship on finance can fruitfully draw on and engage with.

As Germain delineates, there are important foundational influences on Sinclair as an IPE scholar. He retained a focus on the structural power of capital and the social forces surrounding it. He drew on Strange's insights into structural power within global finance, and the interplay of state and non-state actors. His SFA "incorporates the social relations of constitution into structural power" (Sinclair 2021: 76). Strange's thematic focal points on private authority and the role of knowledge in the world economy were all key insights and inspirations for Sinclair's body of work.

Cox, Strange and Gill all, to some extent, shaped the way Sinclair thought about power and authority within world order, and about the importance of knowledge and what we might term "epistemic power". Yet the historical specificity and analytical precision of Sinclair's work on global finance goes beyond the broader brush analyses of towering scholars such as Strange and Cox – albeit still nourished by some of their insights. He was also something of an iconoclast, "coming at" the role of ideas, knowledge, authority and power in political economy in his own distinctive fashion. Although he was very influenced by the ideas of Cox, and indeed Gill, Sinclair stood apart from a generation of Neo-Gramscian IPE scholars.

Sinclair's work explored knowledge, power and the ideational realm, which were also focal points for a Gramscian turn in international studies, and he was mentored by Cox who was a leading light of that approach. Yet, always thinking on his own terms, Sinclair's was a distant relation with Gramscian IPE, and – as Magnus Ryner explores – a complicated one with Marxian scholarship. In relation to Constructivist IPE, too, Sinclair ploughed his own furrow and went about things in his own bespoke fashion.

So much that was central to the politics of finance, Sinclair underlined and understood, played out at the ideational level. Sinclair was a leading exemplar of an approach to political economy that recognizes the independent, causal and constitutive role of ideas in shaping political economic outcomes and practices. As such he contributed to the emergence of a Constructivist IPE tradition (distinct from Constructivism in IR), helping to develop, systematize and operationalize some of the core Constructivist IPE insights. In recognizing "the social nature of global finance" and shining the light on intersubjective practices through which financial actors attempt to make sense of the market, Sinclair's work highlights how a crucial mediating role is played by "the institutions that work to facilitate transactions between buyers and sellers", which "have a central role in organizing markets and, consequently, in governing the world" (Sinclair 2005: 10–12).

His exploration of intersubjective aspects of financial institutions, to look at how key actors "make sense" of their world and to see this as a crucial site of politics, was a key constructivist move. One key locus for this was the "mental frameworks" that actors and institutions used to make sense of finance. Sinclair accordingly explored and attached great significance to "ratings orthodoxy" (see Germain's chapter), and the understanding of state–market relations that it enshrined and reproduced. His work also deepened our understanding of the ways in which finance is "subject to the pathologies of social life", swayed by rumours, norms and "animal spirits", thus "we should expect turbulence and change, euphoria and dysphoria in the [financial] markets" (Sinclair 2021: 79–80).

The constructivist focus on "intersubjective practices through which financial actors" attempt to make sense of the market foregrounds the role, outlined by Watson, of mathematical models. Watson spells out processes of internalizing behavioural norms, wherein underlying understandings of state–market relations get reproduced by being "written into the systems of equations through which the models are constituted". These and other ideational constructs occupied a key place within the routines and practices of the private authorities, vital to shaping global finance, that Sinclair's work did so much to illuminate. CRAs deployed artefactual idealized mathematical models, yet these were often masquerading as representational models with ready applicability to the real world. The massively damaging and destabilizing consequences of this mismatch that Sinclair explored in *To the Brink of Destruction* provides a telling illustration of the enormous ideational power that CRAs wield.

Another theme that was central for his approach to world politics was the social validation of expert knowledge: what made the interventions of certain expert actors or institutions authoritative and legitimate? In the terms of John Searle, a scholar whom Sinclair drew on extensively, CRAs' import was a social fact. CRAs matter because of "what people believe about them, and act on collectively". This rests on "a collective belief that says the agencies are important, which people act upon, as if it were 'true'" (Sinclair 2005: 54). Their epistemic authority is a peculiarly important and significant social fact in the context of the spread of disintermediated markets. Sinclair sheds light on what Clarke terms "the role of knowledge in constituting legitimate authority" by "unpacking how intersubjective meaning and understanding was established and reproduced across different social actors and arenas".

Sinclair forever reminds us that our subject matter is the politics of global finance, and the epistemic influence wielded largely by private authorities in and through the operations of global finance is a crucial site of power. This points to how the ideational realm is important for understanding power dynamics within the global political economy. Sinclair's early work, published in the first edition of the journal the *Review of International Political Economy*, zeroed in on a series hitherto under-explored, perhaps unexplored, intersubjective processes. These were, he went on to demonstrate over much of the next 30 years, hugely consequential. CRAs became ever more crucial as disintermediation became more pervasive within the global financial system, in what Sinclair termed "new global finance" (1994b). The reciprocal feedback loops that characterize these intersubjectivities were always a key target for Sinclair's research effort. Intersubjectivity is a crucial theme running through Sinclair's work and is key to the social character of finance.

Sinclair explored how particular forms of expert knowledge enabled the construction of social fictions. Perhaps the most salient examples are the complex, largely illegible and little understood financial products created in part by CRAs as securitization got out of hand. Watson discusses "CDOs-cubed", which are "a collateralized debt obligation of a collateralized debt obligation of a collateralized debt obligation". These financial products, which became hugely important and widespread, in their construction necessarily bore the imprimatur and seal of approval of CRAs' private authority. They existed only because of "the performative effects of the models which purported to show how they would be profitable".

How knowledge producers' ideas or outputs were regarded by others, and issues of esteem, credentials and repute, were crucial for his account of the politics of global finance. Yet Sinclair's was also distinct from other constructivist work in bringing in other influences. For example, Germain in this volume sees an ideational focus that is "tethered to" a Coxian "historical mode of thought". Sinclair's was an engagement with constructivist ideas and themes, but on his own terms. This distinctiveness was linked to his eclecticism – drawing on a quite wide array of influences. Sinclair's intellectual curiosity and openness to drawing on insights from varied sources and traditions meant he did not take an "off the shelf" approach to understanding ideas, be it Neo-Gramscian or other. Instead, once again, he ploughed his own furrow. All this makes Sinclair all the more interesting as a scholar, one who opens up lots of interesting avenues of inquiry, but also one who is quite hard to pigeonhole, as a number of chapters in this volume explore.

The politics and power of ratings: agencies and practices

Sinclair's SFA, with its attentiveness to the social construction of orthodoxies and pervasive worldviews, underlines two social fictions that surround how global finance is commonly understood and thought about. First, mainstream orthodox work on finance presupposes it to be a mechanical, knowable system that operates according to rationality and efficiency principles in a manner consistent with the assumptions of the efficient markets hypothesis (EMH). These analytical priors are fundamental to how finance is routinely understood and approached within economics or business schools, built into the mathematical models that Watson explores in his chapter. We have already touched on many of the reasons why that kind of account of finance is radically incomplete.

Second, much work on financial expertise assumes that actors have requisite levels of expert knowledge, such that they can "know" about financial market developments. This is where his ground-breaking work on CRAs was so critical. The presumption is that CRAs, using their models and techniques, can discern and accurately gauge the future creditworthiness that their ratings denote. Their workings are presumed from the outside to enjoy something approaching scientific authority. CRAs, as reputational intermediaries, enjoy a level of respect and trade on a repute that treats their pronouncements on creditworthiness as authoritative.

Yet looking up close at how ratings get done, as Sinclair did, reveals that the emperor has no clothes. CRA evaluations are not founded on anything like as sure a footing as "ratings orthodoxy" presumes. CRAs' reputation for accurately discerning creditworthiness is one of the "mutually agreed fictions" that Hozic identities as centrally important within the "deepening of disintermediation". Sinclair's delving into CRAs' workings revealed something interesting about epistemic authority; it can be more apparent than real. Credit ratings, Sinclair points out, "necessarily involve judgement. They are not unambiguous and do not exist independently from interpretation. They are social constructions, products of deliberation ... predicting the future is a task involving great uncertainty" (Sinclair 2021: 158–9).

Watson discerns how Sinclair picks up on multiple forms of moral, epistemic and human fallibility surrounding CRAs' use of mathematical models, for example. This, as Hozic notes, is why these expert understandings and interpretations are a key factor in fuelling the crises endogenous to the financial system. Ratings infer assumptions that CRAs and other reputational intermediaries can "know" about financial market developments through their models and techniques. This, for Sinclair, overstates the legibility and knowability of finance and financial markets. Beneath the veneer of intellectual respectability, these ratings are far from "scientific".

Given the intersubjective nature of global finance, credibility and confidence, CRAs have acquired "an intangible reputation for good judgement" (Sinclair 2021: 19–20), and from this flows their enormous influence on global finance. The merit of their ratings is collectively agreed upon and accepted, even if the ratings themselves are not accurate, and even if their methods and techniques may be questionable. The SFA lays bare in fascinating ways how prevailing understandings within the ratings process are contingent and are somewhat arbitrarily arrived at. Yet at the same time, they really matter for the allocation of global credit (Sinclair 2005: 10–11). Sinclair's work shows us how, to some extent, these are castles made of sand. Yet even though finance cannot be "known" to that degree, there is nevertheless enormous epistemic power wielded by CRAs as authoritative bodies pronouncing on finance.

Sinclair's analytical and methodological move to focus on what Petry terms "the micro-foundations of global finance" was generative of so many insights and proved pertinent to a wide array of debates. Drilling down into the minutiae of how financial markets operate, Petry delineates Sinclair's "attentiveness to the practical and technical workings of global finance", and how this was enormously fruitful, and a move others emulated. A similar analytical move, following in Sinclair's footsteps and pursuing a "bottom-up" focus on particular financial market actors and institutions, is showcased in Dan Wood's chapter. He takes this mode of inquiry forward with his exploration of index providers. Wood notes how index providers' authority and legitimacy rests on "an epistemic claim" to have the "correct procedures". These supposedly enable index providers to "accurately represent 'the market'" in ways that resonate with CRAs and their exercise of epistemic power.

Clarke's chapter on fintech similarly emulates Sinclair's approach, drilling down into and applying SFA insights to the roles of particular actors and their mundane practices. Fintech has "reshaped judgement practices of credit rating in socially and politically consequential ways" – its digital data-rich modus operandi means that user data can be harnessed for credit risk analysis. This has enabled, among other things, commodifying personal data and digital footprints of populations previously too little known or too risky for finance to engage with. An SFA is deployed to demystify "black boxes" of global finance, finding that fintech firms "are more market players than market judges". As an SFA would anticipate, knowledge is a social creation in fintech firms – with new forms of *datafication* seen as a qualitative shift in rating practices wherein *all data is credit data* – with implications for creditworthiness and its assessment. Fintech's implications and ramifications shape and control access to capital within international capitalism, deepening inequalities on a global scale. Some fintech firms' huge market capitalizations are testament to how consequential it swiftly became, with its sizeable displacement within global financial markets.

Sinclair's work analysing ratings agencies and their practices revealed to IPE audiences not only previously neglected institutions but also highlighted the crucial "'reconfiguring' effect that these private authorities and their practices can have on global economic and political life" (Sinclair 2005: 10–11). One important illustration of how consequential this reconfiguration of how private authority can be exercised within global finance was provided in his final book. A foundational contributing factor to the GFC, Sinclair reveals, was when CRAs as reputational intermediaries changed their modus operandi to become market actors as well as market intermediaries, becoming integral to securitization processes (Sinclair 2021). CRAs' authorship role within securitization processes, acting as consultants in the construction of structured finance products, was shaped as Watson notes by their models that engendered "a shared cognitive perspective of safety that wildly overstated the risk-free nature of untested products".

Gotoh, Gaillard and Michalek's chapter follows Sinclair's lead and unearths more aspects of CRAs, their practices and their "reconfiguring" effects. Delving deep into CRA "micro-practices" reveals their role within the increasingly byzantine intricacies of structured finance. As finance has become increasingly not just disintermediated but also securitized, the role CRAs play and the nature of rating judgements and evaluation has also evolved. Gotoh, Gaillard and Michalek chart fascinating evolutions between the "art" and "science" of rating. Ratings were once dominated by qualitative judgement, but with the increasing volume and scale of ratings required for proliferating financial products, techniques of analysis had to keep pace. Increasingly, quantitative approaches were needed as the scale of the workload grew, given the sheer volume of rating acts required by securitization.

Gotoh, Gaillard and Michalek chart the key role of "technological innovations (e.g. securitization and algorithmization)" and the "skyrocketing growth of structured finance". New financial products abounded, including collateralized bond offerings (CBOs), collateralized debt offerings (CDOs), and "special purpose vehicles". In terms of how ratings get done, securitization required and depended on increasing "parameterization" whereby "a transaction's rating became the consequence of identifying and optimizing the key elements of the presented transaction". This reaffirms a key point Sinclair made about how the CRAs themselves played a key role in the authorship of all these innovative securitized assets.

These transformations were part of the highly consequential shift, noted above, wherein CRAs evolved from "conservative financial gatekeepers" to "short-term profit maximizers". The value of these novel securitized assets all hinged on the "imprimatur of a rating by one of the Big Three". CRA agency was in this way crucial within securitization, such that "rating analysts had to invent the wheel", assigning ratings to these novel and hugely complex assets. As securitization advanced to become ever more esoteric, it became further removed from real assets. Gotoh, Gaillard and Michalek's chapter notes how the ratings process "steadily drifted away from qualitative analysis and increasingly focused on quantitative metrics". The zenith, perhaps, was reached with the introduction of what Gotoh, Gaillard and Michalek term "CDOs squared" where the underlying "reference asset" is not a real asset at all, but a securitized confection, a CDO. CRAs were crucial to these innovations and to the authoring of these assets. Yet the extent to which anyone within these agencies or beyond really understood the assets or liabilities, or could hope to gauge their value, was attenuated ever more.

In a Strange-esque *qui bono* sense, there are important distributional and political aspects to the changing incentives and timeframes created by this novel mode of securitized, disintermediated finance. As Gotoh, Gaillard and Michalek underline, the way structured finance issuances operated, banks, originators, CRAs and lawyers were all "paid at the beginning" – so none were concerned about the long-term financial performance of the asset once created. As Sinclair's final book explored so compellingly, the temporality of this incentive structure was the time bomb that detonated the GFC, revealing multiple weak points in an inherently fragile global financial system.

Micro-practices, neoliberalism and the institutions of global finance

Sinclair's approach was to zero in on specific institutions, such as CRAs, and their associated "micro-practices", notably their ratings orthodoxy, at the core of contemporary capitalism (Sinclair 2005: 10–11). The research process drills down into key "micro-processes" of global finance and explores the dominant ideational forms, and the power relations they reflect and reproduce. This is used as a means to tell a much bigger story about state–market relations, and about global capitalism, its instabilities and power dynamics.

In analysing these "micro-processes", identifying the key role of, and power wielded by interpretive frames is one of Sinclair's key contributions. This insight suggests a method of political economy analysis that homes in on these mental schemata and explores how they are arrived at, what ideas feed into them, what they entail and what their political implications are. Sinclair's work illuminated these themes brilliantly in relation to CRAs. Our authors focus on a range of apparently mundane and technical practices (Petry, Clarke, Wood, and Gotoh, Gaillard and Michalek), showing how they play a key role within global capitalism. A number of the chapters, including those by Wood, Clarke, Watson and Petry reflect on the important "bottom-up" methodological move in Sinclair's work to centre on particular institutions, practices and mental schemata, grasping how these can be highly consequential. Petry considers how, in Sinclair's work, these "seemingly mundane practices" in fact "shaped global financial flows and reconfigured power constellations".

Clarke's SFA approach to fintech shows how market authority has been reinvented, including through private authority in new forms of knowledge networks and new processes of passing authoritative judgement on economic matters and creditworthiness. Also at play are changes in where social authority lies in making judgements in finance compared to the financial world of CRAs that Sinclair analysed. "Peer-to-peer" lending, out of which some fintech grew, endeavoured to displace banks as their different form of credit intermediation sought to shift market authority over the social practice of risk assessment. A curious maturation process, perhaps a normalization process, ensued where these financial institutions, often founded as disruptive challengers in rejection of and opposition to traditional banks, either became banks, or became ever more bank-like. Challengers were increasingly co-opted or incorporated into existing financial institutions, and their judging of creditworthiness reverted closer to standard practices of financial institutions. This recalls Sinclair's insights about judgement authorities under disintermediation being subject to a trend towards centralization.

One way to make sense of the import of mental schemata deployed by financial expert bodies is in relation to what we might term the politics of economic ideas or competing political economic worldviews. The focus in the ideational realm central to SFA brought to the fore, among other things, how "ratings orthodoxy" was imbued with particular understanding of appropriate state–market relations. Ratings were one mechanism whereby specific neoliberal views were reproduced as common sense. One strand of Sinclair's work explored "deficit discourse" about public finances and fiscal soundness (Sinclair 2000a), and the particular neoliberal political economic worldviews entailed in its construction. The formulation and promulgation of "deficit discourse" was a key site of politics for Sinclair involving particular understandings of appropriate (and inappropriate) roles for the state in the economy, levels of public spending, acceptable fiscal stances, and so forth. This exposed powerful yet malleable, and to some extent contested, sets of dominant political economic ideas. The way fiscal rectitude is constructed by expert economic bodies is another of those contingent, pliable and changeable ideational forms that pervaded Sinclair's work.

The establishment of "deficit discourse" is revealed as a social process wherein epistemic authority is exercised by both public and private authorities – consistent with the social conceptions of agency and knowledge central to the SFA. Here, too, there were overlaps with much Constructivist IPE scholarship. One of the key "mental frameworks", for Sinclair was "ratings orthodoxy" (see Germain's chapter), which entailed a particular neoliberal worldview. It was, as his books underscored, in the system-wide repercussions and implications of CRA authority, and their mental schemata, that their true significance in shaping the global political economy was demonstrated.

Sinclair's analysis revealed "the way power is exercised" through the social construction of deficit discourse. His work delineated "the main lines of contestation" on deficit matters (Sinclair 2000a: 187). Deficit discourse ramifies widely within the global political economy, "its real significance lies in areas beyond the strictly fiscal" (Sinclair 2000a: 185), shaping governing agendas more broadly. The mental schema for thinking about deficits entail at times "a restructuring of the parameters of acceptable speech surrounding governmental finance and action" (Sinclair 2000a: 192). It "operates in a way, mentally and in practice, of closing off sets of practices from contestation" (Sinclair 2000a: 186).

These are additional areas where the important role of intersubjective beliefs within global finance – what views are considered and accepted as "sound" – can prove highly consequential. Shared views on acceptable deficit levels, propagated by CRAs and others, are more of the key "intersubjective structures" or "interpretive frames [that] actors use to understand the world" (Sinclair 2005: 10–12), which played such a key role in Sinclair's account of global capitalism. Thus "getting control over the process of discourse creation" is "a significant question of power" (Sinclair 2000a: 191). How these dominant fiscal discourses are constructed, and how they shape the possibilities for governments engaged in economic management, are important aspects of the politics of global finance. They feed into "ratings orthodoxy": CRAs and their views on the creditworthiness of government bonds, and as such could be said to police the boundaries of acceptable fiscal policy.

These focal points shed fresh light on the politics and dynamics of global finance. Petry in this volume underlines how Sinclair foregrounded that "the world's dominant rating agencies were not just based in the US but thoroughly imbued with an American character given their origination in US financial systems and worldviews". For Sinclair, it was about a characteristically US notion of "best practice" within an "American-derived, synchronic mental framework" (Sinclair 2005: 17) being reproduced through ratings processes. This creates possibilities for the SFA and Sinclair's work to speak to debates about comparative capitalist restructuring.

An SFA lens, applied to specific practices within global finance, shows how this micro-level focus can also connect to broader meso- and macro-level debates, for example about different national varieties of financial systems and indeed financial capitalisms. American CRAs constitute what Sinclair called an "embedded knowledge network" that continues to dominate aspects of global finance. Floating Moody's on the NYSE in 2000 was a straw in the wind of the increasing dominance of shareholder value and short-term profit maximization over any other concerns. Yet these financial norms are not fully replicated in other financial systems or varieties of capitalism. Gotoh, Gaillard and Michalek's comparative analysis highlights "divergent norms and mental frameworks" between American and "local" CRAs. These ideational dynamics and micro-processes help explain why and how financial capitalisms differ, as revealed in comparative analysis of East Asian and American CRAs.

Ratings shape the ways capitalism works. Indeed, the "tenures of corporate managers have been shortened", Gotoh, Gaillard and Michalek note, as a result of "mounting pressure from institutional investors regarding short-term shareholder returns". These logics are driven in part by the private authorities that Sinclair focused on, and the mental schemata that drove their ratings operations. The shareholder value paradigm, as reproduced in the mental frameworks of the financial professionals in thrall to ratings orthodoxy, increasingly permeates different financial systems and varied kinds of capitalism. Gotoh, Gaillard and Michalek show the fruitful potential of bringing Sinclair's work and framework into conversation with comparative capitalisms and comparative financial systems scholarship (see also Gotoh & Sinclair 2017, 2021). An SFA offers ways to evolve the methodologically nationalist pre-dispositions of comparative capitalisms analysis in a world of disintermediated, securitized, globalized finance shaped by the power and influence of the CRAs.

Gotoh, Gaillard and Michalek show the complexities of these processes, which are not reducible to the external imposition of Anglo-Saxon or US financial norms. An SFA draws attention to the different cultural and societal norms and values reflected in different national financial systems and institutions. These interact with and mediate the US norms of global finance that the CRAs propagate, shaping capitalist restructuring. This approach can be used, as Gotoh, Gaillard and Michalek demonstrate, to explain domestic financial norms being institutionalized in new ways, and also to explore the mediation of global (financial) forces by domestic ideational and institutional factors.

Similar dissonances, this time between CRA logics, rooted in Anglo-Saxon shareholder value capitalism, and European norms of capitalist organization were evident throughout the eurozone crisis. This sparked abortive attempts to construct a European ratings agency, one more attuned to distinctive European capitalist norms. The failure of this European ratings project is explained partly by the fact that European capitalisms are changing, aligning increasingly with the shareholder value norms. The gravitational pull of short-term profit maximization, as it underpins and informs CRAs and their mental schemata, is a powerful transformative force within both global finance and national capitalisms.

Conclusion

One of the things these chapters reveal is how Sinclair's *oeuvre* offers fruitful avenues for other research questions and debates in political economy. The SFA, in its consideration of rating as a site of politics, invites us to think about power in relation to global finance, and how it relates to ideas and to different forms of authority and knowledge. Sinclair's analysis of the constitutive role that ratings play in financial markets, their epistemic power and their sources of authority, are key insights that moved Constructivist IPE forward as it engaged with global finance. The tools Sinclair and his SFA provided can help explore the ongoing evolutions and reconfigurations of power relations and the politics of knowledge within global finance. Foreshadowing what James later termed the "epistemic turn" in IPE (2024), Sinclair was a pioneer charting a path to a more ideationally attuned and contingent account of political economy.

Flawed mainstream market-based approaches to finance, Sinclair underlines, are "premised on utopian notions about markets and how they work", which presume markets to be "spontaneous and natural". None of these are helpful starting points for analysing the real world of global financial markets that are better understood as "social and historical forms of collective human interaction, created, supported, and governed by state and law" (Sinclair 2021: 67). The SFA approach rejected mainstream views that "markets reflect fundamental economic forces, which are not subject to human manipulation" (Sinclair 2005: 5). This was a key politicizing move in how to think about and "come at" global finance. Those approaches that sought to present and discuss financial matters as technical processes had to be countered; indeed, had to be politicized as embodying one contestable worldview.

The SFA illuminates these mundane practices within private market authorities, what drives them and how they are consequential for political economic outcomes. These constitute some of the key contributions that the SFA offers to understandings of world politics and twenty-first-century global capitalism. Chapters in this book apply the SFA to try to make sense of other institutions with increasingly significant roles in global finance, such as bond index providers. Gotoh, Gaillard and Michalek ask whether AI, as it transforms finance, may challenge CRAs afresh requiring them to demonstrate their "added value" in new ways. As scholars enquire into the future role for reputational intermediaries such as CRAs in a financial world increasingly dominated by AI, they would do well to deploy an SFA lens. Another more prominent aspect of global finance is the ecological dimension that the environmental, social and governance agenda reflects. At its most ambitious, this agenda seeks to ensure that every single dollar invested within global finance is not exacerbating climate change or nature loss. What is the role for CRAs in working out how financial market institutions and actors make sense of climate risks?

As the chapters of this book demonstrate, the SFA provides a platform, building blocks and key insights useful for a wide array of exciting explorations of the politics of global finance, and ideational and intersubjective dynamics shaping the role of private authority within global capitalism. Our aim is to honour Sinclair's legacy by showing how others can build on his amazing corpus of work.

References

Clift, B. 2023. *The Office for Budget Responsibility and the Politics of Technocratic Economic Governance*. Oxford: Oxford University Press.

James, S. 2024. "Special section introduction: epistemic politics in international and comparative political economy". *New Political Economy* 29 (6): 835–43.

2

CRAS AND THE IDEA OF HISTORY: THE ROLE OF SYNCHRONIC AND DIACHRONIC MENTAL FRAMEWORKS IN THE WORK OF TIMOTHY J. SINCLAIR

Randall Germain

Introduction: Timothy Sinclair and the idea of history

As a graduate of York University and working under the supervision of two leading scholars in the critical tradition of international political economy (IPE), Timothy J. Sinclair's research bore many of the hallmarks of this scholarship.[1] His work interrogates the conceptual and material anchors of world order and global governance, with a particular concern to outline, trace and track the role of private authority in the construction of governance. Credit rating agencies (CRAs) are his focus of choice, although he also considers debates on public debt, the role of banks and the question of creditworthiness and financial crises more generally. In his two most accomplished publications – *The New Masters of Capital* and *To the Brink of Destruction* – he locates his analytical framework in the constructivist, or what he later calls the social facts or social foundations tradition (Sinclair 2005: 12; 2021: 75–6; see also Chwieroth & Sinclair 2013: 459). In this chapter, I argue that Sinclair's embrace of these approaches is itself tethered to what Robert W. Cox calls the "historical mode of thought", which is a way of thinking about explanation and understanding in terms of a form of reasoning that is neither entirely rationalistic nor subjectivist. I suggest that the historical mode of thought is one way to engage with the idea of history, and that Sinclair uses it to consider how intersubjectivity defines institutional agency in relation to its material conditions of possibility. We can see the idea of history at work most clearly through his conceptual distinction between synchronic and diachronic mental frameworks and how these inform our understanding

1. Sinclair's supervisory committee included Stephen Gill and Robert W. Cox, both of whom are leading lights in the tradition of critical political economy. For considerations of their work within the disciplinary context of IPE, see Cohen (2008: 84–94) and Germain (2009).

of historical structures and the agency of institutions. Indeed, as I shall argue below, Sinclair's social foundations approach (SFA) to finance is predicated on his embrace of a Coxian-inspired historical mode of thought, even if Sinclair emphasizes features that Cox did not.

I consider Sinclair's engagement with the idea of history in three steps. First, I briefly outline what I see to be the intellectual inspiration for his turn to history, which combines insights from the work of Stephen Gill, Susan Strange and especially Robert W. Cox. It is the engagement with Cox above all that cements the importance of the synchronic/diachronic distinction for Sinclair's approach to IPE. Second, I trace the evolution of this distinction across a selection of his published works to detail the increasing analytical weight he places on this conceptual framing. Indeed, *To the Brink of Destruction* employs the synchronic/diachronic distinction as a critical factor in the institutional evolution of American CRAs, which Sinclair suggests led them to help generate the conditions of possibility for the global financial crisis (GFC) that began with the failure of two Bear Stearns hedge funds and the German bank IKB in the summer of 2007 (Germain 2010: 79–87). Third, I track the utility of Sinclair's use of the synchronic/diachronic distinction, both for his explanation of the changing role of CRAs and for the broader question of creditworthiness. I point to where he could have gone further to extend his application of the historical mode of thought in ways that might strengthen the claims he makes about the continuing epistemic authority of CRAs. Like many who have used the idea of history as a foundation for their analytical frameworks, Sinclair's engagement with the historical mode of thought is not without tensions and complexities, even as it stands as a testament to the necessity of thinking critically about social science in historical terms.

Formative influences: Gill, Strange and especially Cox

Although Sinclair cast a wide intellectual net in his scholarship, there is not much doubt that critical anchors of his approach came from the work of Gill, Strange and Cox. From Gill he took the insight that all institutions are grounded in material relations that require a historically sensitive form of analysis to understand. This version of historical materialism is a foundational element in all of Sinclair's early work, whether to understand the structural power of capital (Sinclair 1994b: 146), the changing international structure of authority (Sinclair 1995: 153), or the role of global elites (Sinclair 2000a: 186). What Sinclair seems to have appreciated most about Gill's historically-informed framework is the way it helps to capture the nuanced form of surveillance performed by CRAs, whose decisions radiate outwards to generate a kind of "panopticon" effect (Sinclair

2005: 8). CRAs are institutions that fit their "time", and when times shift their attributes also evolve. The attention Sinclair devoted to what CRAs actually did always included a healthy concern for what we might call their historicity.

From Strange, Sinclair drew inspiration from her depiction of how structural power was exercised in an almost unconscious manner in the contemporary period across a wide swathe of systemically important but nominally private institutions, including CRAs. One of the enduring puzzles that Sinclair pursued throughout his career concerns how rather obscure institutions are able to generate such profound governance effects. He found Strange's insights about power very compelling and returned to them throughout his career as a critical component of his analytical framework. He was especially impressed by her pioneering efforts to understand how knowledge and authority combined to produce structural power. In *The New Masters of Capital*, he insists that Strange's conception of knowledge fills an important gap in the scholarship on epistemic communities, most importantly by revealing how knowledge becomes "socially validated" (Sinclair 2005: 60; cf. Sinclair 1994b: 142–3). He often suggested that her focus on the fusion of knowledge with power complemented other structural accounts that might otherwise partially obscure the role of agency and institutions in social life (e.g. Sinclair 2021: 71).[2]

But it is the work of Cox that occupies the most prominent place in Sinclair's intellectual universe. This is evident from his introductory chapter to Cox's volume *Approaches to World Order*, where he provides one of the earliest and most complete overviews of Cox's method of historical structures (Sinclair 1996; cf. Mittelman 1998; Schechter 2002; Germain 2013). Indeed, as I note below, this is the first time he unpacks the Coxian distinction between synchronic and diachronic modes of understanding, which forms an important part of the bedrock for his later engagement with the idea of history. And he accurately captures in this chapter Cox's debt to a historicist intellectual tradition that is absolutely central to his framework of historical structures, but which predates his better known engagement with Gramsci (Sinclair 1996: 6–8; cf. Mittelman 1998: 66; Germain 2016: 542; cf. Cox 1983/1996). What Sinclair found attractive in Cox's work is precisely the idea of history as a critical form of reasoning, as a mode of thought, which helps to reveal where existing relationships and institutional

2. Interestingly, in the "Beyond Paradigms" workshop on the scholarship of Timothy J. Sinclair, where this chapter was first presented, several participants spoke about his uncanny ability to include references to both Strange and Cox in almost every seminar they took with him over their graduate educations. In part, Sinclair was drawn to the work of Gill, Strange and Cox because for him they spoke to his early career experience of working in the New Zealand Treasury, where he recalled first encountering what he later understood to be "unconscious" power (Sinclair 2005: xi).

configurations are open to contestation and challenge in terms not only of fundamental material relations, but also from rival collective images of social order and identities, or what Cox calls "intersubjectivities". This is where he ends his updated view of Cox's method of historical structures *redux*, and we can see this at work across the arc of his career (Sinclair 2016: 518–19).[3]

The idea of history and synchronic versus diachronic mental frameworks

It is the case that the idea of history was not immediately visible as a key attribute of Sinclair's research on CRAs and global governance. Indeed, his earliest publications do not venture much beyond the injunction to incorporate an historical perspective as a necessary element of critical analysis (Sinclair 1994a, 1994b, 2001b). For example, in his introduction to Cox's 1996 collection of essays *Approaches to World Order* (Sinclair 1996), he touches for the first time on the distinction between synchronic and diachronic forms of understanding in relation to Cox's framework of historical structures. The synchronic "moment" holds a focus on the internal coherence among ensembles of ideas, institutions and their associated material capabilities, while the diachronic "moment" looks for dynamic tensions and contradictions within spheres of activity that might undermine such coherence (Sinclair 1996: 8–10). He notes that this distinction is critical to Cox's deep sense of historicism, and that it operates not only at the level of epistemology and knowledge but also in Cox's ontology and especially in his methodology of historical structures (Sinclair 1996: 14). In effect this engagement is a marker for Sinclair's later application of the idea of history, and it clearly identifies the synchronic/diachronic distinction as part of Cox's approach to world order (cf. Sinclair 2016: 518).

The first application of the synchronic/diachronic distinction to his own research can be found in his contribution to the volume *Approaches to Global Governance Theory* (Sinclair 1999b). While noting Cox's use of synchronic and diachronic in relation to understanding world order, Sinclair also considers this distinction as part of the study of language by Ferdinand de Saussure and elaborates on novel applications of it by social critics such as Georges Sorel and Jean Piaget (Sinclair 1999b: 162–3). The key move Sinclair makes is to connect this distinction to mentalities, which he suggests are anchored in the contemporary era to the principle of the self-regulating market, a reluctance to accept actual historical limitations to social and economic organization, or what we might

3. Sinclair used and engaged with Cox's work throughout his entire career, and this professional engagement was mirrored in their long and warm personal relationship that shared both intellectual triumphs and private adversity.

call a form of idealist thinking, and a tendency to atomize individuals by downplaying their social connections (Sinclair 1999b: 163–4). He argues that late twentieth-century global governance has become "synchronic" in its formulation, reliant on an "infrastructure of the commonplace" that is fused in turn with an intersubjective mental framework which accepts existing arrangements (and their associated institutions) as the only possible choice for economic and political organization. But Sinclair argues that this is problematic as a basis for understanding the deep-seated changes affecting contemporary societies. Instead, we need a much more dynamic and diachronic understanding of global governance, able to identify and respond to the new risks posed by disruptive technologies and economic developments (Sinclair 1999b: 169). Sinclair's use here mirrors Cox's use of this distinction, which parallels the contrast between problem solving and critical theory, where the former takes existing institutions and their arrangements as given, while the latter investigates their points of tension and/or contradiction (e.g. Cox 1981/1996: 100). Here Sinclair is pointing towards how the synchronic/diachronic distinction can be used as a mental framework of understanding, or in other words as a mode of thought.

The historical grounding of this conceptual framework became clearer as Sinclair's research on private authority and credit rating evolved. In a clutch of publications at the turn of the millennium, the idea of a mental framework as a critical feature for understanding the role of institutions gained traction in his work. Like Cox, he continues to distinguish between problem solving and critical theory, using the synchronic/diachronic distinction as a proxy, such as when he observes that CRAs promote the "polar opposite" of thinking about knowledge and authority as socially embedded constructs: CRAs elevate technique and instrumental calculation as a form of knowledge capable of generating actionable risk assessments of future (financial) behaviour (Sinclair 2000a: 163). Their role in extending the framework of international capital mobility he further likened to a rival "collective image" of how the world works, which of course helps to consolidate their own institutional conditions of possibility (Sinclair 2001b: 104–5; cf. Sinclair 2000a: 186). In *The New Masters of Capital*, he articulated this way of connecting the idea of history as a mode of thought to CRAs by identifying what he labels as their "mental framework of rating orthodoxy" (Sinclair 2005: 50). These were the operational principles by which CRAs arrived at their judgements, and they could take either synchronic or diachronic form (Sinclair 2005: 70). To understand what they do, we have to understand how they "see" the world *qua* agents, which is through a "mental schemata" of rating orthodoxy (cf. Chwieroth & Sinclair 2013: 459).

The value of using mental frameworks as a key part of the *explanans* of CRAs is precisely that it recognizes and tracks how institutions view their environment and advance their interests within the context of that environment. Sinclair's explanatory account of CRAs builds on his identification of them as social institutions whose intersubjective sensibility – the collective image held by stakeholders of their institution's role and purpose – holds the key to the epistemic authority they possess and wield (cf. Chwieroth & Sinclair 2013: 458). Sinclair defines CRAs as a very specific type of institution: their purpose is to provide credible and authoritative assessments about the likelihood of repayment of financial assets under set conditions. He identifies their core intersubjectivity as a "mental framework of rating orthodoxy", which he suggests promotes "an American-derived, synchronic mental framework" (Sinclair 2005: 71). But the key takeaway to understand about them as actors is not the singular effect of any individual rating that they might produce, whatever its accuracy. Rather, the critical consequence of the actions of CRAs lies in the system-wide repercussions of their authority, which infiltrates and affects nearly all institutions involved in holding and using debt. As he argues in *The New Masters of Capital*, the "adjustment of mental schemata is the most consequential impact of their work" (Sinclair 2005: 71).[4] It is not so much the behaviour of CRAs that should command our attention; rather, it is how others see their purpose within the broader global political economy that is critical to comprehend. For Sinclair, CRAs had become nothing less than "private makers of global public policy" (Sinclair 2005: 71).

Sinclair's arguments about the significance of CRAs are perhaps his most important contribution to IPE scholarship. His research here makes visible a previously unheralded set of institutions and suggests that scholars need to pay attention to them not so much because of what they themselves produce – ratings on debt issued in capital markets – but because of how others view them and adapt their activities to conform to the operational principles of CRAs, including their "mental schemata". As an integral element of the international organization of capital under conditions of extensive cross-border mobility, CRAs represent a new locus of authority about the veracity of capital, and therefore a new constellation of power. Understanding how this constellation of power is organized requires a form of knowledge that is sensitive to its operational norms and framing. This is where the connection between the synchronic/diachronic distinction and mental frameworks has proven its value.

But this connection was also used by Sinclair in other avenues of his research. It makes a brief appearance, for example, in his 2012 book *Global Governance*, in a discussion about how families are responding to climate change by shifting

4. In his last major publication Sinclair phrases this point in the following manner: "This (social foundations) approach to understanding the agencies suggests that the source of their power is not just the immediate coercive effect on the cost of borrowing, *but their broader impact on ideas and on confidence in markets, institutions, and governments* [emphasis added]" (Sinclair 2021: 75).

their worldviews from short-term to long-term ways of thinking, which are associated with synchronic versus diachronic temporal templates (Sinclair 2012a: 145). In a more systematic vein, in a book co-authored with Lena Rethel (and also published in 2012), the synchronic/diachronic distinction is employed to help account for the differentiation between regulative versus constitutive rules that govern banks (Rethel & Sinclair 2012: 22–9). Regulative rules are those that align banking practices within certain parameters considered in terms of prudential and efficiency metrics. They prescribe behaviour but do not drive its dynamics and are an example of a synchronic logic of rule-making. Constitutive rules, on the other hand, generate behaviour by sanctioning the purposes to which banks as financial institutions may be directed. They consider behaviour in terms of purpose, often allowing for flexibility of means through which this might be achieved. Because this is a developmental approach – focusing on origins and evolution – Rethel and Sinclair identify such rules as exhibiting a diachronic logic. The synchronic/diachronic distinction here reinforces a purpose-led investigation of banks and banking regulation, which calls for more attention to be paid to the social role that banks play in the broader organization of capital, and not simply to how they act to produce a profit (Rethel & Sinclair 2012: 128–30).

In two of his more recent publications, the synchronic/diachronic distinction becomes central to the explanatory account of CRAs. In a 2017 article co-authored with Fumihito Gotoh, American CRAs are indelibly associated with a synchronic form of finance, which is short term in outlook and decoupled from what they identify as the "real" economy (Gotoh & Sinclair 2017: 1041).[5] A synchronic "mental framework" is part of the current DNA of American CRAs. Gotoh and Sinclair contrast this with Japanese banks and Japan's financial system more generally, both of which they characterize as diachronic in orientation, meaning that they are organized to promote long-term interests, and most importantly to connect financial activity to the "real" economy (Gotoh & Sinclair 2017: 1042). They conclude that the synchronic logic of American CRAs, and indeed American finance more broadly, is not as deeply entrenched globally as is often suggested (Gotoh & Sinclair 2017: 1047). For Gotoh and Sinclair, the

5. The term "real" economy is often associated with those economic activities that generate goods and services that are directly consumed and/or used as inputs for other goods and services. Finance directed towards the real economy is often long-term in duration and directed towards productive assets, whether as long-term debt or foreign direct investment. Gotoh and Sinclair contrast this with financial activity directed towards short-term buying and selling of financial assets (Gotoh & Sinclair 2017: 1041). It should be noted that in practice the distinction between the real economy and the financial or "symbolic" economy is very difficult to track clearly (Drucker 1986: 781–6; cf. Sawyer 2013).

synchronic/diachronic distinction does heavy analytical work to ground institutional behaviour to mental frameworks.

And in his follow-up volume to *The New Masters of Capital*, which asks how and why American CRAs continue to occupy an integral place in the global organization of capital, Sinclair further refines the synchronic/diachronic distinction as it applies to the intersubjective sensibilities of American CRAs. *To the Brink of Destruction* argues that the principal reason why American CRAs were associated with the 2007–09 global financial crisis (GFC) involves a wholesale recalibration of their mental framework of rating orthodoxy. Rating has always been an exercise of judgement rather than a technique of analysis, and the purpose to which American CRAs directed their judgements did a 180-degree pivot in the early years of the new millennium. The uncertainty and disruption caused by financial innovation in capital markets led the "Big Three" CRAs (Moody's, Standard and Poor's (S&P) and now Fitch) to abandon their historic role as neutral arbiters of debt and to become instead advisers on how best to issue and structure debt using newly configured financial techniques and instruments. In Sinclair's terminology, their inner sense of purpose shifted from a conservative and diachronic gatekeeping sensibility to a market-making synchronic sensibility (Sinclair 2021: 41–2). Whereas historically the big American CRAs had kept a certain distance between themselves and what they rated, after the 2001 Enron debacle they themselves became deeply involved in the process of financial engineering, helping to create the very debt instruments that they would subsequently rate and profit from. This shift in institutional intersubjectivity put the business model and franchise of American CRAs at extreme risk and directly implicated them in the GFC (Sinclair 2021: 132).

Sinclair's later configuration of the synchronic/diachronic distinction at work in the mental schemata of CRAs modified his earlier account in *The New Masters of Capital*, where CRAs were seen to possess a mental framework of rating orthodoxy that aligned to the organizational principles of American finance. Both, he insisted in the earlier volume, were synchronic in form. But a decade and a half later, in *To the Brink of Destruction*, he revised this to argue that during most of the post-1945 period, American CRAs (most importantly Moody's and S&P; Fitch did not become a major CRA until the 1990s) in fact held a conservative and diachronic mental framework of rating, which allowed them a certain "distance" from the organizations they rated (Sinclair 2021: 61, 85). It was this distance that ensured their judgements were authoritative and beyond reproach, even if on occasion they proved to be incorrect. But this changed after 2001 to become synchronic in form. This historical sensitivity to the evolution of institutional intersubjectivity within CRAs allows Sinclair subsequently to explain why CRAs put their franchise at risk, how they helped to facilitate the GFC, and how they survived intact and even, on some metrics, now play an even more central role in the international organization of capital. This highlights how the synchronic/diachronic distinction came to occupy a crucial place in Sinclair's analytical framework, capable of shouldering significant analytical weight in his explanation of the centrality of CRAs and their particular form of private authority. But it is not without tensions, which I consider below.

I have detailed in this section the evolution of Sinclair's engagement with and use of the synchronic/diachronic distinction, from his earliest to his most recent publications. I have linked this distinction to the idea of history as a mode of thought, most importantly by considering how it informs a critical element of his "mental frameworks of rating orthodoxy". This is an innovative adaptation from Cox's earlier use of the synchronic/diachronic distinction, where it was associated with his well-known contrast between problem solving and critical theory. Sinclair extends Cox's use by emphasizing the utility of the synchronic/diachronic distinction to account for mental frameworks that reflect institutional intersubjective sensibilities. This is where he adds value to Cox's framework of historical structures even as he differentiates a Coxian approach from what by now he called a SFA. Both are of course deeply historical in outlook and orientation, but Sinclair provides a much more granular analysis of institutional form than does Cox.[6] In the next section I ask how effective Sinclair's deployment of the historical mode of thought is for his aim to understand a slightly broader question, namely the theoretical and empirical features of creditworthiness.

Mental frameworks, creditworthiness and CRAs: the value of using the idea of history in social science

Through much of the past 150 years, access to credit has run primarily through banks, which acted as intermediaries to credit in a multitude of ways. Consequentially, creditworthiness has been largely considered in terms of banks and banking systems. Where banks are well capitalized, prudently run and effectively regulated, credit is made available to the economy in a relatively stable and predictable manner. Conversely, when banks stretch their margins, chase returns or try to arbitrage regulatory gaps, financial degradation and crises often

6. Cox of course undertook an in-depth analysis of the International Labor Organization as an institution of American hegemony (Cox 1977/1996), but he is best known for his Gramscian approach to world order more generally, which eschews such detailed analysis of singular institutions (Cox 1983/1996, 1987). We might say the same of Gill and Strange, who despite some very detailed institutional analyses were primarily known for their general approaches to IPE and American hegemony (Gill 1990, 1993a, 1993b; Strange 1987, 1988). In contrast, Sinclair's work was more often grounded in governance processes that were empirically embedded in identifiable institutions.

follow. To investigate creditworthiness under such circumstances is above all to investigate institutions that facilitate financial intermediation, primarily banks (cf. Rethel & Sinclair 2012).

But over the past four decades disintermediation has profoundly altered the functioning of global capital markets, and banks are now merely one of many guardians to credit. Understanding creditworthiness now requires more than shining a spotlight on banks and other non-bank financial institutions. It also requires scholars to explore the role of institutions, which neither have their own capital to deploy nor stand at the nexus of savers and borrowers in the manner of banks. We inhabit a world of disintermediation, where those with capital can look to third-party verification for the certainty of repayment that might unlock their investments. This is what makes CRAs such important institutions today, because they are significant gatekeepers to credit in a world characterized by deep capital markets, international capital mobility and uncertainty over returns on capital. The question of creditworthiness, in other words, has shifted to include institutions other than banks as part of the research agenda.

Where Sinclair's research diverges from much other research in economics, political science and IPE is precisely to locate a significant decision-making apparatus of creditworthiness in a specialized, even unique type of institution. One reason for this is his insistence that financial systems are not efficient markets on their own terms, operating seamlessly under given circumstances. As he continually reminds us throughout both *The New Masters of Capital* and *To the Brink of Destruction*, financial systems are not like ice cream machines and car engines, which are designed to operate independently of their surroundings. Neither machine is designed to shape its environment, whereas certain kinds of financial institutions, such as CRAs, have outsized and cumulative effects on their environment over time. Financial systems and markets are subject to endogenous dynamics that arise out of institutional imperatives (Sinclair 2010d: 95). Such institutions need to be studied in terms of the reciprocity at work between them and their terrain of activity, in terms of their social relations.

A second way in which Sinclair's research is distinguished from other accounts is his further insistence that institutional imperatives are not simply the product of abstract and unchanging preferences; rather, they evolve out of the ways in which institutions and the decision makers that direct them "see" the world around them. Institutions are not mechanistic agents that react to their surroundings automatically. They continuously interpret their surroundings as social facts, with an active and reciprocal feedback loop that both alters and navigates this environment. Chwieroth and Sinclair (2013: 466) point to such "collective intentionality" as a critical feature of the "social facts" perspective, or what Sinclair subsequently called the "social foundations" approach: "This puts the focus not so much on what agencies do, but rather on what people observe and collectively agree they are doing" (Sinclair 2021: 81). The question of creditworthiness, then, becomes defined by the institutions that impact access to credit and capital, among which are CRAs.

I want to suggest that Sinclair privileges agency as the decisional location for the question of creditworthiness because he tethers his SFA to the idea of history as a mode of thought. Here he follows Cox's method of historical structures, which ironically, given its nomenclature, actually defines structure in important ways in terms of institutional form, the most important of which is the state (Cox 1987: 399; cf. Germain 2013: 193).[7] Like Cox, Sinclair pays particular attention to the reciprocal connections between institutions and their environment. Such reciprocity is a paramount reason for considering the constitutive nature of ordering principles that in turn affect the environment for all institutions in a given context: these emerge out of institutional interactions where authority and knowledge flow from privileged institutions and can have system-wide effects (Rethel & Sinclair 2012: 23–4; Chweiroth & Sinclair 2013: 474; Sinclair 2021: 81, 192–4). The key deliberative processes, however, are both located in institutions and are equal parts interpretive and judgemental: institutions make (or fail to make) decisions that reflect their sense of collective identity and self-understanding; in a word their intersubjectivity. This process is grounded historically and needs to be recognized as such.

There are two key strengths to this intellectual anchorage. First, as noted above, it allows Sinclair to connect institutions to their environment through what might be considered their most important deliberative feature, namely the mental frameworks that flow from their dominant sense of intersubjective beliefs. These are always amalgams of multiple intersecting pressures and are often highly contested by the social agents who are constituent stakeholders in an institution. But the key feature to emphasize is that these connections are visible as historical evidence, as products of their deliberations. They leave a record that can be rendered visible through the traditional techniques of social science research, such as interviews, triangulation of documentary evidence and analysis of publicly available economic and commercial data. When this record is put into dialogue with deliberative processes, we can follow the outputs and consider the explanatory power of competing accounts. This provides a rich narrative of causation that is contextualized appropriately to the environment under investigation. And this is exactly how Sinclair pursues his analysis in *To*

7. Gill and Strange could also be interpreted as grounding their understanding of structure in institutional forms, whether in terms of the "new constitutionalism" (Gill 1995) or the durability of *American* hegemony (Strange 1987, 1989/2002).

the Brink of Destruction: he triangulates Congressional testimony, interviews and secondary data analysis to arrive at his conclusions about the changing constitutive role played by CRAs in the international organization of capital over the past two decades.

The second strength is that this use of the idea of history can track and chart distinct changes in the prevailing mental frameworks, which are constitutive of institutional intersubjectivity. By making institutional mental frameworks a chief target of research on CRAs, Sinclair is sensitive to important changes in how they "see" the world. This focus on change is of course a hallmark of the tradition of critical IPE and serves to focus Sinclair's research concerns at multiple levels. CRAs have become important institutions of private authority because of the gathering disintermediation of the global financial system, which is a marked departure in the global organization of finance. The activities of CRAs reflect this change, but they also drive it by virtue of the systemic effects of their behaviour over the past two decades. Indeed, Sinclair lays significant blame on CRAs for the 2007–09 GFC, given that their pivot after the Enron debacle in 2001 laid the groundwork for the systemic disruption of new financial technologies and assets such as structured finance. Big Three support for the financial engineering of these assets played an indispensable role by introducing to an unsuspecting world a level of volatility that was in fact unprecedented (Sinclair 2021: 132). This focus on change at the endogenous, institutional level is a genuine strength of Sinclair's use of the idea of history to help understand how mental frameworks guide the actions of CRAs.

At the same time, there is a curious tension in the evolution of Sinclair's approach to the question of mental frameworks of rating orthodoxy. In *The New Masters of Capital*, Sinclair argues that CRAs were driven by a synchronic framework of rating orthodoxy that was seeping into the global financial system by virtue of the increasingly constitutive role played by American CRAs. These agencies both reflected their environment and expanded their organization and operation: they inhabited an "American-derived synchronic mental framework" (Sinclair 2005: 71) and as such were an important part of the evolving structure of *American* hegemony. But only 15 years later this conclusion is recast. In *To the Brink of Destruction*, Sinclair argues that throughout much of the post-1945 period, American CRAs had in fact acted through the mental schemata of a diachronic worldview; they were conservative, distanced from their clients and able to assess and issue ratings based upon a set of principles that were diachronically informed, for instance, focused on a longer term of investment and geared towards the productive economy (Sinclair 2021: 44). For a variety of reasons their environment changed and they responded in ways which he suggests imperilled their franchise. But the idea that CRAs possessed a "diachronic" mental framework is at odds with his earlier identification of them as possessing an "American-derived" framework that was synchronic through and through. This is a surprising reversal of his earlier account, and points to the complexity of making mental frameworks the singular fulcrum for explanation in social science research.

Rather than introduce a backward-looking reversal of the type of mental framework at work within CRAs, Sinclair would have been on stronger grounds if he had introduced a graduated scale into his use of the synchronic/diachronic distinction. Much like Cox uses this distinction, Sinclair tends to think about it in binary, mutually exclusive terms. But there is no necessary argument for such a binary view. Why not instead conceive of the synchronic/diachronic distinction in terms of a continuum rather than as a mutually exclusive set of attributes? Indeed, this is much more in tune with the idea of history as an exercise in reasoned interpretation of the historical record, informed by multiple points of engagement and open to differences of kind as well as degree. Sinclair had already flagged the benefits of such a non-binary approach in his revised consideration of Cox's method of historical structures, which includes a tighter nesting of problem-solving research within critical or diachronic processes (Sinclair 2016: 518).

Even more importantly, if Sinclair had taken a further step, sometimes associated with those who build on the idea of history as part of the framework of social science, he might have argued that what appeared to be an "American-derived synchronic mental framework" in 2005 – based on research conducted largely prior to Enron's collapse in 2001 – in fact looks very different from the vantage point of 2021.[8] The pivot of the Big Three in their collective intentionality redefined their institutional mental frameworks of rating orthodoxy, but not in a way that necessarily undermines his earlier characterization. It is entirely possible to understand the mental schemata of CRAs as moving from one synchronic outlook to another but built around modified collective images of the dynamics now in force post-Enron. It is not a question of one or the other mental schemata, but of two different types out of a much larger universe of mental schemata. The point here is that the vantage point of engagement is a key attribute of the idea of history considered in terms of a mode of thought, and Sinclair's occlusion of this important consideration restricts his judgement of the types of mental frameworks operative in CRAs over time. It suggests that assessing the constitutive role of CRAs in the international organization of capital requires not only an account of the relationship between CRAs and their broader environment but needs also to include an account of the vantage point of the researcher. To incorporate the idea of history into one's scholarly framework is to be sensitive to shifts in historical points of engagement alongside all of the other social

8. I have explored some of these attributes in relation to Cox's work in Germain (2016).

conditions that Sinclair so correctly identifies. Indeed, we might say that it necessarily historicizes the SFA itself.[9]

Conclusion: mental frameworks and the idea of history

Sinclair's research makes visible a previously neglected set of institutions that came to wield considerable power within the international organization of capital. I suggest that his work provides us with the tools to understand why these institutions wield power, what kind of power they exercise and how it works. He came to call his approach a SFA, which built on recent advances in constructivist and critical scholarship. But it was also inextricably tethered to the idea of history as a mode of thought, which is a research paradigm, or perhaps more accurately a tradition of thinking about social research, which is rarely invoked in the social sciences. He came to this tradition primarily through an engagement with the scholarship of Cox, especially his distinction between a synchronic and diachronic form of analysis. This places Sinclair very firmly in the tradition of critical IPE scholarship, although he also ranged further afield in his intellectual foraging. The key point I would emphasize in relation to my reading of Sinclair, however, is that the historical mode of thought was an integral feature of his research and found expression in his use of mental frameworks as a core frame of reference to understand CRAs and their increasingly constitutive role on the international organization of capital. I believe this lends an enduring quality to his scholarly contributions about CRAs more generally.

On a broader level, Sinclair's research has much to offer social science by virtue of his ability to put three core features of social life into dialogue with each other: a focus on institutions, intersubjectivity and disruptive change. His adaptation of the Coxian synchronic/diachronic distinction helps to locate how mental frameworks align with broader social arrangements and drive institutions to act in particular ways. But Sinclair could also have usefully incorporated a gradient into this distinction, perhaps by considering how mental frameworks do not exclusively capture the collective imagination of an institution but are rather contested both within and against competing rival images. Like much else in our social world, they are not for the most part mutually exclusive. A more permissive appreciation of how mental schemata operate might have led Sinclair to relax his claim about the 180-degree pivot for the constitutive role played by CRAs in the lead up to the GFC. He is entirely correct to centre institutions in his

9. Curiously, Figure 1 in chapter 3 does not include a visual representation of time as a factor in the explanatory frameworks that Sinclair considers, which is unfortunate given the bedrock role played by the idea of history in his work that I have traced in this chapter (Sinclair 2021: 74).

analysis, but it is rare for them to pivot quite so suddenly and dramatically. It is more likely that multiple factors were at play as their authoritative role gathered strength over the past decades, and further research would undoubtedly have pointed this out had he been able to undertake it.[10]

References

Blyth, M. (ed.) 2009. *Routledge Handbook of International Political Economy*. Abingdon: Routledge.

Cohen, B. 2008. *International Political Economy: An Intellectual History*. Princeton, NJ: Princeton University Press.

Cox, R. W. 1977/1996. "Labor and hegemony". In *Approaches to World Order*, R. Cox & T. J. Sinclair, 420–70. Cambridge: Cambridge University Press.

Cox, R. W. 1981/1996. "Social forces, states and world orders: beyond international relations theory". In *Approaches to World Order*, R. W. Cox & T. J. Sinclair, 85–123.

Cox, R. W. 1983/1996. "Gramsci, hegemony and international relations: an essay in method". In *Approaches to World Order*, R. W. Cox & T. J. Sinclair, 124–43.

Cox, R. W. 1987. *Production, Power and World Order: Social Forces in the Making of History*. New York: Columbia University Press.

Cox, R. W. (with Timothy J. Sinclair) 1996. *Approaches to World Order*. Cambridge: Cambridge University Press.

Drucker, P. 1986. "The changed world economy". *Foreign Affairs* 64 (4): 768–91.

Germain, R. 2009. "Of margins, traditions, and engagements: a brief disciplinary history of IPE in Canada". In *Routledge Handbook of International Political Economy*, M. Blyth (ed.), 77–91. Abingdon: Routledge.

Germain, R. 2010. Global Politics and Financial Governance. New York: Palgrave.

Germain, R. 2013. "The making of IR/IPE: Robert W. Cox's *Production, Power and World Order*". In *Classics of International Relations*, H. Bliddal, C. Sylvest & P. Wilson (eds), 187–96. Abingdon: Routledge.

Germain, R. 2016. "Robert W. Cox and the idea of history: political economy as philosophy". *Globalizations* 13 (5): 1–15.

Gill, S. 1990. *American Hegemony and the Trilateral Commission*. Cambridge: Cambridge University Press.

Gill, S. (ed.) 1993a. *Gramsci, Historical Materialism and International Relations*. Cambridge: Cambridge University Press.

Gill, S. 1993b. "Epistemology, ontology, and the 'Italian School'". In *Gramsci, Historical Materialism and International Relations*, Gill (ed.), 21–48.

Gill, S. 1995. "Globalization, market civilization and disciplinary neoliberalism". *Millennium* 24 (3): 399–423.

Mittelman, J. 1998. "Coxian historicism as an alternative perspective in International Studies". *Alternatives: Global, Local, Political* 23 (1): 63–92.

10. This chapter benefited from comments received at the workshop on "Beyond Paradigms: Timothy J. Sinclair's Social Foundations of Global Finance", held 27 June 2023 at the University of Warwick. It has also been strengthened by responding to constructive feedback from Chris Clarke, Ben Clift, Fumihito Gotoh, Katie Lavalle, Robert O'Brien and Dan Wood. It represents a career's worth of engagement with Sinclair's work and ideas that began with our shared experience as doctoral students at York University, extended across our overlapping research agendas, and deepened over three decades of comradeship and mutual respect. He is still dearly missed.

Sawyer, M. 2013. "What is financialization?" *International Journal of Political Economy* 42 (4): 5–18.

Schechter, M. 2002. "Critiques of Coxian theory: background to a conversation". In *The Political Economy of a Plural World*, R. W. Cox, 1–25.

Strange, S. 1987/2002. "The persistent myth of lost hegemony". In *Authority and Markets: Susan Strange's Writings on International Political Economy*, R. Tooze & C. May (eds), 121–40. Basingstoke: Palgrave Macmillan.

Strange, S. 1988. *States and Markets: An Introduction to International Political Economy*. London: Pinter.

Strange, S. 1989/2002. "Towards a theory of transnational empire". In *Authority and Markets*, R. Tooze & C. May (eds), 141–56. Basingstoke: Palgrave Macmillan

3
TIM SINCLAIR'S ICONOCLASTIC RELATIONSHIP WITH MARXISM

Magnus Ryner

September 1989, Toronto, Ontario, Canada in one of the seminar rooms of the brutalist Ross Building, situated in suburban sprawl: After a gap year interrailing in an eastern Europe where communism is crumbling, various volunteer work projects and some genuine blue-collar work in the Purolator sorting depot in Winnipeg, I am excited to be starting my Masters' degree. It is the first seminar with my intellectual hero Robert W. Cox, through whose work I had discovered that you could do International Relations with Gramsci. The topic is Wallerstein's world systems theory. We rehearse the usual strengths and weaknesses. In a group where PhD students predominate, I dare to speak up about the "abstract" nature of Laclau's critique. I immediately face pushback and a Quebecois PhD student, clearly versed in the subtleties of the French structuralist movement, demands that I explain what I mean. In an exchange that includes words such as "overdetermination", "interpellation", "articulation" and "mode of production" versus "social formation", I think I manage to scrape out a draw (a pre-Foucaldian William Walters, still a Marxist then, mutters that we have ignored Robert Brenner). Just then, someone at the other end of the room pipes up in an antipodean accent that "we shouldn't talk in that sort of language". Cox had been stone-faced like the sphinx in the debate, but this draws a wry smile from him – a big fan of E. P. Thompson's anti-structuralist polemic *The Poverty of Theory*. I have just been introduced to Tim Sinclair.

The group adjourned to the graduate student pub afterwards. This was just the first of many iterations of seminars followed by pub visits over the next two years. Tim and I and some others (including Robert O'Brien and Hélène Pellerin) would thereby become fellow travellers through the fields of international relations, international political economy and comparative political economy. Then came comprehensive examinations, research designs, our first conference experiences, vivas, postdocs, job interviews, first posts, and so on. I will forever remember Tim's delicious combination of gruffness, sense of irony and humour, sharp intellect, ability to mediate seemingly irreconcilable contradictions – intellectual and lived ones – and immense generosity and heart of gold.

I remember Tim as an iconoclast of all theoretical traditions. It is therefore completely fitting that he ended up at the Department of Politics and International Studies (PAIS) at the University of Warwick at a time when Susan Strange was still a dominant force there. If we dare to suggest that Warwick at the time was developing a "research programme" wherein Strange exercised leadership, Tim fitted right in. Tim agreed with Strange that the emergence of IPE as a field of inquiry coincided with the development of a radically new globalized world, which required a radical reconsideration of categories and paradigmatic boundaries in the social sciences. This remained a running thread of Tim's throughout his career – as acknowledged in his inclusion in Sil and Katzenstein's (2010) textbook on political analysis "beyond paradigms" (118–25). And finance, the power of knowledge and private authority were central to it all. It was time to wake up and realize that the world had changed. This included, as Strange (1994) had pointed out, neorealism. But it also included Marxism, or perhaps more to the point neo-Marxism, which despite all differences, shared with neorealism a reified conception of the state that was quite out of place in the new times. Related to this was the more fundamental problem – whether it emanated from Louis Althusser or Kenneth Waltz – a reification of the concept of "structure" itself (Sinclair 2016).

In this chapter I explore Tim's iconoclastic relationship with Marxism and how this changed over time. In doing so, I focus on what could be called his (*very*) early work and how it relates to his mature work on bond rating agencies. In interpreting that work, I am aided by the many conversations we had as graduate students and early career academics.

At first glance, this pursuit might seem fanciful. Tim's "social foundations perspective" that gives primacy to the "ideational" and the "intersubjective" is hardly Marxist. True, Sinclair was a disciple of the heterodox historical materialist Robert W. Cox, but it is clearly more the Weberian rather than Gramscian strands of the latter's work that animated Tim. Is there really anything more to say about this than the fact that Sinclair studied in the Graduate Programme at York University in Toronto, which coincidentally happened to be a Marxist hotbed – but most emphatically not only that – in the late 1980s and early 1990s? Tracing back the lineages of the work on bond rating agencies for which he is known to his early work as a graduate student, this chapter argues that there is. In some respects, the conceptual backbone of his work can be read as a – conscious or unconscious – critical debate with Marxism that can be traced back to his Masters' thesis on Marxist theories on the so-called "relative autonomy" of the state. In other respects, Sinclair's substantive analysis retains strong Marxist strands. What are the "new masters of capital" but Milibandian elite networks representing the interests of the capitalist ruling class? Furthermore, his late work, expressing scepticism towards the prospects of regulating finance after the global financial crisis echoes Claus Offe's thesis on the limited capacity of the capitalist state to regulate the economic sub-system in the capitalist mode of production.

Ideal-typical analysis of a "limited totality": the case of bond rating agencies

Tim's work reached a broader audience in the very first issue of the *Review of International Political Economy* (RIPE) (Sinclair 1994b). It presented the original framing of his PhD thesis and some preliminary conclusions based on the interviews that he had started to conduct with bond rating agencies. There are no obvious traces to a Marxist framing in this article. The focus for Tim is not capital or class in any essential sense. Rather, the focus is on the problem of *information bottlenecks* that render the production of *knowledge* an essential determinant of authority. Bond rating agencies become agents of such authority because in an increasingly global, but above all disintermediated, financial system they produce and frame knowledge that connects creditors with debtors. Connecting up with the post-functionalist work of Rosenau (1992), he therefore considered these agencies as symptomatic of a private form of "post-Westphalian" transnational "governance without government". With a clear constructivist inflection, his work suggests that the partially contingent ideas that bond rating agencies, as an elite network with a clear framework of intersubjective meaning have about what makes a debtor credit-worthy, is a determinant with independent causal power that does not merely reflect material interests. Here, he noted a parallel between what he took from Rosenau and what others had taken from Foucault (Miller & Rose 1990). His subsequent work emanating in his magnum opus (Sinclair 2005), which was underpinned with an impressive amount of empirical research – not the least in the form of elite interviews – provided substantiation of that basic position.

There is also very little by way of traces of Marxism in Tim's methodology. His introductory chapter in *Approaches to World Order* – the volume that compiled Cox's key articles and which Tim edited – is highly instructive in that regard (Sinclair 1996). In that chapter, he explicitly states that he regards his work on bond rating agencies as an application of Cox's "method of historic structures". In accord with Strange's sentiment that IPE in a globalized world requires radical departures, Tim considers Cox's method as "unique" and that it "has not been matched elsewhere" (Sinclair 1996: 8). But what does he understand this method to be? He is explicit that this is not primarily about Cox's adaptation of Gramsci; he considers this less innovative as others have written on that too. Rather, the "flexibility" and "adaptability" of Cox's method is due to Cox's "willingness to sample from discordant intellectual traditions". In particular, he stresses Cox's adaptation of Weber's "ideal type method in dissecting ontological constructs". This enables "synchronic" analysis as a "vehicle through which a much more thoroughgoing understanding of intersubjectively constituted entities can be achieved". This is then a "gateway" to "diachronic" analysis where the limitations, contradictions and conflicts that may generate change of those ontological constructs can be identified (Sinclair 1996: 10). Thereby, reification of structure can be avoided as its components can be unpacked and historicized (Sinclair 2016). The relations grasped by this ideal-typical analysis are to be understood as explicitly delineated "limited totalities" that do not incorporate everything but that, in Cox's words, represent "a particular sphere of human activity in its historically located totality". Diachronic analysis then juxtaposes and connects historical structures in related spheres (Cox 1981: 137 cited in Sinclair 1996: 11). The practice of bond rating agencies as analysed by Tim is to be understood in terms of such a "limited totality" (Sinclair 1996: 11–12).

Tim's understanding of the historicist and transient epistemological status of Cox's method should be stressed. In the most abstract form, Cox had conceived of historic structures in terms of two interrelated triads of mutually constituted ideas, material capabilities and institutions, operating at the levels of production, forms of state and world order. In a later piece where Tim reassessed this conception, he argued that while this had been a useful heuristic that had deepened understanding in the immediate post-Cold War era, limitations had also become apparent motivating significant modifications. Part of this was a reflection on the wieldiness or unwieldiness of the Coxian triads as tools of analysis. When deployed by the relatively untutored, it may result in overly structuralist interpretation. Tim sought to rectify this, for instance, by moving intersubjectivity, understood as Searlian "social facts", to the institutional category and by redefining the ideational as being about "competing ideas" (Sinclair 2016: 516–17). Feminist analysis had also made it abundantly clear that the categories of material capability and production ought to be expanded by adding a distinct category of reproduction (Sinclair 2016: 518). Finally, Tim reminds us that the method is not about discovering invariant laws. The current rise of China is certainly intrinsically important to analyse. But from his perspective, possibly with an eye to hegemonic stability theory, he cautions against any attempt to make broader transhistorical inferences.

Tim Sinclair the Marxist

The previous section has summarised the intellectual position for which Tim is well known. I should own up that many of us who were his peers at York at the time found his position provocative – something that Tim clearly enjoyed. We felt that he seemed to go out of his way to underplay the importance of Cox in bringing Gramsci to IPE, together with the likes of Kees van der Pijl and the Amsterdam School, Alain Lipietz and the regulation school, Craig Murphy, Giovanni Arrighi and others. We felt that although Cox was a heterodox thinker drawing on many – indeed discordant – traditions, Gramsci clearly was central to the work of Cox and in the end intersubjectivity was clearly linked to the Gramscian concept of hegemony. For us, it was Gramsci's concepts of hegemony and counter-hegemony that were the foundations for Cox's diachronic analysis (acknowledged in Sinclair 2016: 516). Cox was also highly influenced by British Marxist historians such as Eric Hobsbawm and, as mentioned above, E. P. Thompson. And, in truth, Poulantzas also had an influence on the development of Cox's typology of "modes of social relations of production", as affirmed with his co-author Jeffrey Harrod (2006). Tim nevertheless let slip that his Masters' thesis had been a Marxist engagement with the concept of the "the relative autonomy of the state".

And indeed, Tim's Master's dissertation from the University of Canterbury, Wellington, New Zealand is a document on the public record (Sinclair 1988). It clearly indicates, together with a book review of Ellen Meiksins Wood's polemical monograph *Retreat from Class* (Sinclair 1989) that, at this time, Tim is writing from within the framework of debates of Marxism. In his Master's dissertation, Tim investigated empirically changes in New Zealand's pastoralist sector in the 1980s towards increased commodification. He did so to test whether any of Ralph Miliband's, Nicos Poulantzas' or Claus Offe's theories of the relative autonomy of the capitalist state were adequate in explaining these changes. His findings were that none of them were, but that their shortcomings were of different kinds. Miliband's theory lacks a specification of the functional pressure from the capitalist mode of production that supposedly socializes the state elite and generates relative autonomy. Consequently, contrary to what Miliband purports, relative autonomy is not an explanatory but rather a descriptive category and cannot explain changes in New Zealand pastoralism (Sinclair 1988: 134–5). Tim considered Offe's systems-theoretical account of the "contradictions of the welfare state" more promising, where "positive subordination" through the politico-administrative sub-system of the economic system could generate a counter-reaction of "negative subordination" by the economic system. This was consistent with the fiscal crisis that Tim had observed as an employee at the New Zealand Treasury, and how the fiscal crisis was mobilized to implement neoliberal reforms. But Offe's characterization, lacking any measure of scale of autonomy, was wound up in a theoretical contradiction. It seemed to suggest a return to an instrumentalist state while maintaining that relative autonomy was a constitutive condition of capitalism (Sinclair 1988: 146). Similarly, Poulantzas' formulation of relative autonomy as constitutive left no room for understanding change within capitalism (Sinclair 1988: 158–9) – as we have seen above, Tim would come to consider this an unredeemable limitation.

At the same time, Tim did not outright reject relative autonomy as a concept. Rather, drawing on Derek Sayer's interpretation of Marx's method, he advocated a more systematic deployment of scientific realism to locate the concept of the relative autonomy of the state at the appropriate level of abstraction. Tim argued that the concept should be seen as a concrete observational term rather than as an abstract concept of the mode of production to which is attributed constitutive causal powers. He suggested, in other words, a more pragmatic empirical approach to the question of relative autonomy – or its absence – and that the causal powers in the capitalist mode of production that determined policy outcomes remained to be explored (Sinclair 1988: 165–74). This, it would seem, is exactly what he would subsequently find in Cox's Weber-inspired method of historic structures.

Connecting the dots?

Judged according to the standards of a Master's dissertation, Tim's is absolutely brilliant and could in my judgement, in revised form, have been published as a monograph. It could also have served as the platform for a PhD thesis, and York University in the early 1990s would have been the ideal place to pursue this. I do not know if Tim initially had the intention to do so. Having now read his thesis a long time after we spent our graduate school years at York, I wonder if this was something that a figure like Leo Panitch had hoped that Tim would do.

Clearly, Tim chose another route, and in many respects this is not particularly remarkable. Academic careers and intellectual commitments are not crystallised at the Master's level. Many, if not most, change their minds and perspectives and rightly so. That is certainly my impression in the case of Tim. I did tread some of the grounds to which his Master's dissertation pointed. This included working out a more systematic method of abstraction with the aid of the Japanese Marxist Kozo Uno (two leading Uno-scholars, Robert Albritton and Thomas Sekine, were at York), Bob Jessop's reformulation of Marxist state theory, and the regulation school that sought to theorize capitalist change by incorporating institutionalist concerns with matters such as information asymmetries in a Marxist conception of capital accumulation. However, whereas Tim was a friend and fellow traveller who always gave me the impression that he rated and respected my intellect, he never showed any interest in exploring these avenues.

Is there, then, really anything more to be said then apart from that Marxism was something that interested Tim at an early stage of his intellectual development, which he then abandoned – not exactly an uncommon story, especially not after the events of 1989? I would suggest that there is. Whether this was conscious or not, there are some striking lines of continuity in the concerns that Tim expressed in his Master's dissertation and his subsequent work.

I recall having an explicit discussion with him about this in his bedsit in Kenilworth in 1996. There he told me that he considered a dimension of his work to be an exercise of exposure: that is, exposure of the powerful and a denaturalization of the supposedly "objective forces" of the global market. As such, he told me his work was a contribution to critical theory. Perhaps in the tradition of C. Wright Mills, then, the "new masters of capital" should be seen as a Weberian power elite. Following Cox, or for that matter Ralph Miliband, he perhaps saw no inconsistency in relating such a Weberian idea of elites to capitalist class interests (Sinclair 1996: 9). And after all, going back to his first article on bond rating agencies in RIPE, the other influence apart from Rosenau that he invokes is Stephen Gill (1991) and the idea of bond rating agencies contributing to the "governance without government" in the form of "new constitutionalism" and hence enabling the structural power of capital.

Some of the key problems that Tim had with Marxism are in fact articulated in published form and they seem to be similar to the problems that he had with (neo)realism: the tendency to reify the state. This is evident in a review that he wrote of Joyce Kolko's *Restructuring the Economy* (Sinclair 1992a). While Tim acknowledges that this book has a certain empirical value and evaluates positively her structuring of the book along the lines of global themes, he argues that the explanatory value of the book is shackled and limited by reverting back to reified categories of state, capital and class. Central in this context is the tendency, in relation to the hegemonic stability theory, to see anarchy as the default character of the international political structure. It should be recalled in this context that the key problem that Tim identified in his Master's dissertation was the tendency of theories of relative autonomy to reify the state.

It should further be noted here that Tim concluded his Master's dissertation by suggesting that another source of causal mechanism other than relative autonomy – which was a possible outcome rather than cause – for concrete policy change had to be found. It seems to me that, after tentatively having explored whether Derek Sayer's realism would be productive in that regard, he found Cox's methodology fruitful in his search for these (whether conceived as "mechanisms" or not). A case can be made that his ideal-typical analysis of the "limited totalities" where bond rating agencies were central – the work that predominated in most of his career – was animated by this concern that was evident already in his Master's dissertation. But rather than conceptualizing this in terms of critical realist "mechanisms", Tim came to find his social foundations, as the introduction to this volume suggests, in the lived experience of powerful agents discernible in concrete empirical research.

A final link to his earlier Marxism can be found in somewhat paradoxical ways in his reflections on the global financial crisis, where in some respects he turns his work on bond rating agencies on its head (Sinclair 2009). Whereas it was a key theme in his work that bond raters could not know the risk they rated in any absolute and total sense and hence passed what ultimately was a partially arbitrary judgement, he was also clear that regulators could not know the object that many at the time hoped they would regulate. In many ways, this is reminiscent of Yasmine Hayek Kobeissi and her almost sublime conception of markets as unknowable. But in contrast to Hayek, Tim was very much of the view – and in that sense in line with Keynes, Marx and Minsky – that financial markets were inherently unstable. This combination of a conception of markets as unstable yet operating in a lifeworld-like fashion in terms of complex language games that politico-administrative sub-systems cannot control without unintended consequences, is highly resonant with Offe's (1985) conception and his critique of the limitations of social democratic reformist regulation.

Conclusions

Given the topic of this chapter, it is perhaps apposite to recall that there is a debate over the relationship between an "early Marx" and "late Marx". In other words, is there a contiguous relationship between the early humanistic work of Marx, highly influenced by Hegelian philosophy and his late more "scientific" work informed by political economy? Or is there an "epistemological break"? Similarly, I have explored the question of whether there is a relationship between the "(very) early Marxist Sinclair" and the "late eclectic Sinclair". If so, what is it?

Based on exploring his very early work and reflecting on my own encounters with Tim, I have reached the conclusion that there is a pertinent relationship. His attraction to the Weberian aspects of Cox's work and methodology allowed him to explore the determinants of policy change that he had found wanting in the Marxist literature on the relative autonomy of the capitalist state. A constant theme here is his dissatisfaction with a reification of the state that he found in Marxist as well as (neo)realist theory. Hence, he gave up on the search of critical realist "mechanisms" and instead found the social foundations of finance and indeed change that had produced the global political economy in lived experience of agents – such as bond rating agencies – whose limited understanding of their environment produced pertinent effects on that environment.

That being said, his work on bond rating agencies, though clearly not Marxist, remained concerned with the critical theoretical vocation of denaturalizing social relations and exposing centres of arbitrary power. Here, I have suggested that there are lines of continuity with his Marxist phase. Yet, in line with the spirit of towering pioneers of IPE, such as Cox and Strange, he remained unashamedly iconoclastic in his analysis of these themes.

References

Cox, R. W. 1981. "Social forces, states and world order; beyond international relations theory". *Millennium: Journal of International Studies* 10 (2): 126–55.

Gill, S. 1991. "Reflections on global order and sociohistorical time". *Alternatives* 16 (3): 275–314.

Harrod, J. 2006. "The global poor and global politics: neo-materialism and the sources of political action". In *Poverty and the Production of World Politics*, M. Davies & J. M. Ryner (eds), 38–61. Basingstoke: Palgrave Macmillan.

Miller, P. & N. Rose 1990. "Governing the economy". *Economy and Society* 19 (1): 1–31.

Offe, C. 1985. *Contradictions of the Welfare State*. Cambridge, MA: MIT Press.

Rosenau, J. N. 1992. "Governance, order and change in world politics". In *Governance Without Government: Order and Change in World Politics*, J. N. Rosenau & E.-O. Czempiel (eds), 1–29. Cambridge: Cambridge University Press.

Sil, R. & P. J. Katzenstein (eds) 2010. *Beyond Paradigms: Analytic Eclecticism in the Study of World Politics*. Basingstoke: Palgrave Macmillan.

Strange, S. 1994. "Wake up, Krasner! The world has changed". *Review of International Political Economy* 1 (2): 209–19.

4

DISINTERMEDIATED KNOWLEDGE INDUSTRIES: THINKING ABOUT ACADEMIC KNOWLEDGE PRODUCTION WITH TIMOTHY J. SINCLAIR

Aida A. Hozic

Timothy J. Sinclair entered the field of international political economy (IPE) at the end of the Cold War, after serving for two years – in 1988 and 1989 – as a Trainee Analyst and Treasury Investigating Officer at the New Zealand Treasury. This twin experience – of working in the ideational and policy hub of the New Zealand's neoliberal transformation while simultaneously observing the dramatic global realignment – marked Sinclair's approach to IPE, as the field itself was changed by these events in the real world. In his first published article, in the very first issue of *Review of International Political Economy* (RIPE), Sinclair (1994b) addressed three themes that he saw as crucial in the new era of global capital markets and post-Cold War politics: the nature of the world order, location of authority and conceptual tools needed to address these changes. Focusing on credit rating agencies (CRAs), Sinclair's work would continue to engage with order, authority and knowledge as interrelated phenomena and as the social foundations of global finance.

As noted by other contributors to this volume (editors, Germain), Sinclair's work was influenced by the Neo-Gramscian IPE of Robert Cox and Stephen Gill, as well as by the "genuine heterodoxy" (Murphy & Nelson 2001) of Susan Strange. In the 1990s, Sinclair was also an important contributor to conversations about private authority, first coordinated at meetings of the International Studies Association and then turned into an edited volume by A. Claire Cutler, Virginia Haufler and Tony Porter (Cutler, Haufler & Porter 1999). Enunciating what would later be addressed as an "epistemic turn in IPE" (James 2024), these discussions, conducted amidst rapid globalization, pointed out that periods of major political and economic upheavals presented an opportunity for new knowledge to arise but were also contingent on their own interpretations. There was a tendency in crises, they warned, to limit knowledge – that pillar of structural power according to Strange (1988) – to smaller and smaller circles of experts and by doing so depoliticize the process of dramatic change. Sinclair (2000b) called those circles "embedded knowledge networks" or EKNs and analysed CRAs as illustrative of their exercise of epistemic authority in the world of finance.

This chapter draws on these principal aspects of Sinclair's work – the focus on knowledge, both as a product/commodity in the market and as its constitutive feature, and on the distinction between exogenous and endogenous understandings of crises, in which understanding and interpretation of crises by experts is a key factor of their reproduction. But the chapter also extends Sinclair's sociological analysis of finance, and especially the concept of disintermediation, to the key sector responsible for production of knowledge in and about global political economy: tertiary or higher education. I apply Sinclair's analytical tools onto the Anglo-American academic world, where knowledge and hegemony are still most obviously entwined (Schwartz 2019). Thus, in the first section, I draw on Sinclair's experiences and writings to establish plausible parallels between his analysis of finance with universities in the neoliberal era. In the second section, I examine how disintermediation, driven by the same processes that Sinclair highlighted in his work on CRAs – globalization, financialization and technological change – impacted the academic world. In the third section, I sketch the implications of Sinclair's analysis for academic scholarship, especially IPE scholarship, in the rapidly shifting – and deteriorating – landscape of the Anglo-American academe and the world order with which it has been associated. In the conclusion, I discuss the narrow openings for alternative ways of knowing and doing IPE as a normative legacy of Sinclair's research for his colleagues.

The New Zealand experiment and knowledge production

When Sinclair started as a Treasury Trainee in 1988, New Zealand had already become known as the site of the world's most ambitious neoliberal experimentation, celebrated for its bold market reforms by *The Economist*, by the World Bank and by Organisation for Economic Co-operation and Development (OECD). The reforms were initiated by the Fourth Labour government in 1984, driven by perception that New Zealand's economy had been run to the ground by excessive government interventions "like a Polish shipyard" (Wallis 1997; Goldfinch & Malpass 2007). The perception of crisis was greatly exaggerated but fit the ambitions of a small group of Treasury officials, enamoured with Chicago School of Economics, public choice theory and new managerialism.

The New Zealand Treasury "was the most influential source of policy advice to the government" and promoted an understanding that "market mechanisms tended to be superior to administrative systems for efficiently allocating resources in society" (Mintrom & Thomas 2019: 272). The reforms were self-propelled rather than driven by demands of International Financial Institutions or regime transitions, as in Latin America or eastern Europe, and prefigured what would later be known as the "Washington Consensus". The unique culture of the Treasury Department, and the way in which the sharply focused neoliberal vision was perpetuated among its analysts, have been subject to intense academic inquiry and debate. The "New Zealand Experiment", which Sinclair could closely observe in motion, attracted attention of academics and policymakers precisely because "an elite group of technopols and technocrats" had so successfully managed to seize "an opportunity to 'capture' or 'hijack' the New Zealand policy process and steer it in the direction they intended" (Wallis 1997: 3).

The reforms of the 1980s privatized state-owned enterprises, removed trade tariffs and liberalized financial markets, and promoted flexible labour markets by diminishing trade union power. But, according to Larner and Le Heron (2005), universities – or the "tertiary education" sector, as addressed in New Zealand policy documents – "remained relatively untouched" by that first phase (1984–89) of the New Zealand Experiment. Eventually, however, the intervention in tertiary education would be prompted by the recognition of the close link between education and the labour market, increased attention to the importance of the "knowledge economy" and the exigencies of the new technological environment. The universities, wrote Glenys Patterson (1991: 57), were seen by the Treasury's radical market reformers "as conservative, short on accountability, and as insufficiently responsive to the needs and demands of a rapidly changing modern economy". In 1988, while Sinclair was at the Treasury, the New Zealand Government established the Working Group on Post Compulsory Education and Training, led by Professor Gary Hawke, as a part of its broader social policy reform. The Hawke Report, produced that same year, initiated a period of dramatic changes in education: introduction of competitive market principles into university funding, focus on measurable outcomes, establishment of education benchmarks, recasting of students into customers with immediate effects of increasing student-teacher ratios, incentivizing production of only certain kinds of knowledges and manufacturing new managerial classes of administrators. Larner and Le Heron (2005) characterize these changes as twofold: first, "recoding of diverse elements of university into calculable and comparative terms" and second, "greater internationalization of universities".

Although Sinclair never systematically examined parallels between the expert network of his colleagues from the New Zealand Treasury and CRAs, or between the worlds of finance and higher education, the analogies were not lost on him. Sinclair's work is peppered with illustrations from and parallels to education. "Ratings", he wrote (Marandola & Sinclair 2014), "represent an accepted and reliable reference to financial practitioners just as school grades represent a reference for parents, employers or university admissions offices." On the shifting environments in which rating agencies operate, he quipped (Sinclair 2005: 156) that they "are like an academic who has become recognized for expertise in some area, but who must always look over his or her shoulder anticipating the arrival of a new scholar determined to 'go beyond' …" And further, on the expected objectivity of ratings (Sinclair 2021): "If you think about a professor grading the work of her students, you want that professor to have a certain critical distance from the students … and it is precisely that objectivity, that distance, and that willingness to judge which the market expected the rating agencies to provide." Whatever the outcome, Sinclair (Marandola & Sinclair 2017: 481) concluded, "even though the educational system may be criticized on different levels, professors' authority to give grades is rarely questioned".

These analogies run deep and inform Sinclair's understanding of finance and his analysis of the global financial crisis (GFC) of 2008. Perhaps, the most important metaphor in Sinclair's work is the one he borrowed from John Maynard Keynes. Keynes' tabloid beauty contest metaphor, Sinclair (2010d) believed, perfectly encapsulated the endogeneity of financial crises to the capitalist system. Much like the tabloid readers who were asked to guess the prospective winner of a beauty contest – and therefore not judge the beauty of the contestants, but preferences of other readers – stock market traders chose winners and losers by anticipating choices of other traders. Market valuation, in other words, is not based on fundamentals, as the proponents of efficient market hypothesis (EMH) believe; it is a social phenomenon in which confidence and reputation – both relational concepts – play a decisive role.

The main pillar in Sinclair's analysis of the financial world was the notion of disintermediation: bypassing of traditional institutions, such as banks, in financial transactions due to technological change or shifts in market structures. In the world of disintermediated finance, with multiple actors second-guessing each other and their moves on the market, Sinclair demonstrated how the CRAs' epistemic authority grew exponentially. "In selling their services," Sinclair (2021: 3) wrote, "the agencies are really selling confidence in themselves as experts about what is likely to happen in the future." Even in financial crises, to which they contributed, CRAs successfully reaffirmed their positions. The GFC, Sinclair argued, may have eroded public confidence in CRAs – but the tendency of "politicians, regulators, experts, the financial press, and the wider media" to view crises as produced by exogenous actors, as a few bad apples in a system that is otherwise self-regulating, has ironically reinstated their position as structurally necessary. "Reputation", argued Sinclair (2021), "is exclusive and favours incumbents".

The inside and outside status of CRAs, their constitutive yet presumed-to-be objective role in the market, makes the structural position of the rating agencies – and their epistemic authority – akin to the position of universities in the neoliberal world. As the link between universities and nation state was severed through market reforms, education too became disintermediated. In the globalized and financialized world of multiple knowledge providers, and a myriad of information sources, academic institutions sought to protect their incumbent reputation through benchmarking, rankings and ratings, and measurable outputs. But, as I shall show in the next section, while universities may have themselves become important market players as accreditors of knowledge, including knowledge about the economy, their ability to produce consent and uphold Anglo-American hegemony might have been diminished.

Disintermediated education

Sinclair's Coxian preference for a historical mode of thought, and diachronic rather than synchronic approaches to IPE, places knowledge – not as absolute but as conjectural – at the heart of contemporary global political economy (Germain, this volume). Implicitly, in Sinclair's research on finance, academic scholarship and universities (with their own situatedness, calculable incentives for knowledge production and mechanisms of social validation) both generate and reflect the crisis-prone marketplace itself.

Germain emphasizes the impact of Strange's fusion of knowledge and authority on Sinclair's own conceptualization of structural power. As Germain (2016) pointed out, Strange anticipated two key aspects of the late twentieth-century economy – a shift in the balance between public and private authority and the increased relevance of knowledge industries. According to Strange (1987: 570–1) "three factors have combined to give the United States this leadership in knowledge" – a large home market; big defence budget and, consequently, government's expenditure on research and development (R&D); and, finally, "the great size, wealth, and adaptability of American universities". To this, thanks to the insights of constructivist scholars, we could add a fourth: the ability of the United States to create a narrative about itself – an "autobiographical narrative" (Steele 2007) – that long proved immensely appealing both at home and abroad.

I focus here mostly on the United States' – and by extension – Anglo-Americans' – higher education because of the size of the sector and its outsized influence on the rest of the world. Although glossing over important national differences, it is a shortcut to examine the way that disintermediation of universities might have affected not just the production of knowledge but also the western hegemonic project. Namely, ever since the 1980s, Anglo-American universities have been exceptionally "active agents of globalization and marketization" (Kleibert 2021) – geographically expansive, consumer-driven and internally internationalized and, therefore, also vulnerable to their global operations. As a result of this spatial and symbolic fix, the same forces that have led to disintermediation of the financial sector – globalization, financialization, technological change – have transformed higher education. Forced to compete with other knowledge providers, and in perpetual need of validation, universities have dramatically changed the kind of knowledge that is being produced and recast their role in the sustenance of the global economic and political order.

Namely, globalization has both pushed Anglo-American universities abroad but also made them dependent on international flows of people and knowledge (Bound *et al.* 2021). Breaking out of their spatial constraints, Anglo-American universities have opened numerous branches abroad, building new campuses and outsourcing their faculty (Lewin 2008). This new form of international expansion, especially to the Middle East and Asia, was often subsidized by foreign autocratic governments and quite controversial, not least because of the reported labour abuses in their construction (Ross & Gulf Labor Artist Coalition 2015). The newly built campuses abroad tended to emphasize disciplines that could travel with ease and bolster globalization: business, sciences, technology. Meanwhile, at home, the universities reduced funding for the humanities, shutting down redundant departments and, sometimes, entire colleges. The reliance on student fees for their finances, and different structures of fees for domestic and international students, made home institutions in the Anglo5 increasingly dependent on foreign students – as full tuition payers in undergraduate education and as the core constituency in graduate education.

In the United States, foreign students came to represent the majority of enrolments in STEM graduate programmes – some 70 per cent in electrical engineering, 60 per cent in computer science and over 50 per cent in chemical, materials and mechanical engineering – but also in economics (a non-STEM field) (Anderson 2014). In the UK, anti-immigrant politics and shifting visa regimes exposed the full dependency of the higher education sector on international students, particularly Chinese. With fees frozen for domestic students since 2017, and now worth only 60 per cent of their 2012 value when they were first introduced, UK universities were relying on foreign students to close the gap. Hostile rhetoric and visa restrictions imposed by the Tory governments led to a significant drop in foreign students' applications, bringing numerous universities to the brink of financial ruin by 2024 (Davies 2024). And in Australia, with nearly 25 per cent of international students, also mostly from China, education has become the country's second largest export thus affecting its foreign policy calculus. Starting 2025, the Australian left-wing government plans to cap the number of international students to 270,000 per year, which some universities – fearing for their survival – call "economic vandalism" (Turnbull 2024).

Spatial expansion abroad and internationalization at home have turned some of the best-known universities into global corporate juggernauts, whose administrators and star faculty fly in and out of distant campuses as classroom instruction both at home and abroad is being turned over to part-time and non-tenure track faculty. According to the American Association of University Professors (n.d.), many universities "have invested heavily in facilities and technology while cutting instructional spending" with serious consequences for the quality of education, academic freedoms and faculty governance. Tenure-protections, already unique to North American universities, are unlikely to extend much into the future. Part-time and contingent faculty now represent nearly two-thirds of the workforce in American universities. Precarious academic labour is the key feature of even the most elite institutions such as Oxbridge and the Ivy League. Substantively stretched, faculty and students expressed concerns: "Can an ivory-tower education really be exported around the world like McDonald's or Hollywood, without destroying the original mission?" (Kamenetz 2013).

Globalization and adherence to market principles have also transformed ways in which universities are financed and their accounting practices. But the pressures of corporatization have dramatically increased since the financial crisis of 2008. Some American institutions – most notably Harvard and other Ivy League colleges – have endowments larger than half of the world's economies; while they were hit hard by the financial crisis they mostly recouped their losses by 2015. Others resorted to desperate measures: Brandeis University, whose endowment suffered not only because of the financial crisis but also because it was a part of a Ponzi scheme by investor Bernie Madoff, contemplated selling its precious collection of modern art to prevent massive layoffs of faculty. Brandeis regained its A1 rating from Moody's Investors Service in 2013 [sic!], but financial stability was brought about through cuts to faculty salaries and programmes (Heilman 2015).

Meanwhile, public universities – such as the University of California (UC) system – became poster children for "the financialization of governance" in the American higher education. A team of researchers from the University of California-Berkeley has closely followed the trends towards increased reliance on debt financing in the UC system, and also in American universities more broadly. UC universities have been borrowing to invest "into medical centres, dormitories, and athletic facilities at the same time as core university functions were scaled back due to cuts in state appropriations" (Eaton *et al.* 2016). Faced with these divergent pressures, administrators have "empowered financial managers and recruited Wall Street veterans to positions as senior university executives and members of UC's Board of Regents". As a result, they argued, the university's governance has been closed off "to the broader public and even persons who have formal authority but lack financial expertise". Looking beyond the UC system, the same team has documented widespread and increased costs of institutional borrowing in American higher education, concentrated returns on investment in the wealthiest of institutions, rising financing costs on loans outpacing returns at poorer institutions and the ballooning household spending on interest on student loans (Eaton *et al.* 2016). The bleak picture of American higher education emerging from this research shows a polarized, profoundly unequal knowledge industry, entwined with the financial sector through a series of debt relations – with universities essentially acting as a "student loan broker to arrange financing for households to pay" for "increased tuition, room and board costs".

In the UK, the most contentious issue has been the Universities Superannuation Scheme (USS), the pension scheme of university staff. Created in 1974, the pension scheme was relatively stable until 2011 when major rule-changes led to reduced benefits to its members, forced increased contributions and introduced risks into the members' ability to collect expected pensions at their retirement age. Flawed valuations, excessive pay for fund managers and low interest rates all contributed to USS losses, leading to a series of strikes by affected university faculty and support staff between 2018 and 2023. And while the industrial dispute was ultimately resolved, USS investments in fossil fuels and water privatization are illustrative of the way in which higher education workers remain locked in the matrices of financial capital, regardless of their quest for political and intellectual independence.

The implications of financialization of the Anglo-American academe are wide-ranging, transforming expectations of teaching and learning for students and their professors. As could be expected in the institutionalized webs of financial debt, there is both internal and external pressure to shift academic focus to measurable learning outcomes, employment rates after graduation and alumni salaries. Financialization of universities and their endowments and the completely non-democratic aspect of their investments has now become very public with the wave of student protests and encampments in 2024. The research done by student groups asking for divestment from arms manufacturers is a treasure trove of information exposing the affinity between particular kinds of knowledge produced in universities and the world of conflict and capital in which they are immersed (LSESU Palestine Society 2024). Emphasis on and dependence on techno-capitalism is a part of that same equation – with technology, now including AI, both making and unmaking the universities as we know them.

The vanishing grand narratives

These changes in the social foundations of higher education have had significant implications for hegemonic knowledge production. By measurable outcomes and rankings, Anglo-American universities continue to lead in production and distribution of mediated and/or academic knowledge, including knowledge about international affairs and political economy. However, their once unparalleled ability to control hegemonic narratives about the West and its role in international politics may have been eroded. The loss of control over the global imaginary is less due to the rise of alternative centres of knowledge or image production ("counter-narratives") and more to the contradictory influences of Anglo-American economic master's tools – globalization, financialization and technology. In other words, while the standards of western knowledge may have been diffused, the appeal of the western narrative has been diluted by the very tools that make the continuation of its structural dominance possible.

The symptoms of this malaise are all over. International Relations scholars have spoken of "the end of IR theory" (Dunne, Hansen &Wight 2013) and complained about the dearth of "grand strategy" conversations (Cambanis 2011). The field, especially in the United States, is dominated by "hypothesis-testing" works, mostly quantitative, and no longer identified with any of its great paradigmatic traditions that sought to explain America's role in the world. Ido Oren (2016) explains this move from great theoretical debates to quantitative research in the field of IR by relying on three factors, some of which resonate with what has already been said in this chapter: corporatization of American universities, changing levels of funding for social science research from the national security agencies of the American government and the embeddedness of International Relations within American Political Science.

Citing Lazerson (2010), Oren (2016) noted how faculty "lost power to university administrators and boards" and argued that one of the key consequences of the new culture of productivity and metrics was that "quantitative assessment of research has gained momentum at the expense of qualitative assessment". Just as importantly, he argued, the shifts in federal funding for social science research have greatly affected the type of knowledge about the world affairs produced in American universities. In his view, the dearth of Department of Defence (DoD) funding "in the 1980s and 1990s slowed quantitative IR's momentum considerably and thus helped tilt the professional playing field toward its main intellectual rival: grand theory" (Oren 2016: 15). But after September 11, and as the wars in Afghanistan and then Iraq stretched ad infinitum, "the federal government began pouring money into counterterrorism and counterinsurgency research" (Oren 2016: 16). The type of richly funded, often multi-million dollar projects (equivalent of mega-budget movies for social scientists) that the government agencies support – "Models of Counterterrorism", "Integrated Conflict Early Warning Systems" or "computational model of resources and resiliency", to name just a few – sought "to align the research interests of social scientists more closely with US national security interests" (Oren 2016: 11) albeit not with American meta-narratives in a changing world environment. Finally, embeddedness of international relations within American political science, where neo-positivism and quantitative orthodoxy carry the day, has ensured that "the default intellectual position" of junior scholars is "the rather atheoretical and quantitative mode of analysis that is the gold standard in American political science, especially in American politics" (Oren 2016: 22).

Scientization of knowledge and the vanishing of grand narratives carry consequences for IPE also. Even if wary of reproducing the "transatlantic divide" in IPE (Cohen 2007) in this brief chapter, there is no doubt that in the United States' IPE big picture theories and approaches have all but vanished. Instead, "narrow questions" of causal inference, public opinion research, new behaviourism and experimental models, all conducive to big data and replication, have become the norm. In the journal that was once the principal outlet for North American IPE debates – *International Organization* – only a handful of articles published after 2008 addressed the GFC. As Blyth and Matthijs (2017: 207) noted, it should not be surprising that IPE scholars were caught off guard by Brexit and also the election of Donald Trump. In their view, IPE has "moved away from the traditional 'big questions' toward more micro-approaches". Indeed, as they argued, IPE has become "curiously quiet on the content and consequences of the global macroeconomy when it is not directly looking at moments of crisis per se".

In the UK context, Stockhammer, Dammerer and Kapur (2021) have documented that the Research Excellence Framework (REF)– the main research assessment tool of the universities – marginalizes heterodox economics. Indeed, examining the case of "Modern Monetary Theory"(MMT) as an example of heterodox, "indie" economics, Helgadóttir and Grosen (2024) have demonstrated that MMT's temporary ascendance was mostly due to intense online advocacy rather than its dissemination through well-threaded academic channels.

Increased attention to sociology of knowledge and epistemic politics of IPE indicate that the field itself is not immune to outside reputational pressures and internal boundary making, which have resulted in perennial exclusions of gender and feminism and forgetting of the darker history of colonialism and imperial political economy (Clift, Kristensen & Rosamond 2022). A survey study of IPE scholars in the UK by Nunn and Shields (2022) has shown that the lack of institutionalization of IPE in the UK higher education enables the field to maintain its critical edge but also makes its susceptible to "micro-decisions in relatively few institutions". Seabrooke and Young (2017) describe IPE as a field characterized by niche proliferation as much as polarization – but always driven by (presumably internalized) "competitive exclusion pressures".

The dynamic of academic knowledge production, under the conditions of disintermediation, reveals continued preoccupation with credentials, objectivity and relevance as ways of distinguishing among a variety of actors, institutions, publication venues and claims. As in the policy world, the insistence on expertise affirms authority but – in times of crises and contestation – leaves open the space to alternative post-truth narratives. As Clift and Rosamond (2024) have argued, the deepening of disintermediation of (economic) knowledge – and re-politicization of expert knowledge – have also fuelled populist challenges to technocratic reason. Thus, Scott James (2024) may be right – and Sinclair would approve – it is prime-time "to re-endogenize technocratic power as a set of dynamic and contingent epistemic practices that must be continually reproduced and renegotiated over time". However, to do so, we must be willing to confront the structures of higher education and incentives that define the playing field and continue to reward incumbents, even at the peril of their own extinction.

Conclusion

"Universities, like banks, are too big to fail", wrote Philip Augar (2024), an equity broker who chaired the UK Post-18 Education and Funding Review during Theresa May's government. Sir Augar, who was knighted for his services to education in 2021, was quick to add that "the collapse of even a handful of the UK's 140-plus universities would not have the same cataclysmic effect as a run on the banks". Nonetheless, "institutional failure would leave a nightmare of liabilities".

Sir Augar's crude analogy between the greedy financial institutions and universities as presumed providers of public good might seem scandalous at first but it would not have surprised Sinclair. For decades already, universities have been more concerned with their own reputation than with the world that they purport to interpret and guide. De-funding of higher education, pauperization of all but star faculty, and repression on university campuses are ways in which politicians and administrators seek to re-establish their authority in times of crisis, disciplining knowledge to maintain the status quo. Like CRAs, they are even willing to assume responsibility for political problems that they may or may not have created, just to affirm their indispensable role as adjudicators of knowledge and truth.

But the world we live in, Sinclair would warn, depends – like money – on mutually agreed fictions, not truth. And under the circumstances, academic knowledge might be best able to retain its social purpose if it remains *in*disciplined (Nunn & Shields 2022). Sinclair's legacy demands that we remain suspicious of incentives that maximize our own career returns at the expense of problematizing and exposing the world's most powerful fictions. Instead of reproducing, we should seek to demystify embedded knowledge networks, including those that sustain us.

References

American Association of University Professors (AAUP) n.d. "Background facts on contingent faculty". www.aaup.org/issues/contingency/background-facts.

Anderson, S. 2014. "International students are vital to US higher education". *International Educator* 23 (3): 1–4.

Augar, P. 2024. "Universities, like banks, are too big to fail". *Financial Times*, 2 September.

Blyth, M. & M. Matthijs 2017. "Black swans, lame ducks, and the mystery of IPE's missing macroeconomy". *Review of International Political Economy* 24 (2): 203–31.

Bound, J., B. Braga, G. Khanna & S. Turner 2021. "The globalization of postsecondary education: the role of international students in the US higher education system". *Journal of Economic Perspectives* 35 (1): 163–84.

Cambanis, T. 2011. "In search of a new grand strategy". *The Atlantic*, 12 September.

Clift, B., P. Kristensen & B. Rosamond 2022. "Remembering and forgetting IPE: disciplinary history as boundary work". *Review of International Political Economy* 29 (2): 339–70.

Clift, B. & B. Rosamond 2024. "Technocratic reason in hard times: the mobilisation of economic knowledge and the discursive politics of Brexit". *New Political Economy* 29 (6): 886–99.

Cohen, B. 2007. "The transatlantic divide: why are American and British IPE so different?". *Review of International Political Economy* 14 (2): 197–219.

Cutler, A., V. Haufler & T. Porter (eds) 1999. *Private Authority and International Affairs*. Albany, NY: State University of New York Press.

Davies, W. 2024. "How the Tories pushed universities to the brink of disaster". *The Guardian*, 2 July.

Dunne, T., L. Hansen & C. Wight 2013. "The end of international relations theory?" *European Journal of International Relations* 19 (3): 405–25.

Eaton, C., J. Habinek, A. Goldstein, C. Dioun, D. Santibáñez Godoy & R. Osley-Thomas 2016. "The financialization of US higher education". *Socio-Economic Review* 14 (3): 507–35.

Germain, R. 2016. "Susan Strange and the future of IPE". In *Susan Strange and the Future of Global Political Economy*. Abingdon: Routledge.

Goldfinch, S. & D. Malpass 2007. "The Polish shipyard: myth, economic history and economic policy reform in New Zealand". *Australian Journal of Politics & History* 53 (1): 118–37.

Heilman, U. 2015. "Was Brandeis president Frederick Lawrence doomed by fundraising woes?" *Forward*. https://forward.com/news/214085/beloved-by-students-fundraising-doomed-brandeis-president-lawrence.

Helgadóttir, O. & M. Grosen 2024. "Indie economics: social purpose, lay expertise and the unusual rise of modern monetary theory". *New Political Economy* 29 (6): 900–13.

James, S. 2024. "Special section introduction: epistemic politics in international and comparative political economy". *New Political Economy* 29 (6): 835–43.

Kamenetz, A. 2013. "Should top U.S. colleges expand overseas?" *Newsweek*, 5 March.

Kleibert, J. M. 2021. "Geographies of marketization in higher education: branch campuses as territorial and symbolic fixes". *Economic Geography* 97 (4): 315–37.

Larner, W. & R. Le Heron 2005. "Neo-liberalizing spaces and subjectivities: reinventing New Zealand universities". *Organization* 12 (6): 843–62.

Lazerson, M. 2010. "The making of corporate U: how we got here". *Chronicle of Higher Education*, 17 October.

Lewin, T. 2008. "U.S. universities rush to set up outposts abroad". *The New York Times*, 10 February.

LSESU Palestine Society 2024. "LSE's complicity in genocide of the Palestinian people, arms trade, and climate breakdown". May. https://lsepalestine.github.io/documents/LSESUPALESTINE-Assets-in-Apartheid-2024-Web.pdf.

Mintrom, M. & M. Thomas 2019. "New Zealand's economic turnaround: how public policy innovation catalysed economic growth". In *Great Policy Successes*, P. T. Hart & M. Compton (eds), 264–82. Oxford: Oxford University Press.

Murphy, C. N. & D. R. Nelson 2001. "International political economy: a tale of two heterodoxies". *British Journal of Politics and International Relations* 3 (3): 393–412.

Nunn, A. & S. Shields 2022. "The intellectual and institutional challenges for international political economy in the UK: findings from practitioner survey data". *Review of International Studies* 48 (3): 503–22.

Oren, I. 2016. "A sociological analysis of the decline of American IR theory". *International Studies Review* 18 (4): 571–96.

Patterson, G. 1991. "University 'reform' in New Zealand 1984–1990: policies and outcomes". *Contemporary Issues in Education* 10 (2): 56–70.

Ross, A. & Gulf Labor Artist Coalition (eds) 2015. *The Gulf: High Culture, Hard Labor*. New York: OR Books.

Schwartz, H. M. 2019. "American hegemony: intellectual property rights, dollar centrality, and infrastructural power". *Review of International Political Economy* 26 (3): 490–519.

Seabrooke, L. & K. Young 2017. "The networks and niches of international political economy". *Review of International Political Economy* 24 (2): 288–331.

Steele, B. J. 2007. *Ontological Security in International Relations: Self-Identity and the IR State*. Abingdon: Routledge.

Stockhammer, E., Q. Dammerer & S. Kapur 2021. "The Research Excellence Framework 2014, journal ratings and the marginalisation of heterodox economics". *Cambridge Journal of Economics* 45 (2): 243–69.

Strange, S. 1987. "The persistent myth of lost hegemony". *International Organization* 41 (4): 551–74.

Strange, S. 1988. *States and Markets: An Introduction to International Political Economy*. London: Pinter.

Turnbull, T. 2024. "Australia introduces cap on international students". BBC News, 27 August.

Wallis, J. 1997. "Conspiracy and the policy process: a case study of the New Zealand experiment". *Journal of Public Policy* 17 (1): 1–29.

5

FROM RATINGS TO INFRASTRUCTURES: UNCOVERING THE MICRO-FOUNDATIONS AND GLOBAL POLITICS OF FINANCE

Johannes Petry

Introduction[1]

In recent years, international political economy (IPE) scholarship has increasingly focused on the issue of financial infrastructures. Major IPE journals like the *Review of International Political Economy* and *New Political Economy* saw a great increase in publications on financial infrastructures since the mid-2010s, including the publication of a special issue (Bernards & Campbell-Verduyn 2019) and the identification of this topic as one of the "blind spots" in contemporary IPE research (de Goede 2020). Meanwhile Benjamin Braun's (2020) article on infrastructural power has become one of the most cited articles in *Socio-Economic Review* in recent years. This trend is also reflected in academia widely, as an analysis of journal articles indexed in the Web of Science highlights (Figure 5.1). Financial infrastructures have clearly become a topic of great interest to political economy scholarship.

This infrastructural turn in the IPE of finance often draws on two different intellection traditions.[2] Either scholarship takes inspiration from Science and Technology Studies (STS) and the Social Studies of Finance (SSF) approaches that focus on the micro-structures of markets and emphasize the socio-technical character of financial infrastructures (Bernards & Campbell-Verduyn 2019;

1. I would like to thank Malcolm Campbell-Verduyn for his excellent comments on this chapter as well as Ben Clift and Chris Clarke who went above and beyond in their editorial roles to bring this piece over the finishing line. A great thanks also to Marieke de Goede, Paul Langley, Tony Porter, Nick Bernards, Nina Boy, Benjamin Braun, Barbara Brandl, Philipp Golka, John Morris and Carola Westermeier for offering their perspectives on this matter.

2. There is, of course, also a growing literature that only discusses infrastructures as something purely physical, for example, how fibre-optic cables, microwave towers and co-location make high-frequency trading possible.

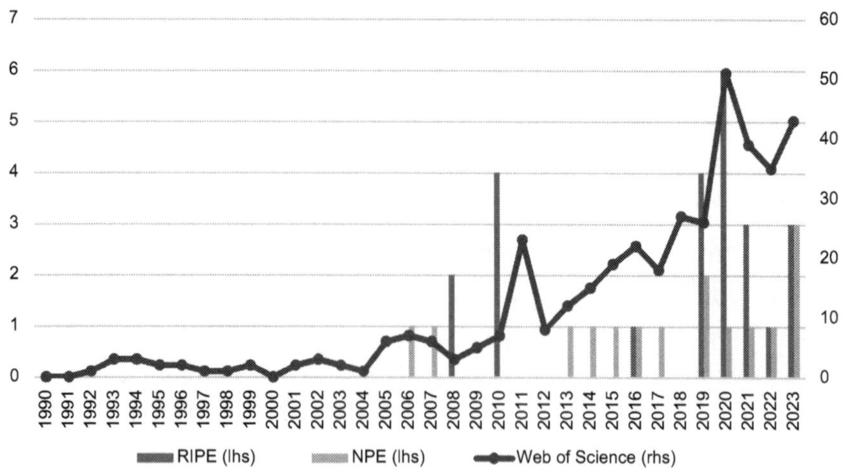

Figure 5.1 Scientific articles on financial infrastructures
Source: Web of Science.

Clarke 2019; Krarup 2019; Pardo-Guerra 2019; de Goede & Westermeier 2022; Campbell-Verduyn & Hütten 2023) or this literature builds upon the concept of infrastructural power by sociologist Michael Mann, a meso-level concept for understanding the power relation between the state and financial actors (Schwartz 2019; Braun 2020; Braun & Gabor 2020; Petry 2020; Green & Gruin 2021; Coombs 2022; Wansleben 2022). These two perspectives on financial infrastructure are also presented in the *Cambridge Global Handbook of Financial Infrastructures* (Westermeier, Campbell-Verduyn & Brandl 2025a), which exemplified the state-of-the-art in this new debate. While many IPE scholars now engage in analyses of financial infrastructures, it often seems as if there is little "home-grown" IPE concepts and scholarship to draw from when studying financial infrastructures.

However, this chapter argues that the scholarship of Timothy Sinclair might actually offer important insights for advancing debates surrounding financial infrastructures. The chapter thus reflects on Sinclair's pioneering role on understanding what is today referred to as the infrastructural politics of global finance. He was one of the first people in IPE to investigate the power and authority of private market actors as well as the role of market ordering devices in mediating their power within the global financial system. His social foundations of finance approach offered a distinctive and telling account of the *politics* of these financial processes. His analysis of credit ratings demonstrated how seemingly mundane practices shaped global financial flows and reconfigured power constellations within the global economy. When analysing his work, we can observe many similarities to the infrastructural turn.

However, while he did have an influence on leading figures in the new financial infrastructure scholarship, there is little broader acknowledgement of his work in this new literature, which either draws on micro-level STS/SSF conceptions of infrastructure or Michael Mann's meso-level concept of infrastructural power. This chapter argues that, by uncovering the global *politics* of market ordering devices, Sinclair's work offers a third perspective for understanding financial infrastructures in IPE. While politics is not absent in the financial infrastructure debate, Sinclair's approach extends the political understanding of infrastructures towards more global phenomenon, demonstrating how seemingly technical activities like ratings influence and shape world order, power and global governance. The aim of this chapter is thus to explore similarities and differences between the work of Sinclair and the current debates on financial infrastructures as well as how his scholarship might extend the thinking about infrastructures with a clearer focus on their inherent politics.

The chapter is structured as follows. The second section attempts to re-read the work of Sinclair through an infrastructural lens; not by crowbarring infrastructure into his work but by highlighting affinities with an infrastructural view and exploring links between CRAs and financial infrastructures, relating Sinclair's own conceptual terminology to the financial infrastructural turn, which he in some sense anticipated. The third section then illustrates similarities with the recent fascination with financial infrastructures within IPE. The fourth section outlines some of Sinclair's influences on this scholarship and proposes how Sinclair's work could potentially advance these contemporary discussions, charting another perspective for analysing financial infrastructures that reconnects micro, meso and macro levels of analysis by foregrounding the broader global politics of financial infrastructures. The fifth section concludes.

The new masters of capital: an infrastructural view of ratings?

In his work, Sinclair has mainly focused on understanding and locating the shifting loci of power within the global economic system as certain actors were able to shape the actions of states and markets alike. Within the context of a changing global financial system – characterized by the phenomenon of growing financial disintermediation – power for Sinclair was increasingly exercised by credit rating agencies (Sinclair 1994b, 2005, 2021). Rather than being coercive, the agencies exercised their power as private market authorities. A useful distinction can thereby be drawn between actors who are "in authority" such as state officials and those who are "an authority": a position derived from their positioning as "legitimate" experts within a given social structure (Sinclair 2005; Lincoln 1994).

With this focus on private authority, Sinclair departed from many of his scholarly peers. While in the 1990s and early 2000s many IPE scholars of global finance focused on the role of states, the state–market relationship and financial globalization (Cohen 1996; Helleiner 1996; Strange 1996; Pauly 1997; Underhill 2000), his work on the rating agencies[3] was different – and also important – in that he was one of the first IPE scholars to investigate the authority of private market actors (see also Porter 1993, 1995; Cerny 1994). His was a more "bottom-up" focus on particular financial market actors and institutions, and their practices, which were often overlooked in much IPE analyses of state actors and actions (Sinclair 1994b).

The medium through which rating agencies exercised authority were credit ratings, a seemingly mundane and technical set of practices that few IPE scholars understood as something political at the time. His work focused on uncovering the politics inherent to these powerful market ordering devices, how seemingly mundane practices shaped global financial flows and reconfigured power constellations within the global economy. Importantly, his approach to understanding the impact and role of credit ratings within global finance thereby shares a lot of similarities with the recent fascination with financial infrastructures in IPE.

As Sinclair (2001a: 442) put it himself, "as a political economist concerned with coming to an understanding of authority in capitalism, I investigate the infrastructure of contemporary commercial life" (also Sinclair 2000b: 489). This focus on infrastructures went well beyond the main focus of IPE debates at the time that largely focused on regulatory aspects – which he thought had severe shortcomings. While Sinclair never really developed the concept of infrastructure, he made the following distinction: for him there was an important difference in that "regulation is concerned with the 'rules of the road', not with the design of the road itself" (Sinclair 2012b: 140). Following John Searle, Sinclair took an interest in the "constitutive rules" that "make the game" of chess, for example. He highlighted how similar "deep, constitutive rules that constitute the markets" are foundational to the financial system (Sinclair 2021: 79–80, 132).

Consequently, he focused on credit ratings as "an important part of capital market infrastructure" (Sinclair 2005: 52). Rather than a purely technical or inconsequential exercise, he analysed ratings as "key benchmarks in the

3. In his broader research agenda, Sinclair also analysed other private market actors like banks (Rethel & Sinclair 2012), capital market development in non-western countries (Gotoh & Sinclair 2017; Sinclair 2011) as well as global governance (Hewson & Sinclair 1999a); this chapter, however, focuses mainly on his work on rating agencies.

cognitive life of these markets – features of the marketplace – which form the basis for subsequent decision-making by participants" (Sinclair 2005: 52). As ratings became something that market actors strategized around (Sinclair 2001a), rating agencies and their activities became "part of the internal organization of the market itself" (Sinclair 2012b: 142), which imbued these bodies with a considerable degree of power and authority.

The source of their authority is the creation, manipulation and presentation of knowledge about the market that takes the form of different credit ratings.[4] In disintermediated capital markets, "market actors are overwhelmed with news and data about prices, businesses, and politics" and have little capacity to make sense of all this information across assets and asset classes. By providing credit ratings, the agencies thus create important "rules of thumb" that make investment decisions (much) less costly for market actors (Sinclair 2005: 52).

In addition, rating agencies are important for investment decisions due to "what people believe about them, and act on collectively" (Sinclair 2005: 54). The social foundation of rating agency power is thus "a collective belief that says the agencies are important, which people act upon, as if it were 'true'". As Sinclair put it, "the AA bond, for example, is just as commonplace – and just as unquestioned – an entity in these markets as a chair or table is in the domestic kitchen" (Sinclair 2001a: 443). This links again to Searle and ideas about "social facts", which are developed further below. Their assessments about the creditworthiness of companies, municipalities or countries as expressed by different credit ratings are thus crucial for enabling the workings of disintermediated capital markets. They have a crucial role in *coordinating* markets, "adjust[ing] the ground rules inside international capital markets and thereby shap[ing] the internal organization and behaviour of those institutions seeking funds" (Sinclair 2001a: 448).

By "constraining thinking to a specific range of acceptable possibilities" and occasionally "exercis[ing] veto over options", rating agencies shape the actions of market actors (Sinclair 2001a: 443). Rating agencies are thus important intermediaries that are "essential to the functioning of the [global financial] system" (Sinclair 2012b: 142). This focus on particular private financial institutions and their apparently mundane, technical practices, and how these a play a key *political* and "market ordering" role, was ground-breaking in IPE. It prepared the foundations in important ways for the infrastructural turn in the study of finance that was to follow many years after Sinclair's first RIPE article in 1994.

4. Susan Strange (1997: 30–31) also highlighted the role of knowledge as a source of power within the global economy that was also interlinked with finance.

Commonalities, ratings and the infrastructural turn

As noted in this chapter's introduction, recent discussions about financial infrastructures are largely informed by two different perspectives, each with a particular understanding of how financial market institutions relate to their wider social context: the micro-level analysis of infrastructures in STS/SFS and the macro-level analysis of infrastructural power in the tradition of sociologist Michael Mann (Westermeier, Campbell-Verduyn & Brandl 2025a). Sinclair's particular understanding and analysis of credit ratings share a lot of commonalities with these two approaches, arguably even anticipating some of the central tenets of the contemporary financial infrastructures literature. Let us take a look at these two perspectives in turn.

The first perspective that informs current discussions about financial infrastructures in IPE takes inspiration from STS (and SSF) literatures. This approach focuses more on "the mundane technical objects that power and process financial transactions, market interactions and monetary flows with distinct modes and rules of operations" (Westermeier, Campbell-Verduyn & Brandl 2025b: 5). This is a methodological focus on particular practices that clearly finds echoes in Sinclair's work on credit ratings agencies. Financial infrastructures are understood here as "the social, cultural, and technical conditions that make [financial markets] possible" (MacKenzie 2005: 12), socio-technical systems that enable the functioning of markets but tend to be taken for granted and assumed (Star 1999; Edwards 2003). Importantly, infrastructures are relational and should thereby not be seen as simply "a thing" (Bernards & Campbell-Verduyn 2019).

This *relational* aspect of financial infrastructures was central to Sinclair's work. His emphasis on the social foundations of finance is mirrored by the contemporary emphasis on infrastructures as socio-technical arrangements that comprise both human activities and non-human objects. The outcome of the ratings process is an alpha-numerical calculation (e.g. AAA, AA, A, BBB, etc.), but it becomes consequential only because other actors view them as important.[5] Drawing on John Maynard Keynes's tabloid beauty contest metaphor, he developed an endogenous understanding of finance and points out that in part rating agencies "have to be considered important actors because people view them as important, and act on the basis of that understanding in markets" (Sinclair 2012b: 141). As noted above, Sinclair was also influenced by the ideas

5. Unlike more STS/SSF-inspired analyses of financial infrastructures, it is important to note that while Sinclair (2005: 30–42) discusses the technical details of the ratings process – from collection different forms of data and information to analytical determination and how rating methodology creates ratings as alpha-numerical outputs of this process – he focuses more on the social aspects of ratings than their materiality.

of Searle, who noted how when particular intersubjective beliefs become sufficiently embedded, they develop the quality of social facts, resting on "collective intentionality" (Searle 1995: 24–5; Sinclair 2005: 53–4). Social facts differ from "brute" facts in that what makes them "true" or "false" is not "independent of anybody's attitudes or feelings about them" (Searle 1995: 8). Rather than "brute" facts like the height of a mountain or "subjective" facts based on individual perceptions, ratings were *social* facts that rested upon "what people believe about them, and act on collectively" (Sinclair 2012b: 141).

Social facts play a constitutive role in shaping political economic outcomes, guiding collective intentionality, shaping the meaning and significance attached to economic phenomena. Social facts can, as in the case of the rating agencies, acquire sufficient influence to profoundly shape material conditions in the political economy. They are key elements of the "intersubjective structures" or "interpretive frames [that] actors use to understand the world" (Sinclair 2005: 10–12). This emphasis on the social dimension of ratings parallels the insistence in more recent work that financial infrastructures are *social* as well as technical systems, and they are inherently relational.

Sinclair's work also anticipated other key elements of the STS approach towards understanding financial infrastructures, which Bernards and Campbell-Verduyn (2019) describe as facilitation, openness, durability, centrality and obscurity. Infrastructures, for instance, enable certain socio-economic transactions to take place (Larkin 2013); financial infrastructures thus need to be in place to *facilitate* market transactions, to make these transactions possible in the first place (Bowker and Leigh Star 1999). They are typically existing and newly emerging socio-technical systems through which "payments are settled, risks are assessed, and prices agreed" (Bernards & Campbell-Verduyn 2019: 777).

This crucial relational aspect of infrastructures is also encapsulated in his conceptualization of rating agencies as embedded knowledge networks (Sinclair 2005, 2000b). The outputs of these networks, credit ratings, "play a crucial role in constructing markets" (Sinclair 2005: 15). Importantly, he demonstrates how rating agencies became more crucial for the organization of markets over time as the nature of financial capitalism changed. While they existed before, it was the shift towards disintermediated markets and debt financing that made them even more pivotal to financial systems. In this "new global finance", as Sinclair (1994b) called it, instead of providing an opinion, they were now considered to "pass judgement". These judgements increase in importance – that is, they have even more power to enable and constrain the behaviour of firms, states, borrowers, and so on – in a world of disintermediated finance.

Rating agencies thereby enabled the functioning of capital markets. As one of the interviewees in his book put it, "Love them or loathe them, if they did not exist, we would have to invent them" (Sinclair 2005: 51–2). Without ratings, participants in disintermediated capital markets would be overwhelmed with information and transactions would not be possible. Ratings thus need to be understood as "key benchmarks in the cognitive life of these markets … which form the basis for subsequent decision-making" – they are "part of the internal organization of the market" (Sinclair 2005: 52). This constitutive role that ratings play in financial markets has affinities with insights from financial infrastructure scholars. Infrastructures are the foundation through which other financial activity is enabled.

Moreover, ratings shape how international capital markets operate; they thus exhibit *centrality*, for instance, shaping the way core functions are undertaken (Bernards & Campbell-Verduyn 2019: 777). This is the embeddedness of Sinclair's embedded knowledge networks (Sinclair 2005: 15) – the role of rating agencies within capital markets as "analytical and judgemental systems that, in principle, remain at arm's length from market transactions" but which are simultaneously "viewed as endogenous rather than exogenous to financial globalization" and thus are "generally considered legitimate rather than imposed entities by market participants". He thereby understands networks more dynamically, as an "organizing logic" (Powell & Smith-Doerr 1994: 368), encouraging scholars to think about what rating agencies "actually do in the social system" (Sinclair 2000b: 490).

Despite being relatively *obscure* compared to many more well-known financial actors, rating agencies have a crucial coordinating function for capital markets. The coordination effect of rating agencies narrows the expectations of creditors and debtors to a well-understood or transparent set of norms shared among all parties, signifying the *openness* feature of financial infrastructures. Thus, the agencies do not just constrain the capital markets but actually provide significant pressures on market participants, contributing to their internal constitution (Sinclair 2005: 15–16). These again are Searle's constitutive rules that make financial markets possible. By setting these "ground rules" within capital markets, rating agencies shape "the internal organization and behaviour of institutions seeking funds" (Sinclair 2005: 15). Notably, in his later work, Sinclair also commented on the *durability* of the rating agencies (Mennillo & Sinclair 2019; Sinclair 2021), since despite receiving much criticism for the financial crisis starting in 2007, they emerged from the crisis in relatively unchanged form, still powerful actors and crucial to a world of disintermediated finance.

A focus on power also largely motivates the second perspective on financial infrastructures. IPE scholars have drawn on the work of Michael Mann (1984: 192) who argued that the ability of modern states to control the basic, backgrounded features of socio-economic life imbued them with infrastructural (in contrast to despotic) power (Konings 2010; Weiss & Thurbon 2018).

The more recent scholarship on infrastructural power in finance has turned this argument on its head. By highlighting states' reliance on particular market-based methods and instruments of economic governance, states have also imbued private financial actors with infrastructural power (Braun & Gabor 2020; Gabor 2020). As Braun (2020) puts it, "the flipside of the infrastructural power of the state is the infrastructural power of those parts of the private sector that serve as the conduits for state agency". While state actors like central banks might have facilitated the growth of financial markets, they are now structurally dependent on these markets (Wansleben 2023).

These insights can already be found in Sinclair's work. By investigating the shift towards debt financing by corporate firms, states and municipalities, the increasing use of these market-based methods of governance can be shown to have increased the power of rating agencies. Sinclair highlights that the authority of rating agencies developed within and was enabled by changing socio-economic structures, for instance, the growth of capital markets and the decline of banks as allocators of credit, which created a demand for rating agencies' services for the functioning of the then disintermediated structures of finance. Therefore, he argues "authority is best understood as an effect of these circumstances, rather than as an entity or a characteristic of an actor or institution" and "its existence is therefore not functional, ... but always contingent on time, place, and circumstance" (Sinclair 2005: 64).

Sinclair's work thereby provides a two-way set of insights for the concept of infrastructural power in finance. On the one hand, he emphasizes how within increasingly disintermediated capital markets the rating process and its centrality within economic governance imbues rating agencies with power over states and municipalities, as well as both financial and non-financial corporate actors. On the other hand, he illustrates how this constellation increases the global power of the US, and American finance specifically. Sinclair was keen to stress the world's dominant rating agencies were not just based in the US but thoroughly imbued with an American character given their origination in US financial systems and worldviews. Rating agencies disseminate *particular* forms of knowledge and financial norms, facilitating the convergence of economic policy around characteristically American "best practice" (Sinclair 2005: 17).

Overall, we can observe that many tenets of contemporary discussions of financial infrastructures in IPE have already been present in Sinclair's highly influential work on the social foundations of finance.[6] Moreover, his rich scholarship provides important and productive starting points for a much more *political* (re-)reading of financial infrastructures.

---

6. As mentioned above, one aspect that Sinclair focused less on was the materiality of infrastructures since he focused more on how they are inherently social constructs.

Learning from Sinclair? Putting (global) politics into the infrastructural turn

Although often not properly acknowledged – Sinclair's work is hardly cited in the literature on financial infrastructures – his way of thinking about global finance has in fact influenced a series of scholars that are now at the forefront of the debate about financial infrastructures. Even if the influence was not always direct, Sinclair's pioneering scholarship, which included an attentiveness to the practical and technical workings of global finance, did much to open up fresh and promising avenues of inquiry and arrange the mental furniture of those who engaged with it to open up new research possibilities.

Malcolm Campbell-Verduyn, one of the leading figures on financial infrastructures, did his doctoral thesis on the private authority of rating agencies and similar financial institutions and was very much influenced by Sinclair's scholarship (Campbell-Verduyn 2016, 2017). In addition, a surprising number of other proponents of the infrastructural turn in the study of global finance spent time in the Politics and International Studies Department (PAIS) at Warwick – often working and engaging directly with Sinclair. Nick Bernards and Chris Clarke work at Warwick, some like Julian Gruin, John Morris and Nina Boy did their postdocs there, while Lorenzo Genito, Benjamin Braun and me all did their PhDs at PAIS. Many of them were inspired by Sinclair's work, be it indirectly or through his mentorship and supervision.

In their respective studies of central counterparties and index providers, Lorenzo Genito and me, for instance, explicitly draw on Sinclair's work when examining the private authority of these infrastructure providers (Genito 2019; Petry, Fichtner & Heemskerk 2021). Other leading scholars in this debate on infrastructures like Paul Langley, Tony Porter or Marieke de Goede had long and deep engagements with Sinclair's scholarship, their approaches in part shaped and influenced by his thinking (see, e.g. Porter 2005).

Overall, Sinclair's approach might even chart another way to understanding financial infrastructures. His open-minded "analytical eclecticism" (Sil & Katzenstein 2010) might be a resource and inspiration on which future work in this subfield can draw. While sometimes crossing levels of analysis and disciplinary boundaries, the two predominant perspectives for analysing financial infrastructures often remain within their separate bubbles, speaking to different audiences and focusing on their respective levels of analysis. As a result of this somewhat siloed thinking, important opportunities for cross-fertilization may be missed, and key aspects of the politics and the social foundations of global finance may get overlooked.

Perhaps most notably, through weaving together the micro, meso and macro levels of analysis, Sinclair's social foundations perspective enables a much more explicit emphasis on the (global) *politics* of finance. As Sinclair (2005: 20) noted, his work "focus[ed] on more than one level of analysis, such as sovereign states [as] the politics of rating pervades the world order" – affecting corporations, national states or municipalities alike. While he did engage in the nitty-gritty analysis of the technical details of the rating process, Sinclair thus always circled back to understanding the politics within ratings and especially their global political implications. As highlighted in Germain's chapter in this book, Sinclair insisted that rating agencies should be understood in terms of their mental frameworks, understood as intersubjective belief systems that tie the mundane practices of rating to the global politics of finance.[7] He talked about how the "mental framework of rating orthodoxy ... hinges around the perceived interests of investors, the actors rating agency officials see as their principals" (Sinclair 2021: 61). This mental framework is also "a feature of the structural power of the agencies" and "incorporates assumptions about knowledge that defines rating as a technical process" (Sinclair 2021: 61). This emphasis on the worldviews of rating agencies gave Sinclair's study of them political agency, linking the analysis to larger questions of power, global governance and world order.

As Sinclair (2001a) noted himself, the rating agencies had become a crucial aspect of the infrastructure of global governance. This "specialized form of intelligence gathering and judgemental determination" was crucial for privatizing policymaking and narrowing the "legitimate sphere for state-led public policy interventions" (Sinclair 2001a: 441), reconfiguring the relationship between states and markets. Moreover, ratings thus facilitated "policy convergence around characteristically American 'best practice'", promoting an "American-derived, synchronic mental framework" (Sinclair 2005: 17). By influencing (potential) debtors and creditors about how to think about creditworthiness along the lines of an "American-derived, synchronic mental framework" (Sinclair 2005: 71),[8] the agencies thus increasingly cemented US power and worldviews globally (see also Cox 1996). The agencies and their mundane practices "should be understood therefore as a crucial nerve centre in the world order, as a nexus of neoliberal control" (Sinclair 2005: 70).

In terms of his approach and focus, then, and Sinclair's way of thinking about global financial institutions and dynamics, his work always foregrounded a thoroughly political reading of market ordering devices. His research on the social

7. While STS/SSF approaches to financial infrastructures might also point towards the politics, they are more minimalistic and unclear about broader, more systematic implications; I thank Malcolm Campbell-Verduyn for pointing this out.
8. As Sinclair noted (2005: 71), "the most significant effect of rating agencies is not therefore, their view of budget deficits or some other specific policy but their influence on how issuers assess problems in general. This adjustment of mental schemata is the most consequential impact of their work."

foundations of global finance resonated with the SSF by the likes of Donald Mackenzie, who considered Sinclair's 2005 book to be the "single best study" of rating agencies (Mackenzie 2011: 1784). Sinclair's social foundations of global finance approach opened a distinctive understanding of the politics of ratings that could provide the basis of further engagement between work on financial infrastructures and cognate traditions, such as SSF and STS.

Concluding remarks

Financial markets, for Sinclair, had to be understood as social and political constructs, and it made no sense to consider them as naturally occurring phenomena. His fundamental point that "financial markets are more social – and less spontaneous, individual or 'natural' – than we tend to believe" (Sinclair 2005: 5) is one that the best work on financial infrastructures keenly appreciates. The crucial mediating role that Sinclair zeroed in on, played by rating agencies as "the institutions that work to facilitate transactions between buyers and sellers", was of huge political significance. Indeed, these apparently mundane, technical practices, Sinclair (2005: 5) revealed, played "a central role in organizing markets and, consequently, in governing the world". What his *oeuvre* did so much to reveal was "the 'reconfiguring' effect these institutions and practices have on global economic and political life" (Sinclair 2005: 10–11).

Sinclair's pioneering scholarship on the social foundations of global finance, and on rating agencies in particular, worked with a conceptual terminology distinct from that developed in recent times by financial infrastructure scholars. Yet Sinclair's focus on rating agencies and processes as "market ordering devices" clearly warrants engagement from those working in that sphere. As outlined above, even though he did not develop the lens of infrastructures at length, Sinclair uncovered the various aspects of the rating agencies that signify their infrastructural qualities: the characteristics of facilitation, openness, durability, centrality and obscurity as well as how they convey and distribute power between state and market actors. This work on the rating agencies then inspired in various ways future scholars working on financial infrastructures, including but not limited to some of the key scholars in this area mentioned above.

Sinclair also had his own approach that was thoroughly political all the way down, which serves as a useful reminder of the importance of the global politics of finance for all scholars looking at the internal plumbing of financial markets. His way of exploring global finance was to look very closely at particular practices and institutions using his social foundations approach that rejected a mainstream view that "markets reflect fundamental economic forces, which are not subject to human manipulation" (Sinclair 2005: 5). This politicizing move was a product of his own intellectual lineage, including the work of Robert Cox. Building on this, Sinclair's work underlined the intersubjective nature of finance, credibility and confidence and was always centrally interested in the (global) politics of finance. What rating agencies say about the state of a firm's or a government's creditworthiness matters, and in this way the ratings process needs to be understood as the site for the exercise of highly significant political power, which significantly impacted global governance and world order.

His methodological move to centre on "specific institutions and associated 'micro-practices' at the core of contemporary capitalism" (Sinclair 2005: 10–11) was a visionary step, foreshadowing the infrastructural turn. Sinclair revealed the fascinating combination of how these hugely consequential institutions, and the prevailing mental frameworks within the ratings process, were both somewhat arbitrarily arrived at, and at the same time, enormously important for the allocation of global credit – for state and market actors alike. These are key insights and fundamental starting points that future financial infrastructures work could pay even closer heed to.

References

Bernards, N. & M. Campbell-Verduyn 2019. "Understanding technological change in global finance through infrastructures". *Review of International Political Economy* 26 (5): 773–89.

Bowker, G. & S. Leigh Star 1999. *Sorting Things Out: Classification and its Consequences.* Cambridge, MA: MIT Press.

Braun, B. 2020. "Central banking and the infrastructural power of finance: the case of ECB support for repo and securitization markets". *Socio-Economic Review* 18 (2): 395–418.

Braun, B. & D. Gabor 2020. "Central banking, shadow banking, and infrastructural power". In *The Routledge International Handbook of Financialization*, P. Mader, D. Mertens & N. Van der Zwan (eds), 241–52. Abingdon: Routledge.

Campbell-Verduyn, M. 2016. "Merely TINCering around: the shifting private authority of technology, information and news corporations". *Business & Politics* 18 (2): 143–70.

Campbell-Verduyn, M. 2017. *Professional Authority After the Global Financial Crisis: Defending Mammon in Anglo-America.* Basingstoke: Palgrave Macmillan.

Campbell-Verduyn, M. & M. Hütten 2023. "Locating infrastructural agency: computer protocols at the finance/security nexus". *Security Dialogue* 54 (5): 455–74.

Cerny, P. 1994. "The infrastructure of the infrastructure? Toward embedded financial orthodoxy in the international political economy". In *Transcending the State-Global Divide: A Neostructuralist Agenda in International Relations*, R. Palan & B. Gills (eds), 223–49. Boulder, CO: Lynne Reinner.

Clarke, C. 2019. "Platform lending and the politics of financial infrastructures". *Review of International Political Economy* 26 (5): 863–85.

Cohen, B. 1996. "Phoenix risen: the resurrection of global finance". *World Politics* 48 (2): 268–96.

Coombs, N. 2022. "Narrating imagined crises: how central bank storytelling exerts infrastructural power". *Economy and Society* 51 (4): 679–702.

Cox, R. W. 1996. "Social forces, states and world orders: beyond international relations theory". In *Approaches to World Order*, R. W. Cox with T. J. Sinclair (eds), 107–11. Cambridge: Cambridge University Press.

de Goede, M. 2020. "Finance/security infrastructures". *Review of International Political Economy* 28 (2): 351–68.

de Goede, M. & C. Westermeier 2022. "Infrastructural geopolitics". *International Studies Quarterly* 66 (3): sqac033.

Edwards, P. 2003. "Infrastructure and modernity: force, time and social organization in the history of sociotechnical systems". In *Modernity and Technology*, T. Misa, P. Bray & A. Feenberg (eds), 185–225. Cambridge, MA: MIT Press.

Gabor, D. 2020. "Critical macro-finance: a theoretical lens". *Finance & Society* 6 (1): 45–55.

Genito, L. 2019. "Mandatory clearing: the infrastructural authority of central counterparty clearing houses in the OTC derivatives market". *Review of International Political Economy* 26 (5): 938–62.

Green, J. & J. Gruin 2021. "RMB transnationalization and the infrastructural power of international financial centres". *Review of International Political Economy* 28 (4): 1028–54.

Helleiner, E. 1996. *States and the Reemergence of Global Finance: From Bretton Woods to the 1990s.* Ithaca, NY: Cornell University Press.

Konings, M. 2010. "Neoliberalism and the American state". *Critical Sociology* 36 (5): 741–65.

Krarup, T. 2019. "Between competition and centralization: the new infrastructures of European finance". *Economy & Society* 48 (1): 107–26.

Larkin, B. 2013. "The politics and poetics of infrastructure". *Annual Review of Anthropology* 42 (1): 327–43.

Lincoln, B. 1994. *Authority: Construction and Corrosion.* Chicago, IL: University of Chicago Press.

Mackenzie, D. 2005. "Opening the black boxes of global finance". *Review of International Political Economy* 12 (4): 555–76.

Mackenzie, D. 2011. "The credit crisis as a problem in the sociology of knowledge". *American Journal of Sociology* 116 (6): 1778–841.

Mann, M. 1984. "The autonomous power of the state: its origins, mechanisms and results". *European Journal of Sociology* 25 (2): 185–213.

Pardo-Guerra, J. 2019. *Automating Finance: Infrastructures, Engineers, and Relation-Making in Electronic Markets.* Cambridge: Cambridge University Press.

Pauly, L. 1997. *Who Elected the Bankers? Surveillance and Control in the World Economy.* Ithaca, NY: Cornell University Press.

Petry, J. 2020. "From national marketplaces to global providers of financial infrastructures: exchanges, infrastructures and structural power in global finance". *New Political Economy* 26 (4): 574–97.

Petry, J., J. Fichtner & E. Heemskerk 2021. "Steering capital: the growing private authority of index providers in the age of passive asset management". *Review of International Political Economy* 28 (1): 152–76.

Porter, T. 1993. *States, Markets and Regimes in Global Finance.* Basingstoke: Palgrave Macmillan.

Porter, T. 1995. "Innovation in global finance: the impact on hegemony and growth since 1000 AD". *Review (Fernand Braudel Center)* 18 (3): 387–429.

Porter, T. 2005. "The new masters of capital: American bond rating agencies and the politics of creditworthiness: Timothy Sinclair". *New Political Economy* 10 (3): 427–31.

Powell, W. & L. Smith-Doerr 1994. "Networks and economic life". In *The Handbook of Economic Sociology*, N. Smelser & R. Swedberg (eds), 379–402. Princeton, NJ: Princeton University Press.

Schwartz, H. 2019. "American hegemony: intellectual property rights, dollar centrality, and infrastructural power". *Review of International Political Economy* 26 (3): 490–519.

Searle, J. 1995. *The Construction of Social Reality.* London: Penguin.

Sil, R. & P. Katzenstein 2010. "Analytic eclecticism in the study of world politics: reconfiguring problems and mechanisms across research traditions". *Perspectives on Politics* 8 (2): 411–31.

Star, S. Leigh 1999. "The ethnography of infrastructure". *American Behavioral Scientist* 43 (3): 377–91.

Strange, S. 1996. *The Retreat of the State: The Diffusion of Power in the World Economy*. Cambridge: Cambridge University Press.

Strange, S. 1997. *States and Markets*. Second edn. London: Pinter.

Underhill, G. 2000. "State, market, and global political economy: genealogy of an (inter-?) discipline". *International Affairs* 76 (4): 805–24.

Wansleben, L. 2023. *The Rise of Central Banks: State Power in Financial Capitalism*. Cambridge, MA: Harvard University Press.

Weiss, L. & E. Thurbon 2018. "Power paradox: how the extension of US infrastructural power abroad diminishes state capacity at home". *Review of International Political Economy* 25 (6): 779–810.

Westermeier, C., M. Campbell-Verduyn & B. Brandl (eds) 2025a. *Cambridge Global Handbook of Financial Infrastructures*. Cambridge: Cambridge University Press.

Westermeier, C., M. Campbell-Verduyn & B. Brandl (eds) 2025b. "Infrastructural gazing on global finance". In *Cambridge Global Handbook on Financial Infrastructures*, C. Westermeier, M. Campbell-Verduyn & B. Brandl (eds), 1–10. Cambridge: Cambridge University Press.

6

THE POLITICAL ECONOMY OF CREDIT RATING AGENCIES: AMERICAN SHORT-TERMIST UNIVERSALISM, EUROPE'S ACQUIESCENCE AND EAST ASIA'S RESISTANCE

Fumihito Gotoh, Norbert Gaillard and Rick Michalek

Introduction

Timothy Sinclair's pioneering works, including "Passing judgement: credit rating process as regulatory mechanisms of governance in the emerging world order" (Sinclair 1994b) and *The New Masters of Capital* (Sinclair 2005), have inspired many studies on the political economy of credit rating agencies (CRAs) (e.g. Gaillard 2011, 2014; Kruck 2011; Paudyn 2014; Helleiner & Wang 2018; Gotoh 2019; Mennillo 2022). This chapter draws on his "social foundations" and "market-centred" approaches and discusses the divergent norms and mental frameworks of American and local (non-American) CRAs. Sinclair (2001b: 109) contended that "international capital mobility is not a law of nature or a machine", and capital's bargaining power vis-à-vis labour and the state is contingent on the state's history and domestic social norms. The Big Three CRAs, namely, Moody's Investors Service (Moody's), Standard and Poor's (S&P) and Fitch Ratings (Fitch), have not only played a critical role in global financialization and financial governance but also contributed to the Asian and global financial crises. As Sinclair argued in *To the Brink of Destruction* (Sinclair 2021), both market-centred (rationalist) and social foundations (constructivist) approaches are needed to explain the American CRAs' significant influence on the global financial crisis (GFC).

In this chapter, first, we elucidate what transformed the American CRAs from conservative financial gatekeepers to short-term profit maximizers, highlighting financial and technological innovations (e.g. securitization and algorithmization) and then argue that the American CRAs' short-termist universalism has been acquiesced to in Europe but has conflicted with social norms and elite interests in East Asia, leading to the establishment of local CRAs. This triptych of Anglo-American, European and East Asian models reprises an early debate about forms of financial systems and capitalism from the 1980s (Zysman 1983; Albert 1993). In the early 2010s, the project of a Europe-wide CRA to defend European sovereign credit ratings failed because of the robust triopoly of the American CRAs and the new key role played by the European Central Bank. In contrast, Japan, South Korea and China established local CRAs to counter the American CRAs because East Asian elites viewed the risks of market failure as larger than those of government failure, prioritized socio-political stability and wanted to restrict the influence of American CRAs. Sinclair (2005, 2021) analysed the two contrasting forms of finance – the synchronic form, which focuses on short-term profit-making in financial markets, and the diachronic form, which links finance with investment in productive assets for the growth of social wealth and criticized the short-termist synchronic mental framework of American CRAs. The American CRAs' ratings undervalue social stability as maintaining such stability competes with debt issuers' repayment capacity (Sinclair 2005). We examine how effective Sinclair's works are in analysing the above research themes and how we could build on his works.

For example, investigating the reasons for varying time preferences by region could develop Sinclair's works (2005, 2021). According to Hofstede (2015), long-term oriented societies, which emphasize perseverance, modesty, pragmatism and thrift include East Asian countries, while short-term oriented societies, which are characterized by the need for instant reactions, self-enhancement and sacrosanct traditions (universal guidelines), and spending and borrowing, comprise the US and other Anglophone countries. Many European countries (e.g. Germany, France, Italy, and Nordic countries) indicate "middle-term" orientation and are situated between the two camps. Therefore, it could be argued that the American CRAs' short-termist universalism is in greater conflict with East Asia's long-term orientation than with Europe's middle-term orientation. However, Hofstede's perspective may be too dichotomous and static, given that culture in a society is not monolithic and evolves over time. He claimed that Confucianism, which stresses virtues of perseverance, modesty and thrift among others, influences East Asia's long-term orientation (Hofstede 2011). Nevertheless, although the South Korean household saving rate was high until the Asian financial crisis (20.4 per cent in 1998), after introducing the promotion of credit card usage to boost domestic demand in 1999, household savings plummeted and household debt soared, which cannot be explained by long-term orientation.[1]

1. Iain Pirie, University of Warwick, raised this point at the conference entitled "Beyond Paradigms: Timothy J. Sinclair's Social Foundations of Global Finance" held at the University of Warwick on 27 June 2023.

Time preference is a significant determinant of human behaviour (Galor & Özak 2016) but is more nuanced and complicated than it looks at first glance. Time preference is a matter of degree, and long- and short-term orientations coexist in most societies. In another chapter of this volume, Randall Germain argues that the synchronic/diachronic distinction can be regarded as a continuum rather than a mutually exclusive set of attributes, and we concur with this view. The US has had both short-termist synchronic and long-termist diachronic forms of finance. Short-term trading of debt and equity exemplifies the former form, while venture capital and private equity investments are classified as the latter form, in which Anglophone economies have taken longer-term risks than East Asia ones.[2] However, the overall characteristic of American finance has become more short-termist. Furthermore, there are trade-offs between the market-based (witnessed in Anglophone economies) and bank-centred (prevalent in East Asia) financial systems: the former's relative inferior stability due to fluctuations in asset values driven by modifications in market information and investors' views, as well as weak risk sharing by investors, offsets its otherwise superior efficiency obtained through wide dissemination of diverse information (Allen & Gale 2001). This suggests that Anglophone economies' short-termism and East Asia's long-termism are linked to the respective preferences for economic efficiency (through individual investors' large risk-taking) and sociopolitical stability.

Since neoliberal policy started promoting financial deregulation in the US and Britain during the 1980s, trading has become the largest profit driver of global investment banks. Moreover, corporate ownership in the US has dramatically shifted from individual to institutional investors, largely pension and mutual funds, while the tenures of corporate managers have been shortened due to the mounting pressure from institutional investors regarding short-term shareholder returns. Rappaport (2011) names the dominance of public companies and the financial markets by corporate and investment managers responsible for other people's money as "agency capitalism" and claims that short-termism is a rational choice for such managers as near-term performance is tied to their job security, labour market reputation and compensation. Against these backdrops, the shift to the issuer-pay model, the sharp expansion of securitization and Moody's listing to the NYSE in 2000 pushed the characteristic of American CRAs towards synchronic short-termism. In the meantime, common law that offers stronger protection for investors than civil law adopted by continental Europe and East Asia (La Porta *et al.* 1998), has enabled investors in Anglophone countries to have strong (long-term and short-term) risk-taking, while the government has used civil law as an instrument for state building and controlling

2. Interview with a venture capitalist in July 2023.

economic life (La Porta *et al.* 1999). Gambacorta, Yang & Tsatsaronis (2014: 24) maintain that "common law systems foster the development of market-based finance, which depends on the efficiency of arm's length relationships between issuers of securities and investors". Confidence in market-based finance hinged on such arm's length relationships and facilitated the transition to short-termism and the exponential growth of structured finance in Anglophone economies. By contrast, East Asian elites are less confident in market-based finance and prioritize the diachronic form of finance (including bank-centred finance) over synchronic finance to maintain socio-political stability and their political and economic interests. Investigating the correlations between the historical development of legal systems and the characteristics of finance in regions could build on Sinclair's works.

The structure of our chapter is as follows. The following section accounts for American CRAs' shift to short-termism as manifested by their concentration on securitization from a former Moody's credit officer's perspective. The third section analyses why Europe has acquiesced to the American credit rating system and has not established a Europe-wide CRA. The fourth section discusses the establishment of Japanese, Korean and Chinese local CRAs to counter the influence of American CRAs. Finally, the concluding remarks refer to the prospect of CRAs, including algorithmization.

American credit ratings agencies' short-termism

Sinclair (2021) convincingly illustrated how the skyrocketing growth of structured finance had influenced the characteristics of the American CRAs and led to the GFC. Nevertheless, if he had analysed the divergent cultures of the corporate credit and structured finance rating divisions within the agencies, it would have provided further explanatory power for his work. The American CRAs' corporate rating divisions traditionally emphasize the "art", for instance, qualitative factors including industry risk, management capability and R&D competitiveness, over quantitative factors (mainly financial ratios) and are long-term oriented, while their structured finance rating divisions focus on the "science" (quantitative factors) and include professionals (e.g. quantitative analysts and lawyers) different from those in the corporate credit rating divisions (Rona-Tas & Hiss 2010). However, credit analysis needs both the art and science.

During the late 1980s and into the 1990s, there was an explosion of residential mortgage-backed securities (RMBS) issuance. This incredible supply was coincident with the failure of the Savings and Loan thrift institutions, and the issuance included securitization from the Resolution Trust Corporation, the US government agency charged with resolving and disposing of the assets of the failed thrifts. The crisis did not go wasted as bankers and their legal counsel found and further developed the use of securitization. The technology was quickly adopted and modified for additional asset classes and for different purposes. Receivables financing, previously delivered through factoring, found securitization to be cheaper and more efficient. And soon after, collateralized bond offerings (CBOs), consisting of pools of corporate bonds, funded by the issuance of a combination of securities. In all such cases, the imprimatur of a rating from one of the Big Three CRAs was indispensable and further reduced the cost of capital for the user (Sinclair 2012b).

By the mid-1990s, law firms that focused on structured finance and securitization were struggling to staff all the billable hours. However, the real acceleration in activity came when the banks, and the "non-bank" originators, embraced the technology and began to employ securitization in new and novel ways. Common law is conducive to the issue of structured finance, in which major American law firms play a key role.

Rating traditional debt issuance involved the analysis of balance sheets, cash flows, profit margins and corporate structures. Analysts were expected to know the issuer, its personnel and its history and to understand and analyse earnings and projections. Structured finance introduced the "special purpose vehicle" (SPV): a legal creation with no actual employees but with a balance sheet and with strict operating instructions designed to fund a "priority of claims" capital structure wherein the most senior claims sold to investors offered the lowest risk, and therefore the highest rating. From the earliest ratings assigned to securitizations, the rating analyst was playing "catch up" to Wall Street and its lawyers. Initially, these offerings were concentrated in CBOs. These structures exploited legal "ring-fencing" and were, by location, tax-advantaged to isolate the originators from consolidation issues (off-balance-sheet financing) and bankruptcy risks. Placing the issuing vehicles offshore, originators (at the instruction of their lawyers) were able to have their "tax-advantaged" cake and eat it too.

Structured finance ratings would only be assigned upon certification that the "ramp-up" was successfully completed.[3] The critical horizon, from the rating agency's perspective, was not upon the ultimate (long-term) performance but upon the initial launch (near-term) of the issuance. Note well the incentives attending these rated structured finance issuances: everyone (but the investors) is paid at the beginning. The banks and originators, who sought to purchase the assets at a discount to their transfer price into the vehicle, were paid from the issuing proceeds. So were the lawyers and the CRA. This fostered the culture of "I'll be gone, you'll be gone" (Knee 2006: xvii, quoted by Sinclair 2021: 184). Provided that the descriptive metrics required of the SPV's indenture were satisfied, the

3. The acquisition of the targeted assets, the revenue from which funded the rated obligations.

subsequent performance of the assets was a matter for the rating surveillance department. The definition of the ratings used in these issuances was carefully crafted to ensure that there could be no expectation that an initially assigned rating offered anything promising the persistence of that same level of risk.[4] Originators experienced with static pools quickly realized a new revenue stream could be had by actively managing the constituent pool of bonds. Originating banks spun off asset manager entities, further distancing the bank from the risk of the issuance (and rating deterioration) but enabling additional profits from management fees. Once again, the rating analysts had to invent the wheel by which the risk to investors of a specific class of securities backed by a dynamic pool of assets could be assigned a rating that was consonant with all the other ratings otherwise available from that CRA. And with every new development in the technology of securitization, the focus tightened on the quantitative models and the math. Rating committees, originally group affairs, slowly devolved into a three-person discussion: the quantitative analyst, responsible for determining whether the in-house quantitative model of the deal was congruent with the internally developed thresholds, the assigned lawyer, responsible for confirming that the terms employed in the described deal (and therefore in the model) were accurately contained in the documentation, and a supervising manager.

The potential of the technology, and the profit margins within the structured derivatives products division, made the privately held Moody's (the division within Dun & Bradstreet responsible for ratings) an attractive candidate for a spin-off and public offering. In 2000, Moody's was spun off from Dun & Bradstreet and was listed on the NYSE.[5] From that point onward, the in-house focus steadily shifted from "protecting the perceived premium" associated with Moody's analysis to the level of its current stock price. This focus was further intensified with the shift in the compensation structure. Managers received additional stock options above those awarded to analysts at the VP level for an increased volume of ratings. Direct and explicit references to market share and "deals lost to the competition" were made and emphasized in group and departmental meetings.

The shift in culture was further evidenced by the emphasis on quantity over quality. In 2002, there were approximately 18 lawyers employed in the structured derivatives group charged with reviewing the documentation presented with the 45–60 transactions seeking Moody's rating. By 2007, despite the number

4. One of the authors (Rick Michalek) was responsible for reviewing and amending the definitions of the ratings found in Moody's structured derivatives indentures, and for advising whether any implication of persistence was legally present.

5. S&P Global was listed on the NYSE in 2013. The third CRA, Fitch Ratings, is owned by the Hearst Corp.

of transactions having increased well over 250 per cent, the number of lawyers increased by only 28 per cent. Direct and indirect pressure was applied to prioritize the issuance, particularly in repeat or "dupe" (duplicated) deals where issuances were offered through a series.

The banks recognized their bargaining power as they saw the competition for market share intensify between the CRAs (Sinclair 2012b). Their lawyers worked to create documentation that gave their clients greater flexibility (looser covenant restrictions) even as the CRA managers were preoccupied with the number of deals being rated (which resulted in larger bonuses). With the rapid acceleration of timelines, analysts were forced to triage their review. Predictably, the pressure to get more deals rated despite the steadily diminishing time available for review resulted in a relative laxity in both qualitative and quantitative analysis. While the rating models used in-house had to be continually fine-tuned to address the evolution of structures presented, the documentation raced ahead, leaving gaps between what the structurers were designing and what the documentation was constraining.

On top of this struggle to accurately evaluate the incoming transactions, surveillance of the performance of existing and rated transactions was also falling behind. As the technology for issuing "second derivative" products (collateralized "asset-backed securities", collectively known as collateralized debt offerings (CDOs)), the importance of accurately rated and monitored underlying issuances became critical. This importance was further amplified by the introduction of synthetic CDOs (in which no underlying pool was actually purchased but only referenced). The penultimate creation prior to the financial crisis of 2008 was the introduction of "CDOs squared" where the underlying or referenced assets were themselves CDOs. While the in-house "rule" was, if the assets were rated in-house there was no need to question the risk of the underlying assets beyond the rating assigned to it, the reality was that many of the assigned ratings were overdue for revision and review.[6]

As noted above, the rating process through the evolution of securitization steadily drifted away from qualitative analysis and increasingly focused on quantitative metrics. The cost structure of the structured derivatives group involved greater investment in quantitative analysts and the development of a surveillance department (wherein the largest part of the work was sent offshore). Extremely talented modellers and statisticians were employed, often trained abroad and working in the US on employment visas and often where English was not their first language. At the height of issuance frenzy, it was occasionally necessary for a rated deal to "share" a lawyer, or in extreme circumstances, go without the benefit of a lawyer's assistance at all. These young "quants" could be found

6. This "trust" in in-house ratings did not extend to competitors' ratings.

alone on conference calls with partners of major law firms on the other end, patiently listening as the partners explained why the proposed documentation was adequate and no further comments were required.

While the great financial recession brought much if not all the excess to a screeching halt, it also brought changes to the rating process. Rating stability following the debacle of 2008, which saw AAA-rated securities drop overnight to junk status, became a proper focus. However, the dominance of quantitative and numerical analysis persists. The reliance on models of economic behaviour, themselves built on sequences of algorithmic logic purporting to describe the underlying elements of the modelled transaction, persists. The time required to accurately and comprehensively identify the variables that may impact a complex structured derivative transaction destroys the economic viability of the product unless it can be commodified and algorithmically modelled.

The exponential growth of the structured finance rating business, the public ownership of Moody's and intensified competition between the Big Three contributed to their short-termist universalism, which has had global repercussions.

Europe's acquiescence to the US credit rating system

The credit rating business was long an industry designed by US experts to provide financial services to US investors (Sinclair 2005). The financial globalization that started in the 1980s enabled the two top CRAs (Moody's and S&P) to expand their operations in other developed countries. For instance, Moody's rated 8 European sovereign debt issuers in 1985, rising to 41 in 2007, and they rated 48 corporate debt issuers in 1985, rising to 1,383 in 2007 (Gaillard's 2011 database; Moody's Investors Service 2008). This growing coverage was boosted by two fundamental evolutions.

The first driver was the increasing indebtedness of European issuers. The total amount of the international corporate and general government debt securities outstanding issued by entities located in the five largest economies of the European Union (EU)[7] at the time (i.e. France, Germany, Italy, Spain and Britain) jumped from $161 billion in 1990 to $6,146 billion in 2007.[8]

The second driver was the extensive use of credit ratings in European financial regulations. More than five decades after their US counterparts, European legislators and regulators – at the national and community levels – implemented new financial rules incorporating credit ratings. For example, in July 1988, the French government enacted a regulation mandating that companies issuing

7. The European Community (EC) was replaced by the EU in 1993.

8. Authors' computations based on https://stats.bis.org.

bonds with a maturity of more than two years obtain a credit rating.[9] Next, in the EU, Council Directive 93/6/EEC of 15 March 1993 on the capital adequacy of investments firms and credit institutions established that the default risk associated with certain debt instruments had to be evaluated by at least two CRAs recognized by the competent authorities.

These regulations paved the way to the overreliance of European policymakers on credit ratings until the 2010s. How can Europe's acquiescence to the US credit risk assessment be explained? In fact, in a context of growing borrowing needs, increasing financial disintermediation and heightened capital mobility, European governments seemed to have an obvious interest in espousing the US market-centred philosophy. They were also satisfied with the sovereign ratings that they were assigned. Eleven of the twelve EC members in 1990 managed either to preserve their very high ratings or to get upgraded by 2007.[10] As a result, it is not surprising that, in 2007, CRAs were free of any direct regulation in the EU.

Following the subprime crisis in 2007–08 and the disclosure of CRAs' wrongdoing (Securities and Exchange Commission 2008; see also United States Senate 2011: 243–317), European legislators started supervising the rating industry. In accordance with Regulation No. 1060/2009 of the European Parliament and of the Council of 16 September 2009, CRAs that issue credit ratings in the EU must be subject to registration. They should also eliminate conflicts of interest, disclose their policies regarding unsolicited credit ratings and make available information on their historical performance data. The amendments introduced by Regulation No. 513/2011 of the European Parliament and of the Council empowered the European Securities and Markets Authority (ESMA) to register and supervise CRAs. Its role may be compared to that of the Office of Credit Ratings (OCR), established within the Securities and Exchange Commission (SEC) by the Dodd-Frank Act of 2010.

The US credit rating system was fundamentally questioned by European policymakers during the eurozone sovereign debt crisis. Between January 2009 and January 2014, the credit ratings of Italy, Ireland, Spain, Portugal, Greece and Cyprus were, on average, downgraded by 5, 8, 9, 9, 11 and 13 notches, respectively (Gaillard 2014). Fitch, Moody's and S&P were held responsible for exacerbating market stress and endangering the eurozone. In reaction, the European Parliament passed a new legislation.

Regulation (EU) No. 462/2013 of the European Parliament and of the Council of 21 May 2013 amending Regulation No. 1060/2009 includes key measures

9. "Arrêté du 21 juillet 1988 portant homologation d'un règlement du Comité de la réglementation bancaire", *Journal Officiel de la République Française du 21 juillet 1988*, 9519–20.
10. Authors' analysis based on S&P sovereign ratings. The exception was Italy.

designed to cut reliance on CRAs, limit conflicts of interests, monitor sovereign ratings and stimulate competition. First, in line with the provisions contained in the Dodd-Frank Act, European regulators are required to eliminate the references to credit ratings in existing rules, guidelines and recommendations.[11] Second, an entity holding at least 5 per cent of either the capital or the voting rights in a CRA cannot enjoy the same position in or exercise a dominant influence over another agency. Third, every year, at the end of December, CRAs should publish a calendar for the following 12 months setting the dates for the publication of sovereign ratings. Those must be reviewed at least every six months. In addition, sovereign ratings and reports should not include any policy recommendations or prescriptions. Fourth, the European Commission encouraged the establishment of a European CRA assigning sovereign ratings. The objective was to "make an impartial and objective assessment of Member States' creditworthiness, taking into account the specific economic and social development". This project was a failure. Conceived amid the eurozone debt crisis in 2010–11, it seemed outdated when the regulation was enacted in 2013. Why? Primarily because of the proactive role played by the European Central Bank (ECB).

On 26 July 2012, Mario Draghi, president of the ECB, declared: "Within our mandate, the ECB is ready to do whatever it takes to preserve the euro. And believe me, it will be enough." This statement marked the beginning of a ten-year accommodative monetary policy that soothed capital markets and CRAs. Concretely, the long-term government bond yields of Italy, Spain and Greece plummeted from 5.49 per cent, 5.85 per cent and 22.5 per cent, respectively, in 2012 to 0.81 per cent, 0.35 per cent, and 0.88 per cent, respectively, in 2021.[12] In the meantime, the ratings of these three countries rebounded, increasing on average by more two notches if one examines S&P ratings. In this new environment, the creation of a "lenient" European CRA had become redundant.

In summary, European policymakers have largely accepted the US rating system, even during the eurozone sovereign debt turmoil. This acquiescence to what Sinclair (2001a) calls a powerful "embedded knowledge network" reflects the deep integration of the EU into the neoliberal globalization that took shape in the 1980s.

11. Although this measure was positive, it was insufficient to address the fundamental issue. Considering their business model and the high degree of financialization of western economies, CRAs are unlikely to become independent and neutral third-party opinions (see Mennillo & Sinclair 2019).

12. Annual average percentages; Oesterreichische Nationalbank's database.

Table 6.1 American rating orthodoxy vs East Asian heterodoxy

	Time preference	*Preferred form of finance*	*Prioritized goal*	*Emphasized risk*
American rating orthodoxy	Short-termism	Synchronic	Market efficiency	Government failure
East Asian heterodoxy	Long-termism	Diachronic	Socio-political stability	Market failure

East Asia's resistance to American rating orthodoxy

In contrast to Europe, East Asian countries established local CRAs to restrict the power of American CRAs, which can be viewed as a manifestation of economic nationalism.[13] Table 1 contrasts the general characteristics of "American rating orthodoxy" (Sinclair's term) with those of "East Asian heterodoxy", although they are not completely dichotomous, and East Asia has been influenced by the synchronic form of finance. Such normative differences, East Asian elites' material interests and the Japanese, Asian and global financial crises have contributed to East Asia's resistance to American rating orthodoxy. It could be argued that East Asian societies' preference for collectivism has rejected the individualist financial norm – but why? Given the diversity of religions (e.g. Buddhism, Confucianism, Daoism, Shintoism, and Christianity) in East Asia, a history of rice farming is a common factor across the region that likely fostered collectivism. Talhelm *et al.* (2014) contend that histories of farming rice and wheat make cultures more interdependent (collectivist) and independent (individualist), respectively.[14] We examine the cases of Japan, South Korea and China, which demonstrate some differences in the reaction to American CRAs. Although Sinclair (2005) conducted extensive fieldwork only in Japan, his social foundations and market-centred approaches are effective in analysing all three countries' credit rating markets.

After the 1984 Japan–US Yen–Dollar Committee reached an agreement on the liberalization of Japan's financial and capital markets, Moody's and S&P opened their Tokyo offices in 1985. Although three local CRAs – Japan Credit Rating Agency (JCR) and Nippon Investor Services (NIS) backed by Japanese financial institutions and the Ministry of Finance (MOF), and Japan Bond Research Institute (JBRI) owned by Nikkei (a media company) – were also established in 1985, more resourceful American CRAs were expected to overwhelm these local CRAs. Before the early 1990s asset bubble burst, many Japanese banks and

13. Interview with a Fitch official in July 2023.
14. However, southern and northern China have respective traditions of rice and wheat agriculture.

companies enjoyed high credit ratings by the American CRAs. Furthermore, the merger of JBRI and NIS to form Rating and Investment Information (R&I) in 1998 signalled the local CRAs' defensive position. From an Anglo-American perspective, the local CRAs with ties to financial institutions and the government are compromised institutions. In Japan, regulatory authorities provide financial institutions and companies with administrative guidance on matters unstipulated by law, and local CRAs assign high credit ratings for industries and companies highly connected with the government and financial institutions.[15] Such relations sometimes cause moral hazard (Gotoh & Sinclair 2021).

Observing Japan's financial deregulation and crisis during the latter half of the 1990s, the American CRAs expected the convergence of the Japanese credit market with the American market (shrinking government and bank support for corporate borrowers) and drastically downgraded many Japanese banks and companies from the mid-1990s until the early 2000s (Gotoh & Sinclair 2021). However, the massive downgrading made Japanese borrowers antagonistic to the American CRAs, and as public capital injections resuscitated major banks, which in turn supported financially troubled companies, most of those downgraded borrowers did not go bankrupt (Gotoh & Sinclair 2021). Additionally, the GFC damaged the credibility of both securitization ratings and the judgement of the American CRAs. Consequently, since the mid-2000s, the American CRAs have been marginalized in the Japanese market, now dominated by the local CRAs. This is because of the conflict between the synchronic nature of the American CRAs and Japanese society's preference for diachronic finance.

Three local CRAs, National Information & Credit Evaluation (NICE), Korea Investors Service (KIS) and Korea Ratings (KR), equally divide the domestic South Korean credit rating market (Joe & Oh 2017). In the 1980s, under administrative guidance by the Korean government, NICE, KIS and KR were established by the banking industry, the Korea Development Bank, and 70 non-bank financial institutions, respectively (Mitsui 2012). After the Asian financial crisis, the Korean government allowed foreign capital to hold stakes in local CRAs by implementing the Enforcement Rule of the Use and Protection of Credit Information Act (Oh 2014). Fitch started purchasing stakes in KR in 2001, which increased to 54.44 per cent in 2007 and to 73.55 per cent in 2008. Meanwhile, the Korean government allowed Moody's to acquire only 50 per cent + 1 share in KIS in 2001.[16] However, in 2016, Moody's obtained full ownership of KIS by purchasing the rest from NICE Infra (NICE's subsidiary).

The American CRAs have not directly entered the domestic rating market, and despite their ownership of the local Korean CRAs, Moody's and Fitch have

15. Interview with Yoshitaka Kurosawa, Nippon University in July 2023.

16. Interview with a Korean CRA official in June.

not been involved in KIS's and KR's credit assessment.[17] The American CRAs focus on high financial returns (dividends) from their Korean subsidiaries and have avoided friction with South Korea, whose sovereign and corporate ratings were massively downgraded by the American CRAs during the Asian financial crisis.[18] Like in Japan, the Korean local CRAs' corporate ratings take into account substantial implicit government and bank support for borrowers, but many major borrowers (e.g. Daewoo, SsangYong and Hanjin Shipping) went into default. Joe and Oh (2017) claim that from 2002 to 2013, the local CRAs' rating quality deteriorated despite the American CRAs' increased ownership of the local CRAs. South Korea's virtual restriction of American rating orthodoxy in the domestic market and the American CRAs' focus on financial returns reflect their respective diachronic and synchronic characteristics.

China is the world's second largest bond market, just behind the US, but its domestic credit rating market faces several issues, including conflict of interests between local CRAs, and central and local governments, systematic rating inflation, implicit government guarantees for state-owned enterprises (SOEs) and increasing bond defaults. Five of nine Chinese local CRAs are at least partially state-owned, while SOEs' representation in the bond market is very high (Lin & Milhaupt 2017). From the 1990s until 2013, the Chinese government consistently bailed out any potential default on SOE and non-SOE bonds for three motivations: "too big to fail" (systemic risks and financial contagion), "too connected to fail" (issuing firms' or their owners' strong political connections) and "too many to fail" (losses to too many retail investors causing potential social unrest). The first non-SOE and SOE bonds were allowed to default in 2014 and 2015, respectively (Lin & Milhaupt 2017). Issuers put more pressure on CRAs to assign AAA to mitigate the increased funding costs after the no-bailout reform, enhancing the proportion of AAA bonds despite the weakened implicit government guarantee (Mo, Gao & Zhou 2021). However, government support for SOEs has persisted, leaving productive and profitable non-SOEs lacking government support and disadvantaged in funding.

After the GFC, China's Dagong Global Credit Rating Agency attempted to expand into the US and Europe to challenge the Big Three dominance and pursue China's geopolitical interest, but its attempt failed because Dagong could not comply with the American and EU regulations (Bush 2021). Furthermore, in 2018, Chinese authorities suspended Dagong's domestic operation for one year due to misconduct, including conflicts of interest with debt issuers, poor internal governance and defective rating models (Mennillo 2022). Until then,

17. Interview with a Fitch official in July 2023.
18. According to Joe and Oh (2017), the respective KIS's and KR's dividend payout ratios as of 2013 were 90 per cent and 65 per cent, respectively.

non-Chinese CRAs were granted access to the domestic rating market only through joint ventures with local CRAs, but with the domestic rating market liberalization, Chinese authorities approved S&P's and Fitch's wholly-owned subsidiaries to rate domestic bonds in 2019 and 2020, respectively. The arrival of American CRAs would have competitive effects on local CRAs to improve domestic market governance.[19] However, given SOEs' critical importance for the party-state, the motivations for implicit government guarantees would persist, while American CRAs face rating shopping due to excess competition. The Sino-American normative difference is the largest obstacle for American CRAs to succeed in China.

Conclusion

Our analyses in this chapter demonstrate that both social foundations and market-centred approaches are indispensable to elucidate the American CRAs' short-termist universalism, Europe's acquiescence to the American credit rating system and East Asia's resistance to it. The analyses suggest that the American CRAs' power is dominant but may not be as global as typically viewed in the West (Gotoh & Sinclair 2017). To build on Sinclair's works, the origins of varying economic behaviour and time preferences by region need to be grasped, while the synchronic/diachronic distinction should be loosened. We have examined these origins from various angles including legal systems, religions and thoughts, and agricultural production, but further investigation is needed. Besides, while beyond the scope of this chapter, it may be worth considering whether the embedded moral hazard created by repeated government bailouts has laid the foundation for Wall Street's blind faith in its ability to recover from any market failure (Gaillard & Michalek 2019).

The American CRA's rating process has been shifted from the art to the science. Looking forward, the American CRAs and, to a certain extent, their European counterparts, are faced with addressing a historical dilemma. The choice of short-term profit maximization with its attendant culture as described in section 2 has diverged significantly from the relationship-driven and investment-focused diachronic path favoured by East Asia. As the technology of securitization developed, there was an increasing dependency on "parameterization": a transaction's rating became the consequence of identifying and optimizing the key elements of the presented transaction. Profitability depended less on value added, and more on volume added. Now, with the advent of AI steadily encroaching on

19. Interview with a former Moody's official in June 2023.

all things finance, the CRAs will, if not already, be faced with demonstrating where their added value lies. AI is already in use by the investor community, culling through databases of deal documentation to identify those provisions most favourably aligned with optimal returns for a targeted class. Whether such methodology is directly marketed, or whether the issuer community is willing to advertise an unrated but "AI optimized" transaction generating risk-levels designed and represented to be equivalent to those which would otherwise bear a CRA's label may be a question soon facing the rating agencies.

References

Albert, M. 1993. *Capitalism Against Capitalism*. London: Whurr.

Allen, F. & D. Gale 2001. *Comparing Financial Systems*. Cambridge, MA: MIT Press.

Bush, C. 2021. "The rise and fall of Dagong Global Credit Rating Agency: a geopolitical challenge for the rating industry". *Journal of Financial Regulation* 7 (2): 319–24.

Gaillard, N. 2011. *A Century of Sovereign Ratings*. New York: Springer.

Gaillard, N. 2014. "How and why credit rating agencies missed the eurozone debt crisis". *Capital Markets Law Journal* 9 (2): 121–36.

Gaillard, N. & R. Michalek 2019. "How and why moral hazard has distorted financial regulation". In *The Failure of Financial Regulation: Why a Major Crisis Could Happen Again*, A. Hira, N. Gaillard & T. Cohn (eds), 111–51. Cham: Palgrave Macmillan.

Galor, O. & Ö. Özak 2016. "The agricultural origins of time preference". *American Economic Review* 106 (10): 3064–103.

Gambacorta, L., J. Yang & K. Tsatsaronis 2014. "Financial structure and growth". *BIS Quarterly Review*, March.

Gotoh, F. 2019. *Japanese Resistance to American Financial Hegemony: Global versus Domestic Social Norms*. Abingdon: Routledge.

Helleiner, E. & H. Wang 2018. "Limits to the BRICS' challenge: credit rating reform and institutional innovation in global finance". *Review of International Political Economy* 25 (5): 573–95.

Hofstede, G. 2011. "Dimensionalizing cultures: the Hofstede model in context". *Online Readings in Psychology and Culture* 2 (1): Article 8.

Hofstede, G. 2015. "National differences in communication styles". In *Culture's Software – Communication Styles*, D. Brzozowska & W. Chlopicki (eds), 1–15. Newcastle upon Tyne: Cambridge Scholars.

Joe, D. Y. & F. D. Oh 2017. "Did foreign ownership of Korean credit rating agencies improve their ratings?". *Contemporary Economic Policy* 35 (1): 193–200.

Knee, J. A. 2006. *The Accidental Investment Banker: Inside the Decade That Transformed Wall Street*. Oxford: Oxford University Press.

Kruck, A. 2011. *Private Ratings, Public Regulations: Credit Rating Agencies and Global Financial Governance*. Basingstoke: Palgrave Macmillan.

La Porta, R., F. Lopez-de-Silanes, A. Shleifer & R. W. Vishny 1998. "Law and finance". *Journal of Political Economy* 106 (6): 1113–55.

La Porta, R., F. Lopez-de-Silanes, A. Shleifer & R. W. Vishny 1999. "The quality of government". *Journal of Law, Economics, and Organization* 15 (1): 222–79.

Lin, L. & C. Milhaupt 2017. "Bonded to the state: a network perspective on China's corporate debt market". *Journal of Financial Regulation* 3 (1): 1–39.

Mennillo, G. 2022. *Credit Rating Agencies*. Newcastle upon Tyne: Agenda Publishing.

Mitsui, H. 2012. "Korea". In *Capital Market and Rating Agencies in Asia: Structuring a Credit Risk Rating Model*, Y. Kurosawa (ed.), 17–42. New York: Nova Science Publishers.

Mo, G., Z. Gao & L. Zhou 2021. "China's no-bailout reform: impact on bond yields and rating standards". *Journal of Banking & Finance* 133: 106–282.

Moody's Investors Service 2008. "European corporate default and recovery rates, 1985–2007". *Special Comment*, March.

Oh, F. D. 2014. "Assessing competitive conditions in Korea's credit rating industry after the 1997 financial crisis". *Economics Bulletin* 34 (2): 1114–21.

Paudyn, B. 2014. *Credit Ratings and Sovereign Debt: The Political Economy of Creditworthiness through Risk and Uncertainty*. Basingstoke: Palgrave Macmillan.

Rappaport, A. 2011. *Saving Capitalism from Short-Termism: How to Build Long-Term Value and Take Back Our Financial Future*. New York: McGraw Hill.

Rona-Tas, A. & S. Hiss 2010. "The role of ratings in the subprime mortgage crisis: the art of corporate and the science of consumer credit rating". In *Markets on Trial: The Economic Sociology of the US Financial Crisis: Part A*, M. Lounsbury & P. Hirsch (eds), 115–55. Bradford: Emerald.

Securities and Exchange Commission 2008. *Summary Report of Issues Identified in the Commission Staff's Examinations of Select Credit Rating Agencies*. www.sec.gov/files/craexamination070808.pdf.

Talhelm, T. *et al.* 2014. "Large-scale psychological differences within China explained by rice versus wheat agriculture". *Science* 344 (6184): 603–08.

United States Senate 2011. *Wall Street and the Financial Crisis: Anatomy of a Financial Collapse*. Permanent Subcommittee on Investigations, Committee on Homeland Security and Governmental Affairs. Washington, DC: US Senate.

Zysman, J. 1983. *Governments, Markets, and Growth: Financial Systems and the Politics of Industrial Change*. Ithaca, NY: Cornell University Press.

7

MANAGING MULTIPLE AUDIENCES: THE IMPORTANCE OF LEGITIMACY FOR BOND INDEX PROVIDERS AND THE POLITICS OF BOND INDEXING

Dan Wood

Introduction

The notion of legitimacy is one that is implicit, but crucially important, in the work of Tim Sinclair. For Sinclair (2021: 81), understanding institutional relationships is not just what institutions say they do, but "what people observe and collectively agree they are doing". In this way, intersubjective agreements of audiences are crucial in understanding the form institutions take. The actions of these audiences are shaped by sets of constitutive rules that produce identities and behaviours (Sinclair 2009). Here, I apply Sinclair's (2021) ideas to understanding bond index providers. The case of bond indexing is particularly complex. Passive investing is much less advanced in bond indexing than stock indexing, with Bloomberg estimating that about half of US stock assets are managed passively, compared to a third of the bond market. Therefore, it is more complex for bond index providers to maintain legitimacy in their procedures and outcomes than stock index providers because there are multiple, contradictory audiences that they seek to maintain. Of the three prominent bond index providers, Bloomberg, J. P. Morgan and FTSE Russell, only FTSE Russell are recognized as one of the "Big Three" index providers alongside Standard and Poors (S&P) and Morgan Stanley Capital International (MSCI). I argue that the work of Sinclair is instructive in explaining how bond index providers' exercise of their authority over bond indices is shaped by maintaining the legitimacy with their multiple audiences.

Index providers claim legitimacy on two grounds. The first is a procedural claim, that they have the correct procedures to interpret markets. The second is an epistemic claim, that, through their procedures, they are able to provide truthful, accurate access to "the market". There are three primary audiences index providers need to legitimize themselves with: active managers, passive managers and those who use indices as a source of market information and data. For active managers, indices need to represent a specific market to support claims that active managers are able to outperform "the market", which justify the high fees they charge investors. Whereas, for passive managers, indices need to accurately reflect "the market" to ensure that passive investors who track the market receive the market average return and evidence passive managers' claim that markets cannot be consistently outperformed in the long run. The third audience are those who use indices as a source of information on "the market" either in the media or financial participants who pay for the data that index providers have on "the market". What unites all uses of indices is the belief that indices are the correct procedure to obtain accurate representation of "the market".

There is a growing international political economy (IPE) literature on index providers. Here, indices are seen as financial infrastructures that significantly mediate financial relations (Petry 2021). Index providers exercise private authority over these infrastructures and are gatekeepers of financial claims over issues such as domestic financial regulation and investor access and set standards over whether and how these should be reflected in their infrastructure (Petry, Fichtner & Heemskerk 2021; Fichtner, Heemskerk & Petry 2022), for example in relation to the ESG agenda (Fichtner, Jaspert & Petry 2023). The rise of passive management strategies that track indices means index providers steer where capital is allocated (Petry, Fichtner & Heemskerk 2021; Fichtner, Heemskerk & Petry 2022), which Cormier and Naqvi (2023) confirm in the case of J. P. Morgan's Emerging Market Bond Index Global Diversified Index. This leads to a significant puzzle. How are index providers able to maintain their legitimacy to three different audiences, while at the same time, their claim to epistemic legitimacy, that indices represent "the market", is threatened by the very success index providers have had in legitimizing themselves? My contribution to the IPE literature on index providers is to demonstrate the importance of maintaining procedural and epistemic legitimacy to bond index providers and the politics of the bond market.[1] To undertake this analysis, I use policy documents and methodology documents as well as public statements from actors involved.

The chapter proceeds as follows. The following section explains how legitimacy can be understood as important to understanding authority and infrastructures using the work of Sinclair. The third section develops an understanding of how the varied constitutive rules of the audiences of bond index providers shapes their requirements of index providers. The fourth section explains how bond index providers seek to maintain their legitimacy and how they work with their

1. I use the term bond market for consistency with existing IPE literature. Index providers tend to use the term "Fixed Income".

audiences to do so. The final section concludes by explaining why this is important for IPE analysis going forwards.

Legitimacy, authority and bond index infrastructure

The bond market is much more complex than the stock market for index providers. The reason for this is that while a company ordinarily has one stock listing that is valid in perpetuity, companies typically have multiple bonds each with different interest rates, credit ratings and maturity dates (see Tran 2023). These different corporate bonds mean that bond indices need to be constantly adjusted, in a way that is not necessary for equity indices. In addition to these corporate bonds, there are bonds for central and local government, as well as government agencies. Government bonds are often issued in multiple currencies and index providers also need to be aware of changing foreign exchange rates. Therefore, how bond index providers exercise their authority over their index infrastructure is significant, given its centrality to contemporary bond markets. Just one bond index provider (not the largest) calculates over 6,000 bond indices reflecting $100 trillion in debt (ICE 2023). Issuers are ultimately subjects of index providers and have little say in their actions; decisions of inclusion/exclusion or weighting given to each issuer are decided by index providers. But index providers are constrained actors. They must ensure that their audiences, who pay to access and use their indices, view them as legitimate; otherwise these audiences could go to their competitors. The key aspect of this section is to link related concepts of legitimacy and authority and show how these are important to bond index infrastructure.

Legitimacy is particularly important in the case of bond index providers as there are three different audiences, with contradictory perspectives of index providers. Existing IPE literature on legitimacy in finance has focused on state-level architecture (Mügge 2011) or power (Seabrooke 2006), whereas Rethel (2011) examines the importance of legitimacy to alternative financial practices in the case of Islamic finance. In both cases, there is discussion of input and output legitimacy, where input legitimacy refers to the quality of procedures and outcome legitimacy to the perceived success of the outcome (see Mügge 2011; Rethel 2011; using the terms popularized by Scharpf 1999). For clarity, I refer to these as claims for procedural and epistemic legitimacy for greater specificity into both what index providers seek to provide and what their audiences are looking for. In this context, epistemic legitimacy refers to the quality of access, or perceived truthfulness of indices that their audiences seek: that indices represent "the market". Legitimacy is not something possessed, it is the result of social processes of construction. It is important here to differentiate between legitimacy and authority. As Seabrooke (2006) notes, legitimacy is a two-way street because it requires actions to confer it on behalf of the audience. In this case, paying to use a specific index or actively engaging with index providers' market consultations. However, authority is a one-way street, because it does not require a confirmatory action, which differentiates a subject of authority and an audience.

Authority is a core concept IPE has used to conduct analysis of index providers so far (see Petry, Fichtner & Heemskerk 2021). Petry, Fichtner and Heemskerk (2021) explain how authority is established by the first mover advantage leading to capture of major national or regional indices as well as the importance of the major index providers' brand identity. They further outline how the growth of passive investment has empowered index providers to directly steer capital, for example, through the inclusion or exclusion of companies or entire markets, including states, from indices (Petry, Fichtner & Heemskerk 2021). While this analysis importantly highlights the authority that index providers have over their infrastructure and through that their subjects, it neglects an understanding of the constraints of that authority and how index providers' audiences affect how they exercise authority. It is also limited to equity indices where passive investment is much more dominant compared to other audiences in the more contested bond market.

I suggest Sinclair's work helps to understand the constraints of the authority of index providers. Sinclair does not make extensive use of legitimacy as a concept. Instead, drawing on Lincoln (1994), Sinclair considered epistemic authority of institutions to mean the capacity to produce consequential speech that wins the trust of audiences (Sinclair 2005; Rethel & Sinclair 2012). Here, I use epistemic legitimacy to emphasize the confirmatory action from the audience. Sinclair's (2005: 15) clearest use of legitimacy comes in *The New Masters of Capital* where credit rating agencies (CRAs) were viewed as legitimate if they could be seen as endogenous to financial markets rather than an imposed, exogenous force, which gives them a central mediating role in markets. Therefore, the key is to understand how the intersubjective views of audiences are formed, to be able to explain why they view index providers as central, legitimate actors in the bond market.

Following John Searle, Sinclair adopts a distinction between regulative and constitutive rules (Sinclair 2009; see also Rethel & Sinclair 2012). Regulative rules are those that limit specific forms of action, such as laws or formal standards (Sinclair 2009). These are largely irrelevant to the relationship between index providers and their audience at present as the industry is largely self-regulated and promotes compliance with IOSCO (International Organization of Securities Commissions) principles (IOSCO 2013), which the Index Industry Association endorse (IIA 2023b). Although, both the SEC (2022) and the EU Commission

(2022) are consulting on more formal rules, which index providers are resisting (see IIA 2022a, 2022b respectively).

In contrast, constitutive rules represent the social foundations of markets that creates specific collective rules that produce specified forms of behaviour (Sinclair 2009). In effect, constitutive rules are intersubjective understandings that produces the behaviours that unites the actions of that group. I suggest each audience of index providers has their own set of constitutive rules that produces their form of behaviour and defines the way in which they interact with infrastructures. It must be noted that Sinclair (2009) developed the distinction between constitutive and regulative rules from the work of Searle. While Searle confines this analysis to institutions specifically (see Searle 2005), Sinclair uses it more expansively given his intersubjective understanding of institutions. One of the main differences between the CRAs that Sinclair analysed and bond index providers is the multiple, contradictory audiences of the latter. These multiple audiences have their own constitutive rules including their relationship to index providers and their infrastructure. This is important because it is these constitutive rules that produce the actions of these audiences that legitimates index providers as endogenous to bond market infrastructure and fundamental intermediaries to their access to the bond market.

Sinclair's analysis of synchronic and diachronic mental frameworks, following Piaget and Cox, is useful to explain the relationship between index providers and their audiences. As Germain highlights (this volume), Sinclair changes exactly what he means by synchronic and diachronic over time for analysing different problems. I choose to use the most recent of these. In this case, synchronic referred to the maintenance of existing systemic logics that separated the financial economy from the real economy and that eliminated the distance between CRAs and the subjects they were analysing (Sinclair 2021). Whereas the diachronic was a form of distance between CRAs and their subject with the ability to provide a longer-term perspective with more of a reference to the productive economy (Sinclair 2021). While there is much to commend such analysis, I agree with Germain (this volume) that a binary between the synchronic and diachronic is not as useful as a spectrum of possible positions. As outlined in the next section, the audiences of index providers have various positions along a synchronic/diachronic spectrum. This shapes what these audiences view as procedurally and epistemically legitimate.

This constrains index providers who must maintain the legitimacy of their index infrastructure. To do this I draw on literature based on Science and Technology Studies of infrastructures. Infrastructures are not "a thing" but are relationships (Star 1999; Bernards & Campbell-Verduyn 2019). These are complex relationships between individuals and systems, and the material and ideational. Bernards and Campbell-Verduyn (2019) set out key characteristics of infrastructures: facilitation, openness, durability, centrality and obscurity. I choose to use this specific invocation of the concept of infrastructures because it provides a useful foundation to explain bond market infrastructure and the power within it.

The first aspect of infrastructures identified by Bernards and Campbell-Verduyn (2019) is facilitation, by which they mean that infrastructures do not technically take actions themselves; they are supposed to make the actions of others possible. Indices do not directly invest capital but facilitate the processes of capital allocation of their audiences who decide how to manage their investments based upon indices. Indices are comparatively open pieces of infrastructure. There are rules over the transparency requirements of indices. The IIA (2023a) requires the methodology for all indices to be publicly available. Using indices as part of an investment product by either active or passive managers requires paying licensing fees to use the name of the specific index and news organizations, like the *Wall Street Journal* (2023) pay to be able to report the levels of the indices. The requirement for indices to meet the needs of their various audiences gives indices durability. Bernards and Campbell-Verduyn (2019: 777) suggests the centrality of infrastructures means they "shape the way core functions are undertaken". For investment-based audiences they cannot carry out these functions without reference to indices. Passive investors must track an index, which means that to maintain an index fund tracking the Bloomberg US Aggregate Bond Index, they must follow all the changes Bloomberg makes to that index. Active managers need indices as benchmarks for their performance and as evidence for their claims to be able to outperform the market. The last criteria is obscurity that happens through a form of "black-boxing" of index providers' technical systems, which might seem counter intuitive given they must make their methodologies open as part of the IIA (2023a). The choices index providers make remain invisible in the technical language, which means these choices are understood via technical rather than political or social means.

Indices are not unchanging pieces of infrastructure. Index providers must choose how they wish to manage or change their infrastructure. Changing infrastructures "takes time and negotiation, and adjustment with other parts of the system" (Star 1999: 382), which is why maintaining legitimacy of audiences is important for index providers. Figure 7.1 provides a summary of index infrastructure and the relationships of legitimacy and authority that connect it. The forms of legitimacy are marked with double-ended arrows to show the two-way street of legitimacy in contrast to the single-ended arrows for authority. The figure shows the mediation of bond index infrastructure between subjects of index providers on the right in issuers and audiences on the left. Audiences are connected to this infrastructure by two forms of legitimacy. They need to believe that index providers have the correct procedures to be able to assess the

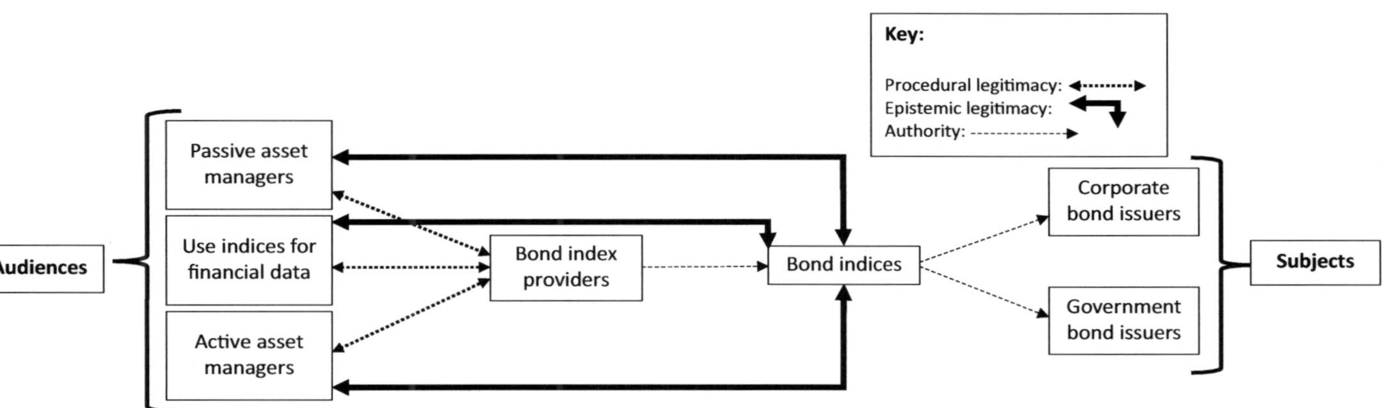

Figure 7.1 The forms of legitimacy and authority connecting audiences and subjects through bond index infrastructure

market and they also need to believe that indices are epistemically legitimate as accurate representations of the bond market. Index providers therefore need to actively cultivate their procedural and epistemic legitimacy to ensure that their audiences continue to believe these things about them. Therefore, the way in which index providers exercise authority over their indices is shaped by trying to maintain their audiences. Relatedly, the changes index providers make to their procedures also affects how bond indices treat corporate and government bond issuers. But these are ultimately subjects of bond index providers. While they can change how they issue bonds, it is ultimately the index provider that decides if and how to include these bonds in their indices. Whereas, if the audiences of index providers are unsatisfied then exit is a possibility for them. It is for this reason that index providers will try to govern themselves and their indices in a way that retains their audiences.

Understanding the constitutive rules of bond index providers' audiences

This section explores the constitutive rules of audiences of bond index providers and how these audiences view bond index providers as part of their constitutive rules. This is important because it demonstrates the differences in how various audiences view index providers and outlines why it is challenging for index providers to unify these audiences. I explain how the constitutive rules are unified around two themes. The first is the procedural claim to legitimacy of index providers. The second is the epistemic claim to legitimacy that indices represent the market.

The first audience are active asset managers. Active management is an investment strategy that seeks to outperform the market average rate of returns. This is not a united strategy as different active managers have different ideas as to how and why the market can be outperformed. It should also be noted, as Gotoh and Sinclair (2017) highlight, that there are different forms of constitutive rules across investment cultures with America more synchronic and Japan more diachronic in outlook, for example. For active managers, ties of constitutive rules are comparatively weak given the diffuse nature of active management and the numerous centres through which these rules are produced. It is important to note the context that active management is operating in. Active management has struggled to compete against passive management, particularly in equities, since the global financial crisis. Bloomberg find 50 per cent of assets invested in stocks in the US are managed passively, compared to about one-third of the bond market (Bloomberg 2021a). A reason for that is that bond indices have not beaten active managers to the same degree as stock indices. To take one example, in S&P's SPIVA data (S&P Index versus Active) found that from 2020 to 2023, 79.8 per cent of active managers underperformed the S&P 500 stock index, versus 38.13 per cent that underperformed the Bloomberg US Aggregate Bond Index[2] (S&P 2023a).

This context influences the types of procedures that are acceptable. While acknowledging differences within active management, it operates on the more synchronic end of audience perceptions than passive management. This is because active managers need index providers to be engaging from a synchronic basis to be able to make its own forms of judgements and interventions into markets, without distance from that which it is judging. Custom indices are where the audience works with the index provider to construct an index that meets their needs. To give a sense of how many bond indices there are, ICE produces 6,000 indices (ICE 2023) and Bloomberg over 40,000 (Bloomberg 2021b). Index providers work with active managers to ensure their indices are seen as representative benchmarks to judge the performance of active managers. See, for example, FTSE Russell and their Principles for Building a Better Fixed Income benchmark (2021). Active managers require intervention into indices to regard them as procedurally legitimate.

The difficulties of passive managers in outperforming bond indices shapes the epistemic legitimacy demanded by active managers. To this end, indices need to accurately represent markets to support active managers claims that they can outperform them. This is what Fidelity do, for example, when outlining their investment strategy in the bond market by first outlining data supporting their claim that they can outperform the market (O'Neil & Muñoz 2022). They then explain how they are able to do this by trying to find value in the aspects of the bond market not included in indices (for example, the bond's credit rating may be too low for inclusion) or to focus on a specific sector that indices do not have flexibility to do so (O'Neil & Muñoz 2022). Custom indices are actively designed to meet these performance claims.

The second audience are passive asset managers who construct bond index funds and ETFs. Passive investment is more internally unified in its constitutive rules than active management, given the concentration of passive management into the Big Three. The bond index market is concentrated further into BlackRock and Vanguard. By 2018, 58 per cent of bond index fund assets were managed by Vanguard and 24 per cent by BlackRock (Bogle 2018: 211). Passive investing involves tracking an index, which means passive funds track indices aiming for the market rate of return but charging low fees. Passive managers need index providers to be diachronic through a detached, long-term perspective of markets, so that they can accrue the long-run benefits of the market.

2. These were chosen for comparison as these represent the most well-known US indices for the stock and bond market, respectively.

John Bogle, the founder of Vanguard, wanted to embed his bond funds[3] with "relative predictability" (Bogle 2018: 63, 134–5, 192). By that, he meant being able to manage future returns so these were not determined by speculative forces, but by the genuine value created in the market. In this way, passive investment could remove the possibilities of volatile returns through the aim for average returns embedded into market indices in the long run. The second aspect of maximizing returns for investors was lowering costs and the key advantage of index funds is the removal of fees investors would otherwise have paid for advice or to execute trades. Therefore, procedurally passive investment requires neutral index construction, from a detached perspective to be able to have low fees, whether these are directly payable to the index provider or in trading to track their decisions. The epistemic claim is that indices must be seen as representing the market to guarantee long-run consistent returns.

The last audience are those who use indices for data and market information. The most well-known example of this is in forms of financial news, whether on television or newspapers, for example, on dedicated sections of sites like the *Wall Street Journal* (2023). This is unsurprising given the history of index providers that arose out of being sources of financial information. It is not just the media who pay for these insights, other financial actors pay to access index information. This is big business for index providers who made $1.7 billion from these subscriptions in 2021 (Swink 2022). The move to passive investing has reduced slightly how important this audience is for index providers, as over half their revenue comes from licensing fees for investment products (Swink 2022). For example, in 2012, subscriptions for access to MSCI data made up 74 per cent of its revenue, whereas in 2021 it was 45 per cent (Swink 2022). While this audience is diffuse, and its importance shrinking, the principles of accurate, timely information are long-lasting and relatively concentrated. There are a variety of synchronic/diachronic mental frameworks involved here. But, following Germain's suggestion (this volume) to consider the synchronic/diachronic as a spectrum, they are in between active and passive managers in terms of how they view bond index providers. On the one hand, they need bond index providers to have some distance from the market to neutrally evaluate it. But on the other, they need more active forms of engagement to advise how to make the most of index infrastructure to be able to assess the market more effectively.

These constitutive rules influence the ways in which this audience conceives procedural and epistemic legitimacy. Procedurally, index providers still need to be seen as neutral and accurate in producing these indices. This audience is particularly concerned with how it can access this information and the procedures

3. When Vanguard first created their bond funds, they were actively managed, launching their first bond index fund in 1986. Vanguard still has actively managed bond funds to this day.

through which it is communicated to them. Different index providers have different sources of data so often want to explain how their data can be integrated with other parts of their infrastructure such as Bloomberg, with the Bloomberg Terminal (2023a). These can be supplemented with technical advice over how to get the best use out of their infrastructure. For example, Bloomberg (2023b) offer advice on how to counter currency risk in bond portfolios when investing in emerging markets. In this way, index providers can provide epistemic access to the market by shaping the way those who are using their data, services and information can access the market. For media organizations who report the level of indices, it matters that their readers believe that indices represent the market.

Clearly, there are differences internally within these audiences as well as between them on their constitutive rules, synchronic/diachronic perspective and how it affects their requirements for procedural and epistemic legitimacy. A summary of this is presented in Table 7.1. The audiences are comparatively united in their requirement for epistemic legitimacy that index providers must ensure that their indices accurately represent "the market". What is interesting is that these audiences have different understandings of the procedures that lead to that. It is therefore likely there will be more tension for index providers in maintaining procedural legitimacy than epistemic. These are important constraints that index providers must consider when exercising authority over their indices.

How bond index providers maintain procedural and epistemic legitimacy

The challenge for bond index providers is to maintain their audiences given their contrasting views and requirements for index providers. This is particularly difficult given the key aspect that unites these audiences, of indices accurately representing "the market", is undermined by their own practices and interventions

Table 7.1 How the constitutive rules of audiences affects their perception of legitimacy

	Active Asset Managers	*Passive Asset Managers*	*Use Indices for Market Data*
Concentration of constitutive rules	Comparatively weak	Comparatively strong	Relatively strong
Synchronic/ diachronic outlook	More synchronic	More diachronic	Mixed
Requirement for procedural legitimacy	Active decision-making to order Indices	Indices calculated neutrally and dispassionately	Indices calculated via correct market ordering process
Requirement for epistemic legitimacy	Indices accurately represent "the market"	Indices accurately represent "the market"	Indices accurately represent "the market"

into the market. I explain how index providers construct claims to procedural and epistemic legitimacy and the challenges they face in each.

The first way in which index providers ensure procedural legitimacy is with regular forms of engagement with their audiences. FTSE Russell engages in regular consultations on the changes they are considering for their indices and asks their audience for feedback on the changes before deciding which version to implement (FTSE Russell 2023a). J. P. Morgan has an annual governance consultation meetings for its indices (J. P. Morgan 2023) and Bloomberg has an Index Advisory Council to consult on changes to its indices (Bloomberg 2020). As an example of how these consultations work, in 2023 FTSE Russell launched a consultation with market actors on whether they should adopt new standards for their ESG Government Bond Index Series, which they then adopted (FTSE Russell 2023b). These consultations also occur over issues of country inclusion/exclusion from indices. In engaging with China, India (see, e.g. Bloomberg's engagement described in Berkley 2019) and South Korea (FTSE Russell 2023c), index providers make clear that they engage with their audiences so that issues of inclusion/exclusion are meant to reflect market sentiment. In this way, the procedures of index providers are regularly endorsed by their audience. Index providers are also obliged to follow western sanctions on China and Russia (FTSE Russell 2023d). It must be remembered that indices themselves cannot be invested in, so measures that make index providers remove companies removes them from measurements of the market rather than actually changes where investment happens directly. It would be possible to keep the companies in indices as measures but prevent the audiences of index providers from investing in the companies under sanction. But audiences of index providers would not want such a scenario as it would lead to tracking error: a distortion between the level of the index and the market investors are able to track.

These procedures are important because these are the ways that indices are seen as "the market". Therefore, these procedures are highly important because they reflect what these audiences agree are the legitimate procedures to measure and codify the market. All indices involve forms of country classification, often that is to limit an individual index to one specific country like the United States. Index providers like FTSE Russell (2023c) also classify countries based on whether they are developed, emerging or frontier markets. These labels are used to determine whether countries' government bonds, or the bonds produced by companies from that country, are included or excluded from certain indices and therefore the investable products produced by active or passive managers. Similarly sector classifications, such as the Global Industry Classification Standard developed by S&P and MSCI (S&P 2023b) assign a sector. Bond indices are generally capitalization weighted (see Bloomberg 2021c), which means the most indebted issuers are weighted more highly when calculating the value of the index. All of these are ostensibly technical, procedural issues in index governance, but have significant impact on what is and is not included in definitions of "the market". Some of these issues are decided in consultation with the audiences as outlined above and audiences consider these factors when deciding which index or index provider they choose. In custom indices, normally for active managers, index providers work closely with their audience to design the procedures for the index (see Bloomberg 2023c) to help achieve the desired outcome.

While there is a lot of agreement between index providers and their audiences, it is not absolute. The forms of engagement between them do present an opportunity to raise these disagreements although it is difficult to know the significance of these. The most direct challenge that audiences could use to challenge index providers is to move to a different index provider. The most high-profile case of this came in the equity, rather than bond market. In 2012, Vanguard moved 22 funds from tracking MSCI's indices to FTSE or the University of Chicago's Centre for Research on Security Prices (CRSP), a move which then FTSE chief executive Mark Makepeace credits for elevating FTSE into the "Big Three" with MSCI and S&P (Makepeace & Ashton 2020: 164–5). Vanguard's reasoning was MSCI's high fees, which undermine the procedural requirements produced by passive investment's constitutive rules. While such a challenge has not happened yet in the bond market, it is shows that asset managers moving index provider is a potential index providers must consider when governing their indices.

The related claim to procedural legitimacy is epistemic legitimacy and that index providers' procedures can accurately produce an index that represents the market that investors can track. With audiences needing to be able to invest in the underlying markets that indices measure, this has a significant impact on how index providers create and apply their criteria. Makepeace highlights that when creating indices, index providers want to be assured that the market is liquid enough for the underlying assets to be traded and that the index can be used as the basis for an investment product (Makepeace & Ashton 2020). Index providers see themselves as protectors of investors' rights. It is for this reason that they are concerned with the degree of controls that countries place on capital and the rights they have over their investments when making decisions of whether to allow countries into indices or not (Bloomberg 2021c; FTSE Russell 2023c). Therefore, one of the key epistemic functions of index providers is to ensure that they produce a version of the market that is easily and predictably investable.

The second aspect is to make that infrastructure as easy to use as possible. Indices are an embedded infrastructure with various factors designed to make them legible in a particular way. Using a base number and calculations in points makes comparisons across time and space easier, supplemented with green and red arrows on tickers to show if the market rose or fell. Index providers take great effort to ensure that results of their indices can be calculated whenever and wherever markets are open and to be able to ensure that their indices can still be calculated, even under times of financial stress or ultra-high trading volumes (see Makepeace & Ashton 2020). Therefore, a key part of epistemic legitimacy is making the market legible and interpretable either for investors or for financial news and those who are using indices for market data.

In this area index providers are without challenge. This is not necessarily because there is perfect agreement that indices accurately represent the market. Like with the CRAs analysed by Sinclair (2021), there is no other form of organization that offers to their audience what they do at the level that is required. Therefore, procedural disagreements, even those that can be seen as index providers intervening into the market they are supposed to be measuring, can be forgiven if the result is an intersubjectively held view that indexing as a practice produces the closest result to the market. Unless this changes the most likely challenge is not to indexing as a practice, but to individual index providers like MSCI. The biggest threat index providers face is not that their audience will leave indexing, but that they will go to a competitor.

It is for these reasons that index providers govern their indices in a way to maintain the procedural and epistemic legitimacy of their audience. Therefore, the way in which bond index providers govern their indices is shaped by the intersubjective views of their audience. This means that IPE should consider the deeper networks of power involved in index infrastructure. This is not to devalue existing analysis of index providers in IPE, which importantly highlights the power that index providers and their indices can exert (Petry 2021; Petry, Fichtner & Heemskerk 2021; Cormier & Naqvi 2023). However, it suggests that this power is a conditional one and it is necessary to consider how that power needs to be legitimized for it to be exercised. Moreover, there is significant value in understanding indexing as part of a process which, in the words of Sinclair (2021: 81), reflects "what people observe and collectively agree they are doing".

Conclusion

Legitimacy is not a concept that Sinclair used extensively. However, understanding it as a process through which market actors are seen as endogenous rather than exogenous to markets is important in opening up analysis of the relationship between procedural and epistemic legitimacy and the authority exerted by institutions. The bond market is particularly important as it operates at a point of growing tension in the debate between active and passive managers. This makes things particularly difficult for index providers to maintain the legitimacy of themselves and their infrastructure to both these audiences. Using Sinclair's ideas of constitutive rules and synchronic/diachronic outlook helps to explain the procedural and epistemic grounds through which audiences view bond index providers and their indices as legitimate. While lacking formal challengers to indexing, competition among index providers means the way in which they govern their indices is shaped by maintaining the legitimacy of their audience. Sinclair's framework would also be a useful starting point for future research on index providers and how they legitimize themselves to prevent state regulation, as well as to understand the political implications inside the "black box" of index providers' procedures. Understanding the social foundations of markets must involve moves to remove the technical façade from financial infrastructures to examine the political relationships that it facilitates and embeds.

References

Berkley, S. 2019. "The road ahead for India's bond market". Bloomberg. www.bloomberg.com/professional/blog/indian-bonds-could-well-be-the-toast-of-global-investors/.

Bernards, N. & M. Campbell-Verduyn 2019. "Understanding technological change in global finance through infrastructures". *Review of International Political Economy* 26 (5): 773–89.

Bloomberg 2020. "Bloomberg announces changes to Bloomberg Barclays Fixed Income Indices". Bloomberg. www.bloomberg.com/company/press/bloomberg-announces-changes-to-bloomberg-barclays-fixed-income-indices/.

Bloomberg 2021a. "Passive likely overtakes active by 2026, earlier if bear market". Bloomberg. www.bloomberg.com/professional/blog/passive-likely-overtakes-active-by-2026-earlier-if-bear-market/.

Bloomberg 2021b. "Bloomberg Fixed Income Indices: the global leader in fixed income indexing". Bloomberg. https://assets.bbhub.io/professional/sites/27/Bloomberg-Fixed-Income-Indices-Overview.pdf.

Bloomberg 2021c. "Fixed Income Index methodology". Bloomberg. https://assets.bbhub.io/professional/sites/27/Fixed-Income-Index-Methodology.pdf.

Bloomberg 2023a. "Bloomberg Indices Terminal Functionality: Bloomberg Professional Services". Bloomberg. www.bloomberg.com/professional/product/indices/bloomberg-indices-terminal-functionality/.

Bloomberg 2023b. "Bloomberg Index Research: Bloomberg Professional Services". www.bloomberg.com/professional/product/indices/bloomberg-index-research-reports/.

Bloomberg 2023c. "Bloomberg Fixed Income Indices: Bloomberg Professional Services". www.bloomberg.com/professional/product/indices/bloomberg-fixed-income-indices/#/.

Bogle, J. C. 2018. *Stay the Course: The Story of Vanguard and the Index Revolution.* Chichester: Wiley.

Cormier, B. & N. Naqvi 2023. "Delegating discipline: how indexes restructured the political economy of sovereign bond markets". *Journal of Politics* 85 (4): 1501–15.

EU Commission 2022. "Consultation document: targeted consultation on the regime applicable to the use of benchmarks administered in a third country". https://finance.ec.europa.eu/system/files/2022-05/2022-benchmarks-third-country-consultation-document_en.pdf.

Fichtner, J., E. Heemskerk & J. Petry 2022. "The new gatekeepers of financial claims". In *Capital Claims: Power and Global Finance*, B. Braun & K. Kroddenbrock (eds), 107–28. Abingdon: Routledge.

Fichtner, J., R. Jaspert & J. Petry 2023. "Mind the ESG capital allocation gap: the role of index providers, standard-setting, and 'green' indices for the creation of sustainability impact". *Regulation & Governance* 18 (2): 479–98.

FTSE Russell 2021. "Principles for building a better fixed income benchmark". https://content.ftserussell.com/sites/default/files/principles_for_building_a_better_fixed_income_benchmark.pdf.

FTSE Russell 2023a. "Market consultations". www.lseg.com/en/ftse-russell/governance/market-consultations.

FTSE Russell 2023b. "Evolution of Sovereign Risk Monitor ESG data used in FTSE ESG Government Bond Index Series". https://research.ftserussell.com/products/index-notices/home/getnotice/?id=2608344.

FTSE Russell 2023c. "FTSE Fixed Income Country Classification for Nominal Fixed-Rate Government Markets". www.lseg.com/content/dam/ftse-russell/en_us/documents/country-classification/ftse-fi-country-classification-for-nominal-government-markets.pdf.

FTSE Russell 2023d. "FTSE Russell treatment of sanctioned equity index constituents: ground rules". www.lseg.com/content/dam/ftse-russell/en_us/documents/policy-documents/ftse-russell-treatment-of-sanctioned-index-constituents.pdf.

ICE 2023. "Fixed Income Indices". www.ice.com/fixed-income-data-services/index-solutions/fixed-income-indices.

IIA 2022a. "Re: Request for comment on certain information providers acting as investment advisers" [Release No. IA-6050; File No. S7-18-22; 87 FR 37254]. www.indexindustry.org/wp-content/uploads/IIA-Response-to-Comment-Request-Final-Signed.pdf.

IIA 2022b. "Considerations in response to the targeted consultation on the third country regime under the benchmark regulation". www.indexindustry.org/wp-content/uploads/110822_IIABMR_Final.pdf.

IIA 2023a. "IIA best practice guidelines". www.indexindustry.org/iia-best-practice-guidelines/.

IIA 2023b. "IOSCO principles". www.indexindustry.org/insights/iosco-principles/.

IOSCO 2013. "Principles for financial benchmarks: final report". www.iosco.org/library/pubdocs/pdf/IOSCOPD415.pdf.

J. P. Morgan 2023. "J. P. Morgan Global Index research". www.jpmorgan.com/insights/global-research/index-research.

Lincoln, B. 1994. *Authority: Construction and Corrosion*. Chicago, IL: University of Chicago Press.

Makepeace, M. & J. Ashton 2020. *FTSE: The Inside Story of the Deals, Dramas and Politics that Revolutionized Financial Markets*. London: Nicholas Brealey Publishing.

Mügge, D. 2011. "Limits of legitimacy and the primacy of politics in financial governance". *Review of International Political Economy* 18 (1): 52–74.

O'Neil, F. & C. Muñoz 2022. "Why bond investors may benefit from Actively Managed Mutual Funds and ETFs". https://institutional.fidelity.com/app/proxy/content?literatureURL=/9860202.PDF.

Petry, J. 2021. "From national marketplaces to global providers of financial infrastructures: exchanges, infrastructures and structural power in global finance". *New Political Economy* 26 (4): 574–97.

Petry, J., J. Fichtner & E. Heemskerk 2021. "Steering capital: the growing private authority of index providers in the age of passive asset management". *Review of International Political Economy* 28 (1): 152–76.

Rethel, L. 2011. "Whose legitimacy? Islamic finance and the global financial order". *Review of International Political Economy* 18 (1): 75–98.

S&P 2023a. "Spiva Data". www.spglobal.com/spdji/en/research-insights/spiva/.

S&P 2023b. "Global Industry Classification Standard (GICS®) methodology". www.spglobal.com/spdji/en/documents/methodologies/methodology-gics.pdf.

Scharpf, F. 1999. *Governing in Europe: Effective and Democratic?* Oxford: Oxford University Press.

Seabrooke, L. 2006. *The Social Sources of Financial Power: Domestic Legitimacy and International Financial Orders*. Ithaca, NY: Cornell University Press.

Searle, J. 2005. "What is an institution?" *Journal of Institutional Economics* 1 (1): 1–22.

SEC 2022. "Request for comment on certain information providers acting as investment advisers". www.sec.gov/files/rules/other/2022/ia-6050.pdf.

Star, S. L. 1999. "The ethnography of infrastructure". *American Behavioural Scientist* 43 (3): 377–91.

Swink, S. 2022. "Index providers take record $5bn in revenue in 2021". *Financial Times*, 24 May. www.ft.com/content/595c3c18-7c13-4e33-9a68-f82f558b7ad6.

Tran, L. A. 2023. "How active is your passive bond fund?". Morningstar. www.morningstar.com/etfs/how-active-is-your-passive-bond-fund.

Wall Street Journal 2023. "Bond benchmarks". *Wall Street Journal*. www.wsj.com/market-data/bonds/benchmarks.

8

THE SOCIAL FOUNDATIONS OF FINTECH

Chris Clarke

Sinclair's last book *To the Brink of Destruction* (2021) dealt with the causes and dynamics of the global financial crisis 2007–09. That crisis involved developments to which Sinclair had drawn attention throughout his work. The role of financial disintermediation, the trend towards an increasingly synchronic mental framework (on behalf of both financial market actors and governance institutions) and an endogenous tendency towards crisis within financial markets had all been significant (Sinclair 2021: 8, 37, 61). Arguably, these developments have continued since the crisis, with influential international political economy (IPE) assessments of global financial governance stressing that it was more of a status quo event than a transformative one (Helleiner 2014). For instance, following the crisis, the authority of the credit rating agencies (CRAs) as private governance institutions remained intact (Mennillo & Sinclair 2019: 267).

Yet the post-2008 world of global finance has distinct characteristics even as some of these longer-standing trends remain in play. Chief amongst them is the rise of "fintech" and its role in reshaping financial markets, practices and regulation (Arner, Barberis & Buckley 2016). Research on the politics of global finance, and related subjects, has sought to understand and critique the emergence of fintech, drawing attention to, among other things, its implications for retail money and credit, including reintermediation and centralization trends (Langley & Leyshon 2021), the forms of governance that fintech underpins, including financial inclusion for global development (Bernards 2019; Natile 2020), and the advent of a "fintech–philanthropy–development complex", responsible for producing digital systems that monetize digital data trails (Gabor & Brooks 2017).

The purpose of this chapter is to mobilize Sinclair's social foundations of finance approach to add to those endeavours, to sketch a political and social analysis of the increasingly important role of fintech in global finance. In the first section, I situate fintech within the contemporary political landscape of global finance, drawing attention to the successes and failures of the new "judgement practices" it produces. In the second section, I emphasize the social power of fintech actors using a social foundations of finance approach, which involves two key steps. The first is to explicate the *private authority* fintech actors enjoy and the second is to *denaturalize* claims to tech expertise.

Sinclair was keen to stress, as influential scholars of fintech have also pointed out (Arner, Barberis & Buckley 2016: 6), that financial markets and technological development have had a co-constitutive relationship throughout history. Indeed, financial markets *are* a form of technology in a significant sense. Given Sinclair's training in and development of a historical method of inquiry (see Sinclair 2016), he was cautious against uncritical acceptance of the latest slogan used by financial insiders and business commentary about them without considering the political, ideological and social context in which they emerge. As a scholar of the long history of global finance, he viewed claims to novelty and innovation through a historical lens.

Sinclair did not write directly about fintech, but we know from his lecture notes for his Masters' level course taught at the University of Warwick, *Critical Issues in the Politics of Global Finance*, that he used the term with a degree of critical reluctance. On the one hand, Sinclair recognized that the trends and emerging technologies associated with fintech innovation could not be ignored. Over the last two decades, they have become increasingly important in restructuring financial markets and their governance. On the other hand, Sinclair was also acutely aware that claims in finance to "disruption" and "democratization", and so on, had been heard during previous waves of innovation and should be treated with a dose of healthy scepticism. For him, an ongoing process in global finance of real consequence was *disintermediation* (Sinclair 1994a: 448; 1994b: 137; 2000b: 491; 2001a: 444), which notably is a central issue that has been problematized in relation to whether this is what fintech achieves (Langley & Leyshon 2021: 381).

Fintech can be understood as the "marriage of financial services and information technology" (Arner, Barberis & Buckley 2016: 3). This chapter uses the term to refer to the firms (typically start-ups, but also "big tech" corporations and incumbent banks as they further move operations online and to apps) and the financial practices (including lending, payments, insurance and investment) associated with emerging digital technologies applied to financial market activity in the last two decades. This has been referred to as "fintech 3.0", acknowledging the fact that finance has been intertwined with technological developments in preceding periods (see, e.g. Cerny 1994; Preda 2006). For Arner, Barberis and Buckley (2016: 6–10), "fintech 1.0" (1866–1967) was a period of *analogue* finance that involved the combination of finance and technology in a first period of financial globalization (driven by colonial and imperial expansion, it should be added), while "fintech 2.0" (1967–2008) was a period of *digitalized* finance (at least in the countries of the rich world) designated roughly by innovations such as the first ATM in the late 1960s.

The key difference Arner, Barberis and Buckley (2016: 14) mark out for fintech since 2008 (fintech 3.0), is that it is not just the traditional regulated financial industry firms now using digital technologies in the provision of financial services. In this new era of fintech, they write, "there has been a rapid expansion in the types of businesses that create and deliver technology to provide financial services and products, in addition to increasingly rapid and pervasive technological developments" (Arner, Barberis & Buckley 2016: 6). In other words, fintech in the more recent era is as much about non-traditional financial firms, such as tech start-ups and big tech firms, engaging in financial markets and providing financial services, as it is about regulated financial firms becoming ever more digitalized in their operation, though this is still part of the story. Shifting patterns of inclusion, exclusion and wealth ownership in global finance therefore require investigation into the social foundations of both "the financial" and "the technological" of fintech.

This chapter moves away from broad generalizations about fintech to better specify and highlight the character and agency of fintech actors. In a partial and provisional form, it echoes Sinclair's work on the CRAs by considering examples of fintech in institutional terms. The chapter provides illustrative vignettes of a fintech lending firm (LendingClub) and a fintech payments firm (Stripe). Fintech refers to a much broader set of firms and practices than the ones these actors represent, not least in the world of blockchain-based cryptocurrencies. Nevertheless, the goal is to focus in on specific institutions that illustrate key issues in the changing political economy of fintech and sketch out what might be said about this from a social foundations of finance perspective. The chapter offers a draft of a future research agenda.

Sinclair was primarily interested in the major US rating agencies, as little known and poorly understood actors who played an outsized role in global financial markets. By contrast, many fintech firms are household names and the subject of much attention across multiple academic disciplines and media commentary. Yet, up to now, they have not been analysed in terms of an explicit social foundations of finance approach focusing on judgement, private authority and the social power of specific institutions. The gambit of this chapter is that this can provide purchase in better specifying and understanding the role of fintech firms as actors of *political* significance in financial markets. This involves, I suggest, analysing fintech in terms of both judgement in finance and its specific form of private authority.

Fintech as judgement

One of Sinclair's major contributions was to highlight that CRAs wielded private authority due to the authoritative judgements they produce. Before his work this form of private authority had not been fully appreciated. Sinclair sought to demonstrate and understand the nature of CRA authority by closely investigating precisely what they do in financial markets. In this endeavour, Sinclair was sympathetic to calls to "open the black boxes" of global finance (MacKenzie 2005). In fact, MacKenzie (2005: 558) cites Sinclair's work on the CRAs as an example of how social scientists can demystify a black box in the context of global finance.

Inside that black box, Sinclair found both the politics of the mundane and the politics of the globalizing economy. With respect to the mundane, it turns out that rating activities are less about pure technical analysis in the pursuit of "correctness" and more about knowledge as "a social creation", complete with all of the social and political complexity and contestation that this implies (Sinclair 2005: 19). With respect to the globalizing economy, it turns out that their activities are not just consequential for knowledgeable market insiders but profoundly important in controlling access to capital on a global scale, which has social and political consequences "affecting work life and democracy in places touched by financial globalization" (Sinclair 2005: 174). Unifying Sinclair's analysis was an emphasis placed on the CRA's *judgement role*. He writes, "[t]he judgements produced acquire the status of understood facts in the markets – even when analysis shows they are at times faulty – because of the authoritative status market participants and societies attribute to the agencies" (Sinclair 2005: 17). Sinclair developed his social foundations approach (SFA) to unpack how judgements in financial markets came to be hierarchically structured and how market participants come to accept the dictates of CRAs *as* authorities.

At first glance, judgement in financial markets might seem to be of little relevance for an analysis of fintech. A comparison of CRAs and fintech firms directly might seem impossible. Not least because fintech constitutes a much greater and more varied array of entities and sets of financial practices compared to the very small number of highly influential (and typically American) rating agency firms. As Sinclair was keen to stress, the whole business of the specialist CRAs was the provision of judgements for other market participants. This idea takes centre stage in his later work, in which Sinclair (2021: 12) argued that the agencies had gone from being *judges* in the ratings process to *advisers*, essentially reneging on their commitment (or pretence) to impartiality. Fintech actors do not have such a coherent collective identity. What Sinclair (2021: 12) described as "the role of referee or judge in debt markets" could not meaningfully apply to most fintech firms. Instead, in short, fintech firms develop digital technological products and practices that, at least in principle, serve to reshape the largely retail financial service activities of, among other things, lending, payments, insurance and investment. In this sense, they are market players not market judges.

However, there is another side to this story worth reflecting upon from a social foundations of finance perspective. Such an approach can take stock of the ways in which fintech firms, in multifaceted ways, have been involved in social contest over the *practice* of making authoritative judgements about the allocation of credit and the determination of creditworthiness. In other words, the digital technological developments with which fintech is associated have reshaped judgement practices of credit rating in socially and politically consequential ways. For instance, in a global development context, fintech credit scoring is involved in the construction of new "calculative infrastructures" through which unbanked populations can be rendered visible to assess creditworthiness from non-traditional data sources (Aitken 2017: 284). Fintech has been identified as part of a "digital revolution" in financial inclusion for development based on a "commodification" of a new class of personal data, such as digital footprints, enabling lenders to "map, know and govern 'risky populations' " (Gabor & Brooks 2017: 425). Indeed, more broadly, fintech firms are often built on a platform model of organization that depends on a digital data-rich mode of interaction with "users" so that user data can be harnessed for credit risk analysis (O'Dwyer 2019: 145; Langley & Leyshon 2021: 382). Meanwhile, working against the tech utopianism found in many insider accounts of fintech, it should be emphasized that the new forms of credit scoring fintech produces have the potential to enable both authoritarian governance (Gruin 2019) and the deepening of inequalities on a global scale, including relations of neo-colonialism (Langley & Leyshon 2022).

Building on Arner, Barberis and Buckley's (2016) periodization of fintech, a distinction can be made between the application of digital technologies to expand and expediate existing "traditional" forms of credit risk analysis (more akin to fintech 2.0) and the application of digital technologies to produce novel means through which "non-traditional" data is translated into credit data (more akin to fintech 3.0). The former we might call the *digitalization* of rating practices typically carried out by regulated financial services firms, while the latter we might call an extension of the *datafication* of rating practices typically pursued by technology-driven start-up firms. Digitalization of ratings refers to evolutionary changes in underwriting loans, while more intense *datafication* of rating practices marks a qualitative shift in the data sources going into the ratings process. It appeals to the evocative idea that became common parlance at fintech industry conferences in the 2010s: given the rapid expansion of mobile and platform forms of economic interaction around the world *all data is credit data* (see Aiken 2017; O'Dwyer 2019). Considered as a social practice involving judgements about credit and creditworthiness, then, there is little doubt that fintech firms have been experimenting with significant new forms of credit rating in recent decades (Clarke & Tooker 2018: 8).

The San Francisco based LendingClub is a useful case in point. Although founded in 2006, the firm's debut on the stock market in 2014 was second only to Alibaba that year in terms of IPO size, and was described by former US Treasury Secretary, Lawrence Summers (who sat on the company's board until 2018) as "a good day for LendingClub" (Alloway & Platt 2014). It shot to a valuation of $8.5 billion on the first day of trading after a frenzy of interest on Wall Street (rather ironically given its intentions to disrupt the established banking industry) and proceeds from the deal reached around $1 billion. Google had already bought an 8 per cent stake in LendingClub in 2013, but a month after the IPO it announced a tie-up with Google to provide small business loans to the tech group's partners (Alloway 2015).

LendingClub (2024) describes itself as a "full-spectrum fintech marketplace bank". Unpacking this claim takes a bit of linguistic and historical excavation. The fintech element is relatively straightforward in the sense that it provides "a broad range of financial products and services through a technology-driven platform" (LendingClub 2024). The "marketplace" descriptor evolved from earlier designations of what such online platforms are doing. Having originated over $6 billion in loans in the US, mostly used to either refinance debt (60 per cent) or pay off credit cards (22 per cent), LendingClub was the biggest player in the "peer-to-peer" (P2P) lending industry in 2014 when it decided to drop the "P2P" label in favour of "marketplace lending" (Alloway & Dunkley 2015). The reason for this rebranding was the fact that in the online lending sector the business model of *directly* connecting borrowers and lenders (that is, the "P2P" element) was falling out of favour, and partnerships with major banking institutions were becoming more common. The fact that LendingClub now calls itself a "bank" is also significant and reflective of the fact that partnerships with regulated banks alone were ultimately insufficient for its activities. Despite being set up to "disrupt" bank lending, in the end, it became a bank.

With regards to the theme of judgement in finance, what is interesting about LendingClub, and the US P2P/marketplace lending sector that it once led, is that, at least initially, it was designed to perform credit intermediation in a way that was different to regulated banks. Having established a P2P loan network on Facebook, LendingClub launched an online intermediary that served to match borrowers and investors outside of the banking system. Borrowers were assigned a credit rating by LendingClub, based on its proprietary data analysis techniques, and were also able to signal their creditworthiness by submitting further information about their position and projected use of requested loan money (Nowak, Ross & Yencha 2018: 318). Investors (the individual lenders) were able to use LendingClub's website to decide which borrowers they would like to include in their portfolio of investments (who they would lend to directly) based on the designated credit score and any further information about borrowers. As with several other P2P lending experiments around the world at this time, credit decisions (judgements) were, at least in part, taking place outside of the established bank channels. The model built on and emulated broader "crowdfunding" modes of financing that were becoming popular with the rise of social media, such as GoFundMe and Kickstarter. For advocates, LendingClub's P2P model of providing a marketplace for credit was "at the forefront of a technology-led revolution" offering better rates for all parties by disintermediating bank lending (Alloway & Dunkley 2015). For detractors, it was an incredibly risky form of financing and, in its position as a non-bank lender without formal deposits, LendingClub had no real stable source of funding. Either way, the crucial role of *judgement* in lending was, at least in part, being experimented with by LendingClub and other fintech firms using the original P2P model. In a sense, these firms were seeking to shift market authority over the social practice of risk assessment, typically wielded by traditional banks (Rethel & Sinclair 2012: 27), to allow investors and borrowers to engage in a form of (albeit very limited) dialogue over lending decisions.

LendingClub's idealized disruption of bank lending, if it ever fully manifested itself, did not last very long. By 2015, institutional investors such as hedge funds and investment trusts became heavily involved in the sector, buying around 80 per cent of loans available on the US platforms, undermining the P2P model by making the platform much less about individuals lending and borrowing from each other (Gapper 2015). In 2016, LendingClub's founder and CEO was forced to resign following a governance scandal and the broader US marketplace lending industry faced a significant downturn. In 2020, LendingClub closed its platform completely to retail investors, effectively ending the P2P model (Renton 2020), and in 2021 the firm acquired the digital bank Radius in a move that allowed LendingClub to obtain a banking charter, issue loans directly and avoid having to partner with banks, which lowered its funding costs (Armstrong 2021).

The story of LendingClub – from a fintech platform with an experimental credit intermediation model to a more conventional loan provider built on institutional funding and a banking charter – illustrates several issues about fintech *as* judgement. First, much emphasis was initially put on the digital technology at the heart of the intermediation offered by fintech firms such as LendingClub. Yet, while innovative in the sense of being a "digital-first" start-up firm, engaging users via simple website interaction, LendingClub perhaps represents more of a further *digitalization* of consumer credit intermediation (that is, moving it further online) as opposed to a more extensive *datafication* of the ratings process itself. Viewed in this light, the novelty of many of the claims to technological innovation by fintech firms like LendingClub ought to be better unpacked and scrutinised; their tech-utopian claims to expertise *denaturalized* and situated within existing social relations of finance.

Second, although the original ratings process in the P2P model invited a somewhat novel means of making judgements about credit from the position of investors, LendingClub's evolution and its ultimate exclusion of individual investors showed the very restrictive limits to that model as a fintech firm attempts to scale (Arner, Barberis & Buckley 2016: 37). Even the very invocation of "peer" status between lenders and borrowers, fragile as it was in the first place, was expunged completely from LendingClub's presentation of itself to the wider world by the time of its IPO (Alloway & Dunkley 2015). Finally, thinking through the implications for where social power lies in making judgements in finance, it is notable that LendingClub emerged as a P2P lending platform seeking to disintermediate bank lending, but then ended up abandoning the P2P model and energetically seeking to establish itself as a bank.

The case of LendingClub shows that – institutionally and reputationally – it is extremely difficult to shift judgement practices in the world of credit. Existing social norms are deeply entrenched, especially in US finance. Institutional actors, including established banks and major investment firms, were able to capture the loan activities generated by LendingClub as a new fintech firm and essentially reconsolidate the financial channels involved. At this point Sinclair's (2000b: 491) argument that, in a disintermediated financial environment, judgement authorities will trend towards centralization is prescient. Of course, Sinclair was referring to CRAs as the institutions that have developed to provide centralized authoritative judgements on creditworthiness. Yet the parallel with fintech firms attempting to disintermediate banks via novel means of credit intermediation at their core is striking. LendingClub is just one fintech firm among many, its story of growth and transformation into a bank reveals the difficulties involved in establishing new forms and sites of authoritative financial judgement. On this issue, Sinclair (2021: 153) wrote about the significant *reputational* entry barriers to the business of providing authoritative judgements, and indeed how reputation itself is "inherently exclusive and not necessarily meritocratic and sensitive to performance". LendingClub attempted to navigate a difficult path between inviting individual lenders to judge loan decisions for themselves, while endeavouring to grow the business based on its own "disruptive" reputation beyond a scale that realistically individual lenders could finance. When LendingClub loans became attractive to larger financial market players, these institutional investors sought ways to "plug directly into the marketplace lending platforms, creating high-speed algorithms that comb through reams of loan-level information to make their investment decisions" (Alloway & Dunkley 2015). The practice of judging creditworthiness via LendingClub reverted to something much closer to the standard practices of the financial institutions that it was initially claiming to disrupt. The social and political significance of the LendingClub story is thus perhaps best understood in terms of a "reintermediation" and "consolidation" of financial channels (Langley & Leyshon 2021).

Fintech as private authority

An organizing feature of Sinclair's (1994b: 134) early research agenda was the question of how non-state power or private authority in the world economy would be exercised in the emerging post-Cold War order characterized by rising international capital mobility. The IPE scholarship to which Sinclair contributed was interested in how the more globalized economy emerging from the 1970s onwards was not, in fact, driven by waves of pure market forces, ruthlessly destroying all forms of political authority. Rather, authority was being reinvented in various ways, including via new forms of knowledge networks and new processes of passing authoritative judgement over economic policymaking and government action (Sinclair 2000b: 487; Chwieroth & Sinclair 2013: 459).

In more recent decades, new forms of private authority are still of vital concern for IPE scholars and others interested in the politics of the world economy (e.g. Campbell-Verduyn 2017). Of particular note, those studying the politics of "big tech" firms have drawn attention to how, by acting as "central intermediaries in the economies of the advanced industrial democracies", a number of these firms have what has been called "platform power" (Culpepper & Thelen 2020: 289). Put another way, a handful of big tech firms have become "the decisive interfaces for ever-growing numbers of economic processes" and this reconfigures how private authority is exercised in the world economy (Staab 2024: 3).

The term "big tech" is at once arresting and problematic. Typically used to refer to the "big five" US corporations[1], it draws attention to the entities that dominate stock market valuations and their status as technological giants. The most pressing political issues concerning large technology platform companies relate to, among other things, data privacy, market power and electoral interference (Atal 2021: 336). These concerns do not play out in precisely the same way across all fintech firms. However, there are considerable points of commonality when it comes to issues of platform power, especially given the centrality of the platform model to both big tech and many (though not all) fintech firms. To develop a SFA to understand the private authority of fintech, the discussion here focuses on one of the most visible points of intersection between big tech and fintech: the realm of payments.

1. Alphabet (Google), Amazon, Apple, Meta (Facebook) and Microsoft. At the time of writing, Tesla, Nvidia, Baidu, Alibaba and Tencent are also companies often considered part of big tech.

The payments sector is attractive to big tech and fintech firms because of the new "raw material" it produces in the form of transactional data (Culpepper & Thelen 2020: 289; Brandl & Dieterich 2023: 549). In recent decades, a "platformization of financial transactions" has taken place as big tech firms integrate payment systems into their platforms to harness the monetization possibilities of the transactional payment data generated (Westermeier 2020). Apple (originally a consumer electronics firm) and Google (originally a search engine firm) are now household names for payments, not least because of the dominance of their "digital wallets", the payment apps which feature on their operating systems making up approximately 28 per cent and 70 per cent of the global smartphone market share respectively. Meanwhile, Meta (the social media network) and Amazon (originally an e-commerce website) are deeply embedded within new models of "platform capitalism" that seek to monetize data flows, and they have been involved in cryptocurrency and payments projects. Amazon, with its digital wallet "Amazon Pay", is particularly interesting given the extent to which the firm has entered financial services in many countries around the world, engaging in activities such as the provision of payments, credit, insurance and even cash deposits. As one of the "meta-platforms", such moves increase Amazon's control of more aspects of economic activity enabled by its platform and position it as a gatekeeper to the commercial internet (Staab 2024: 5). Despite platforms offering an image of decentralization, such a position involves "a deeply centralized model of power" (Atal 2021: 337).

Recent interest in how platforms have become the central enabling device for much economic activity echoes Sinclair's (2000b: 489, emphasis in original) call to recognize the importance of investigating "the *deep infrastructure* of contemporary commercial life". The concept of financial infrastructures has received much attention in IPE in recent years (see Petry, this volume; de Goede 2021), and the infrastructural power derived from being "the decisive interface" is foundational to the private authority of many fintech and big tech firms (Staab 2024: 4). Yet authority for Sinclair (2021: 81) always had a crucial epistemic dimension as well: it was about the capacity of an institution to make authoritative judgements and their audience perceiving these judgements to be legitimate. By centring how knowledge constitutes private authority, his social foundations of finance approach goes beyond conceptions of authority in terms of "power over" other actors and instead incorporates "the social relations of constitution into structural power" (Sinclair 2021: 76). In other words, for Sinclair (2021: 76), an analysis of the role of knowledge in constituting legitimate authority involved unpacking how intersubjective meaning and understanding was established and reproduced across different social actors and arenas.

Sinclair talked about embedded knowledge networks (EKNs) in several of his contributions as "private institutions that possess a specific form of social authority because of their publicly acknowledged track record for solving problems, often acting as disinterested experts in assessing high-value transactions and in validating institutional norms and practices" (Sinclair 2001a: 441). The term "embedded" refers to the point that EKNs are endogenous rather than exogenous to financial markets (Sinclair 2000b: 489). Rather than governing markets from the outside, this meant that for Sinclair (1994b: 448) it was the CRA's role in the structuring of information that gave them such power and authority in the context of more mobile financial flows. Using a term that Sinclair (2000b: 488) deployed in relation to the CRAs, is it useful to conceive of fintech actors, especially in the payments sector, as "important private makers of global public policy"? If some fintech firms constitute new forms of private authority, how much of this authority is built on establishing and harnessing EKNs? Further, is it possible to conceive of the "tech-solutionism" of fintech firms as a form of EKN? The remainder of this chapter examines the private authority fintech actors wield by focusing on the fintech payments firm Stripe, seeking to denaturalize claims to tech expertise by drawing attention to the social constitution of the knowledge claims surrounding the payments industry.

Stripe (2025a) describes itself as "a technology company that builds economic infrastructure for the internet" by offering software to companies "to accept payments and manage their businesses online". Essentially, Stripe's software allows "any website or app to accept payments without having to obtain their own licences or strike deals with the many different banks and card operators that the company has already integrated" (Bradshaw, Megaw & Kruppa 2021). Stripe (2025b) claims to provide "the backbone for global commerce" and to make "moving money as easy and programmable as moving data". The comparison between money and data is no mere metaphor. As noted above, treating "money as data" is at the heart of the business model that fintech firms pursue (Westermeier 2020). This model in the payments sector requires the development of "strong network effects" and as such creates, and in fact depends on, market consolidation (Brandl & Dieterich 2023: 549). Examples of Stripe's expansion include a partnership with Klarna (a "buy now pay later" payments provider that peaked in 2021 as Europe's most valuable fintech company) and a $1.1 billion acquisition of Bridge (a start-up firm specializing in stablecoin infrastructure). Stripe has become known as "a Silicon Valley bellwether" and reported $1 trillion in payment volume in the year 2023 (Hammond 2024).

On one level, the authority that Stripe wields is built on its staggering pace of growth in global payments market share. Stripe claims to serve over 135 currencies and payment methods (Stripe 2025a) and one co-founder stresses that, since the payments infrastructure is global, the firm must also have a "global perspective" (Bradshaw, Megaw & Kruppa 2021). The scale and reach of private firms in the establishment and provision of financial infrastructures here is significant because of the way in which platforms do not merely act as market players, they *become the market* (Stabb 2024). This calls to mind Sinclair's (2001a: 442, emphasis in original) study of the infrastructures of global finance, which he describes as a move away from state–market debates and "in the direction of understanding authority *in* markets (rather than *over* markets)".

On another level, a SFA further centres how fintech firms constitute new forms of knowledge authority via this infrastructural position. This can be explored by paying attention to the social construction of fintech expertise, which is typically built on what might be termed the "tech-solutionism" of platform capitalism. Stripe's evolution is again illustrative of this issue. Founded in 2010, Stripe was born out of a pitch by the Irish brothers Patrick and John Collison to Peter Theil, the early Facebook backer and PayPal co-founder. Along with other major platform firms such as Uber and Airbnb, Stripe was therefore backed by the "PayPal Mafia", a network of founders including Thiel and Elon Musk with a group net worth estimated at $310 billion (in 2024) and so called because of their "tight-knit nature and outsized influence on the start-up ecosystem" (da Costa 2024: 20).

The epistemic authority enjoyed by this investor group – the ability to create and reproduce what it means to have the correct approach to investment, infrastructures, the roles of technology and the state, and more – is notable because it is explicitly acknowledged and indeed embraced by the fintech payment firms under its stewardship. These firms adopt an expansive approach to positioning themselves as infrastructure and take self-conscious efforts to shape meaning and understanding about their role at the centre of market capitalist life. Indeed, Stripe is particularly interesting because it has its own publishing house, Stripe Press, which republishes books and talks from people such as the former vice chairman of Berkshire Hathaway (da Costa 2024: 20). On the publishing house website it explains, "Stripe partners with millions of the world's most innovative businesses. These businesses are the result of many different inputs. Perhaps the most important ingredient is 'ideas'" (Stripe 2024). Moreover, Stripe (2025c) offers educational resources on its website, including a "Global Payments Gateway 101", which are framed as articles "for general information and education purposes" but are also clearly geared towards promoting its products. These are explicit attempts to establish intersubjective meaning and understanding about payments infrastructures to further legitimate the epistemic authority Stripe enjoys.

Moreover, a member of the group involved in seed funding for Stripe explains how crucial it is for entrepreneurs to be successful in "converting people to believe in your start-up and its culture", which involves practices "not so different from a cult" (da Costa 2024: 30). A diverse array of strategies and techniques are to be deployed, including even the careful choice of the type of building a company chooses to operate within to display its "key cultural principles" (da Costa 2024: 30). The EKN represented by Stripe is perhaps best characterized by Silicon Valley start-up culture; emphasizing individualism, libertarianism and tech-solutionism, even when it often results in new concentrations of market power and monopolistic conditions. Thiel (cited in Staab 2024: 45), for example, is well known as something of an ideologist, who defends the monopolistic and oligopolistic markets of digital capitalism arguing in a lecture series that "leading companies of the internet are 'creative monopolies' ... [which] are socially desirable ... because their systematic integration of products and services drives efficiency and innovation in ways that a decentralized internet cannot". Expert claims to knowledge are mobilized here as a form of legitimation technique for market "concentration and closure" on behalf of internet giants (Staab 2024: 61).

By paying attention to the epistemic authority that fintech actors wield and project, the SFA to fintech can better identify the ideological and deeply social position that allows dominant fintech actors to emerge. The technological expertise on which fintech firms are built no doubt plays a role in their success, but it is often overstated and obscures the social relations that allow the major private fintech firms to exist in the form they do. Stripe would not have gained its global market share of online payment processing, second only to PayPal, if it had not attracted the support of the very group of asset owners who backed PayPal in the first place. The business relationships built on the "grandiose" vision and ideology that Stripe's founders managed to communicate – "to increase the GDP of the internet" (Bradshaw, Megaw & Kruppa 2021) – were crucial to its success. Meanwhile, as industry insiders have stressed, Stripe's company (like many other fintech firms) was essentially built by "piggybacking" on existing platforms (da Costa 2024: 227–8). In other words, while there is a high degree of tech-solutionism dominating the outlook of firms in the fintech payments industry and the business commentary about them, this EKN obscures the extent to which the business proposition of fintech payments firms is often not as novel as typically claimed but is always necessarily built on the back of numerous successive waves of experiment and innovation, including from the state and public sector.

In this regard it is notable that recent IPE scholarship has drawn attention to how, despite the outlook of firms tending to express the opposite view, money is *not only data* or "a simple written entry in a ledger" but is "a complex bundle of rights that are closely tied to the nation state or currency area" (Brandl & Dieterich 2023: 551). This means that, as with Stripe, "the vast majority of attempts by tech-driven companies to transform the payment industry only affects the front-end of banking [that is, the customer experience on an app] and therefore leaves the role of major banks untouched" (Brandl & Dieterich 2023: 551). Despite claims to disruption, innovation, and so on, the impact of fintech payments firms in reshaping the broader social foundations of finance is remarkably limited.

The case of Stripe shows that the processes of change for which fintech firms are responsible is much more than just a technical innovation story. Stripe builds on relatively straightforward software developments to capitalize on the benefits of capturing network effects in the realm of payments. Such a capture is made possible by firms such as Stripe gaining mass adoption with relatively low running costs (even if loss making at early stages), and of course by the significant backing of early investors who have the reputational authority to grant legitimacy and bring attention to new companies (Bradshaw, Megaw & Kruppa 2021). Using the work of Sinclair allows for an analysis of fintech payments that draws attention to the social foundations of this story: how powerful private actors are able to hold influence in the world economy; how claims to expertise and calculative practices are never simply technical but involve political and ideological judgement; and how social conventions and collective understandings – not least swings of excess and dearth in confidence (Sinclair 2009: 453) – dominate the valuation of firms and assets in financial markets.

Conclusion

This chapter has sketched an analysis of the social foundations of fintech by spotlighting illustrative cases from the worlds of fintech lending and fintech payments. There is much more work to be done. Overall, extending Sinclair's approach to fintech enables a better understanding of the roles of fintech firms as actors of political significance in financial markets. The themes of judgement and private authority in financial markets are just two of the many possible directions that this extension could take. Other cases of fintech contest over judgement practices and other examples of reconfiguration in private authority driven by fintech developments in global finance could no doubt be subjected to investigation from a social foundations of finance perspective.

The examples discussed in this chapter show not only the lasting insight that can be developed from a SFA, but also the political urgency of better understanding – from the inside – the firms, actors and practices that make financial markets and their influence possible. The re-election of Donald Trump in 2024 and his close association with big tech has raised these concerns to new heights, depicted by *The Economist* (2024) in terms of how "The PayPal Mafia is taking over America's government". As is becoming increasingly apparent across national contexts, fintech and big tech firms are social and political actors, oftentimes with oversized roles in passing ostensibly authoritative judgement over economic policymaking and government action. The SFA reminds scholars of the importance of denaturalizing their claims to expert knowledge (over an increasingly expansive realm of social action touched by digital technologies) and subjecting it to political contestation and mobilization. Sinclair (2010d: 104) criticized approaches that were built on a "utopian image of finance as a smoothly functioning machine" and demanded a political interpretation of markets sensitive to the operations of power and authority. This call remains urgent and will continue as his legacy.

References

Aitken, R. 2017. "'All data is credit data': constituting the unbanked". *Competition & Change* 21 (4): 274–300.

Alloway, T. 2015. "Google in peer-to-peer lending venture". *Financial Times.* www.ft.com/content/fe0e1ca4-9cc3-11e4-a730-00144feabdc0.

Alloway, T. & E. Dunkley 2015. "Democratising finance: P2P lenders rebrand and evolve". *Financial Times.* www.ft.com/content/eed90b1e-9c13-11e4-a6b6-00144feabdc0.

Alloway, T. & E. Platt 2014. "LendingClub banks 56% surge on debut". *Financial Times.* www.ft.com/content/0a25d3e8-8148-11e4-896c-00144feabdc0.

Armstrong, R. 2021. "Investors warm to LendingClub, the fintech that became a bank". *Financial Times.* www.ft.com/content/fc762619-c4ae-4335-ae6f-841ad58e7e93.

Arner, D. W., J. N. Barberis & R. P. Buckley 2016. "The evolution of fintech: a new post-crisis paradigm?" UNSW Law Research Paper No. 2016-62.

Atal, M. R. 2021. "The Janus faces of Silicon Valley". *Review of International Political Economy* 28 (2): 336–50.

Bernards, N. 2019. "Tracing mutations of neoliberal development governance: 'Fintech', failure and the politics of marketization". *Environment and Planning A: Economy and Space* 51 (7): 1442–59.

Bradshaw, T., N. Megaw & M. Kruppa 2021. "How Stripe became Silicon Valley's most prized asset". *Financial Times.* www.ft.com/content/9bfda026-df9d-42e4-8679-c26a072e0522.

Brandl, B. & L. Dieterich 2023. "The exclusive nature of global payments infrastructures: the significance of major banks and the role of tech-driven companies". *Review of International Political Economy* 30 (2): 535–57.

Campbell-Verduyn, M. 2017. *Professional Authority After the Global Financial Crisis: Defending Mammon in Anglo-America.* London: Palgrave Macmillan.

Cerny, P. G. 1994. "The dynamics of financial globalization: technology, market structure, and policy response". *Policy Sciences* 27 (4): 319–42.

Clarke, C. & L. Tooker 2018. "Social finance meets financial innovation: contemporary experiments in payments, money and debt". *Theory, Culture and Society* 35 (3): 3–11.

Culpepper, P. D. & K. Thelen 2020. "Are we all Amazon Primed? Consumers and the politics of platform power". *Comparative Political Studies* 53 (2): 288–318.

da Costa, J. 2024. *Fintech Wars: Tech Titans, Complex Crypto and the Future of Money.* London: Kogan Page.

de Goede, M. 2021. "Finance/security infrastructures". *Review of International Political Economy* 28 (2): 351–68.

Gabor, D. & S. Brooks 2017. "The digital revolution in financial inclusion: international development in the fintech era". *New Political Economy* 22 (4): 423–36.

Gapper, J. 2015. "The lenders of the revolution look familiar". *Financial Times.* www.ft.com/content/8663e89e-1420-11e5-9bc5-00144feabdc0.

Gruin, J. 2019. "Financializing authoritarian capitalism: Chinese fintech and the institutional foundations of algorithmic governance". *Finance and Society* 5 (2): 84–104.

Hammond, G. 2024. "Stripe in 'no rush' to go public as cash flow turns positive". *Financial Times*. www.ft.com/content/63f33d03-fc82-4383-b64f-dc3ca52c6e5f.

Helleiner, E. 2014. *The Status Quo Crisis: Global Financial Governance After the 2008 Meltdown*. Oxford: Oxford University Press.

Langley, P. & A. Leyshon 2021. "The platform political economy of FinTech: reintermediation, consolidation and capitalisation". *New Political Economy* 26 (3): 376–88.

Langley, P. & A. Leyshon 2022. "Neo-colonial credit: FinTech platforms in Africa". *Journal of Cultural Economy* 15 (4): 401–15.

LendingClub 2024. "About LendingClub: helping Americans meet their life goals". www.lendingclub.com/company/about-us.

MacKenzie, D. 2005. "Opening the black boxes of global finance". *Review of International Political Economy* 12 (4): 555–76.

Natile, S. 2020. *The Exclusionary Politics of Digital Financial Inclusion: Mobile Money, Gendered Walls*. Abingdon: Routledge.

Nowak, A., A. Ross & C. Yencha 2018. "Small business borrowing and peer-to-peer lending: evidence from LendingClub". *Contemporary Economic Policy* 36 (2): 318–36.

O'Dwyer, R. 2019. "Cache society: transactional records, electronic money, and cultural resistance". *Journal of Cultural Economy* 12 (2): 133–53.

Preda, A. 2006. "Socio-technical agency in financial markets: the case of the stock ticker". *Social Studies of Science* 36 (5): 753–82.

Renton, P. 2020. "LendingClub closing down their platform for retail investors". Fintech Nexus. www.fintechnexus.com/lendingclub-closing-down-their-platform-for-retail-investors/.

Staab, P. 2024. *Markets and Power in Digital Capitalism*. Manchester: Manchester University Press.

Stripe 2024. "Stripe Press: Ideas for Progress". https://press.stripe.com/.

Stripe 2025a. "About Stripe: Our mission is to increase the GDP of the internet". https://stripe.com/gb/newsroom/information.

Stripe 2025b. "Financial infrastructure to grow your revenue". https://stripe.com/gb.

Stripe 2025c. "Global payment gateways: what they are, how they work, and how to choose one". https://stripe.com/gb/resources/more/global-payment-gateways-101-what-they-are-how-they-work-and-how-to-choose-one.

The Economist 2024. "The PayPal mafia is taking over America's government". *The Economist*, 10 December. www.economist.com/business/2024/12/10/the-paypal-mafia-is-taking-over-americas-government.

Westermeier, C. 2020. "Money is data – the platformization of financial transactions". *Information, Communication & Society* 23 (14): 2047–63.

9

THE QUEEN AND THE PERFECT BICYCLE

Timothy J. Sinclair

As even the most ardent republican would acknowledge, Queen Elizabeth is not one to make flippant comments about grave matters of public policy. So when, perfectly capturing the mood of public exasperation, she asked an economist why his profession had not seen the crisis coming, it became a serious matter for the British establishment. The response, which came at the end of July in the form of a letter to Her Majesty from that august institution, the British Academy, suggested that everyone had been doing their individual jobs correctly, but as a group economists had missed the big picture of a "series of interconnected imbalances". If economists were guilty of anything, the letter suggested, it was "a failure of the collective imagination of many bright people … to understand the risks of the system as a whole".

What the letter revealed was that economists are willing to take the blame for not thinking big enough, but they are not willing to accept that their "perfect bicycle" is in need of any serious repair. This perfect bicycle is the term applied by the young Paul Samuelson, who went on to become one of the most celebrated economists of the twentieth century, to the mathematical equilibrium economics that has dominated the profession for much of the past 50 years. But it may be that the assumptions and implications of this approach to economics and to financial markets, summed up in the efficient markets hypothesis (EMH), are the problem, and that the failure to think about the system as a whole follows from this approach.

Like another famous way of thinking about economics, monetarism, the EMH originates at the University of Chicago. The basic idea is that because prices for stocks, bonds, derivatives, and so on are always based on a large body of information analysed by a large number of buyers, they will therefore reflect the fundamental value of these securities. Securities will trade at an equilibrium between supply and demand, and markets will therefore operate efficiently. It is a remarkable claim about information and how it is incorporated into market prices.

The case for EMH is built on three assumptions, suggests Harvard economist Andrei Shleifer. First, investors are said to be rational and to value their potential purchases rationally. So investors are not likely to buy before finding out about what they are buying and thinking about how to maximize their return. Second, even if some investors are irrational their random trades will cancel each other out, leaving prices unaffected. Irrationality is the exception and it is of no consequence. Last, even if there is a consistently irrational approach to investing among a group of investors, based on the mating cycle of cane toads for example, rational arbitrageurs will meet them in the market and eliminate their influence on prices.

The EMH has two main implications for financial markets, argues the economist Richard Thaler. First, "The Price is Right": asset prices for stocks and bonds incorporate all information, providing very accurate signals to buyers and sellers. If this is correct, asset price bubbles are simply not possible. The very notion of a bubble or inflated price cannot survive the three processes Shleifer identified. The second implication, suggests Thaler, is that there is "No Free Lunch" because traders cannot beat the market. If everyone in the market has the information then any cheap or expensive assets will rapidly be identified by traders and arbitraged away. Just as it is difficult to beat the house at roulette, it is hard to beat the market under these assumptions.

What are the general problems with the EMH? Samuelson's perfect bicycle of financial engineering is sustained by the "ergodic axiom", which underpins the EMH. In economist Paul Davidson's words, the ergodic axiom holds that the future is "merely the statistical shadow of the past". In other words, financial economists calculate probable future risks based on historical data. Unfortunately, human societies are not, to use Robert Skidelsky's phrase, "a stable and repetitive universe". Our communities are more like living things than automobile engines. They grow, change, adjust and over time are transformed. They are non-ergodic. Adopting a fundamental axiom more appropriate for the physical world than the social world seems like a bad start.

Eliminating uncertainty from the lexicon of the financial markets has arguably been a mistake. EMH encourages altogether too much confidence in financial engineering. If more of our financial activities assumed uncertainty, and therefore that we would have to be more risk-averse, we would live in a world of more conservatively managed companies, governments and individuals. Of course, the trade-off would be a society more like that of our grandparents, in which getting a mortgage was a struggle and the standard of living was much lower. But the global financial crisis (GFC) has forcibly recreated that world for many people in any case.

The EMH leads to neglect of the regulation of the key institutions like banks and credit rating agencies that actually make our markets work. It encourages this neglect because it says that information works automatically to impose the disciplines of the market, a bit like an operating system in a computer. But in a non-ergodic world institutions are fundamental to instilling confidence about the future in market participants. In an uncertain world we need institutions we feel we can trust in order to engage in financial transactions.

What specific role did the EMH play in the GFC? The EMH led policymakers to ignore key market processes. Financial market participants do not merely integrate information coming from outside the markets in the wider, real economy, but are focused on what other traders are doing, in an effort to anticipate their buy/sell activities, and thus make money from them (or at least avoid losing more money than the average). In this sense, rumour, norms and other features of social life are part of their understanding of finance.

Keynes provided what remains the best intuitive illustration of the importance of this understanding of finance and financial crises in his tabloid beauty contest metaphor, first published in 1936. Keynes suggested that finance is not, as the EMH supposes, a matter of picking the best stocks, based on an economic analysis of which should rise in value in the future. Anticipating what other traders in the market were likely to do was actually more relevant. Keynes compared finance to beauty contests that ran in the popular newspapers of the time. These contests were not, as might be assumed, about picking the most attractive face. Success was achieved by estimating how *others* would vote and voting with them – although, as Keynes pointed out, others would be trying to do the same, hence the complexity of the financial markets. The point is that policymakers were focused initially on fundamental issues rather than, as Keynes suggested, on what traders were doing. As time moved on, of course, the policymakers had to abandon the EMH-type approach and focus squarely on anticipating traders.

EMH led to a misunderstanding of the initial episode of the crisis, when securities markets came to a halt in late 2007 and early 2008. This was not caused by "toxic" subprime loans. Given that the subprime securities market was worth only $0.7 trillion in mid-2007, out of total global capital markets of $175 trillion, the supposed impact of subprime assets is out of all proportion to their actual weight in the global financial system. This strongly suggests that another explanation for the GFC is needed. The paralysis or "valuation crisis" that came over global finance in 2007–09, in which banks were unwilling to trade with each other or lend money, had no specific relationship to subprime lending. It was a crisis of confidence in the non-ergodic social foundations of global finance.

Given all this, what could replace the EMH? The great attraction of the ergodic axiom and the EMH is that it allows for the construction of human behaviour models. These models are deeply embedded in the training of the economics discipline, and many economists will be very reluctant to give them up. A more modest worldview, which allows uncertainty back into the story of financial markets, as seems necessary, would imply a more inductive approach in which experimental and other empirical techniques become more important. A great deal of research into the social foundations of finance, including trust and how institutions work, seems vital, given the experience of the crisis. Rather than focus on the little pieces of the world, economists may feel compelled to undertake more holistic studies into how things actually fit together.

The EMH, as it has been taken up in the financial markets and by policy-makers, is clearly implicated in the GFC of 2007–09. Two very different understandings of financial crisis compete. The first, the exogenous approach in which the EMH is king, sees finance itself as a natural phenomenon, a smoothly oiled machine that every now and then gets messed up by the government or by events that nobody can anticipate, like war or famine. The other perspective, critical of the EMH, argues that the machine-like view of finance is mythic. Like all other human institutions, finance is a social world made by people, in which collective understandings, norms and assumptions give rise periodically to manias, panics and crashes. On this account, financial crises are normal.

While truly global financial crises are fortunately rare, we understand so little about the mechanisms that cause them that much greater modesty about how finance works seems sensible than is evident in the EMH. We should abandon Samuelson's perfect bicycle and embrace the lesson of Keynes's beauty contest and the valuation crisis of 2007 – financial markets are social phenomena in which collective understandings, especially confidence, are vital. Perhaps then economists will not have to explain themselves to the Queen.

This piece was originally published by Timothy J. Sinclair on 12 August 2009 in Inside Story, *an Australian independent, non-profit magazine. https://insidestory.org.au/about/*

10

OF MARKETS AND MODELS: THE EXTENDED REALM OF THE MUNDANE IN THE SOCIAL FOUNDATIONS OF FINANCE APPROACH

Matthew Watson

Introduction

My abiding memory of Tim Sinclair the academic is that I wish he had written more. This phrase has been lodged somewhere in one of the more obscure reaches of my mind for a quarter of a century because my PhD supervisor had used it in relation to one of Tim's erstwhile Warwick colleagues, Jim Bulpitt (Marsh 1999: 269). I did not recognize its full significance back then, but I think I am beginning to do so now. I certainly look back over the intervening period and conclude that I have written too much, pushing myself to commit to paper a number of things that I would almost definitely have been better advised to have left unsaid. Not so Tim. If he ever gave the impression that he was on a publishing treadmill, then he was always sure he remained fully in control of both its velocity and its ultimate destination. He was never one to aspire to the next publication just for the sake of it, and the rest of us would do well to continue asking ourselves whether we are ever guilty of knowingly falling into such a trap. The whole of the Sinclair *oeuvre* consists only of things that he felt really needed to be said.

In this chapter, I want to provide some sense of what he might have committed himself to saying next had circumstances allowed. I will use, as the basis for my thoughts, the last few research-based conversations we enjoyed in the final 12 months before he died. There is an obvious danger that I am reading too much into these discussions, and that what I might wish to interpret as potential new directions in his research were nothing more than friendly chats in his mind. However, I did get a clear feeling of how our respective research interests seemed to be coming together, where we were picking each other's brains about what might be learnt if we placed in dialogue his storied career researching credit ratings agencies (CRAs) and my relatively recent work on the epistemic function of economic models. We never got close to agreeing to write anything together on topics where these two agendas most clearly converged, but the conversations were always as stimulating and as thought-provoking as I had come to expect from him.

In an attempt to bring at least the essence of these conversations to life, my chapter asks whether Sinclair's social foundations of finance approach can be usefully widened by incorporating into it a rather more systematic study of financial models. It is often suggested today that economics has become a modelling science (Niehans 1990). As the economics mindset has increasingly replaced context-heavy professional experience as the preferred way of "reading" financial markets (e.g. Mehrling 2005; MacKenzie 2006), it should therefore come as little surprise that the broader financial environment is now awash with the use of hypothetical mathematical models (Patterson 2010; Kanaris Miyashiro 2025). A good case can hence be made that models now provide the primary means of visualization whenever the employee of a financial firm seeks to persuade a colleague that the gap in the market they have identified for a new product is "real". If a model can tell them that there is money to be made from structuring trades in a novel way, then this is usually all the convincing that is required.

The mundane and the esoteric therefore now coalesce in interesting new patterns in the social foundations of finance. Financial models have become increasingly abstract, increasingly complex, increasingly otherworldly, and they can tax even the most experienced market watcher when it comes to translating their findings into what is known about actual pricing dynamics. At first glance, this can appear far removed from Sinclair's stated objective to bring greater clarity to the mundane in discussions of contemporary finance (on which, see the chapters in this volume by Petry, Clarke, Wood, and Gotoh, Gaillard & Michalek). But interaction with hypothetical mathematical models of the market environment is now a routine part of the day-to-day activities of so many of the employees of financial firms, however removed those models have become from instinctive everyday understandings of the generic category of finance. My final research-based conversations with Sinclair revealed his growing appreciation that a more expansive understanding of the mundane might require engagement with the increasingly esoteric mathematical content of many of the industry's most frequently replicated models.

The following pages sketch the case for a research agenda of this nature. In honour of Sinclair's intellectual legacy, I focus wherever possible on the actors he knew best as a researcher, the global CRAs headquartered in New York: Standard and Poor's (S&P), Moody's and Fitch. I proceed in three stages. In the first section, I emphasize one aspect of the social foundations of finance that is likely to come more to the fore with further dedicated work on financial models. This is the question of human fallibility. Epistemic fallibility follows from financial actors choosing to hear only the version of the story they want to be told, while conveniently overlooking the relationship of that version to the model's assumptive base. Moral fallibility follows in the rush to cover up what has gone wrong when firms pay inadequate attention to the severely restricted circumstances in which the model's predictions will be born out in practice. The remaining sections make use of these conceptual developments. Section two shows how CRAs' changing modus operandi placed them at the heart of contagious human fallibility in the run-up to the global financial crisis (GFC). They gave very low risk ratings to increasingly ethereal securitized products, thus licensing huge trading sums on assets that ultimately proved to be almost completely worthless, at least in part, it seems, on the basis of exaggerated faith in the underlying models' predictive capacity. Section three refers to the philosophical literature on hypothetical mathematical modelling in an attempt to explain how this extreme level of misplaced confidence might have originated. Purely artefactual models – creations of the mind that depict knowingly idealized circumstances – are all-too-readily confused with representational models that have as an explicit goal the need to speak directly to real-world experiences.

Sinclair and the social foundations of finance approach

As each of the contributions to this volume makes clear, the mark of a Sinclair output was to enforce recognition that financial outcomes are always the creation of human systems. They result from the interaction between people's cognitive perspectives for reading the market environment, an intersubjective relationship emerging from acculturation to industry-standard behavioural norms (Sinclair 2005: 10; 2009: 451). However, there was a tendency before his writing career began three decades ago to position finance as a structure, almost entirely impervious to progressive change and almost always capable of overwhelming all challenges. It was a structure, in other words, that could act as an agent to always ensure that it got its own way. Indeed, there is still a tendency for researchers to default to constructions of this nature, even though Sinclair had used the intervening period to demonstrate again and again that it was always a mistake to have done so (Chwieroth & Sinclair 2013). As such, finance still all-too-often gets conceptualized as a structure with curious agential characteristics, being written about as if it has a will of its own and the ability to act upon that will to ensure that its interests are served (Watson 2007). Yet the actual agents whose activities propel specific financial outcomes are rendered invisible in explanations of this kind. Sinclair's (2010d) work acts as an instruction sheet to place them centre stage once more. There are real people involved in the creation and evolution of financial firms; in the creation and evolution of their business models; in the creation and evolution of the often opaque trading positions they take as they try to turn a profit; in the creation and evolution of the goals to which the sector is oriented at any given point in time; in the creation and evolution of critical tendencies that often spill over into fully fledged crisis moments. All of these – as well as much more besides – are better viewed as manifestations of distinctly human systems than of economic structures.

Strong hints exist throughout Sinclair's work of the merit in understanding these systems through the lens of human fallibility. He never went so far in explicit terms, but we can think in this regard of both epistemic fallibility and moral fallibility. Financial firms are typically unforgiving environments, in which it does not pay any individual to admit what they do not know. Enron's infamous "rank and yank" system is a particularly extreme example of such a tendency, in which employees would attempt to bluff their way through personal review meetings as they sought to avoid being one of the near 50 per cent of the workforce who were only one further poor performance review from being set on the road towards dismissal (Fusaro & Miller 2002: 51). The performance of conscious self-reflection by any individual operating within such a system is likely to prove self-defeating for them personally, because if it provides the merest evidence of errors during the previous review period then they are likely to appear lower down on the grading curve than someone else who just chooses to brazen it out. The rank and yank system encouraged each individual to think of themselves as being in direct competition with every other employee for a coveted place towards the head of the grading curve, embedding what Robert Dipboye (2018: 566) has described as "a 'win no matter what' mentality" in which the creation of self-serving truths mattered more than the effects that wide-ranging dissimulation was having on the firm. Scaled up from individual employees to the company as a whole, it is little wonder that Enron developed a pathology against telling market analysts about the skeletons it was aware existed within its cupboard. The pretence of a healthy financial bottom line could be maintained for a while but was unsustainable in the long run.

Corporate cultures appear to work best in contexts in which employees are encouraged to share concerns about where their knowledge is least advanced. It is only when incentives to keep such anxieties secret are tackled head on that support structures might be put in place to help bridge inevitable knowledge gaps. However, financial firms tend to prefer to allow employees to consider each of their colleagues as a rival for preferment (Bolman & Deal 2003: 168). In such circumstances, everybody has a motivation to cover up their existing lack of knowledge because the philosophical good of epistemic humility is instead regarded as an admission of personal failings. "It is clear", write Peter Fusaro and Ross Miller (2002: 52), "that Enron's management regarded kindness as a show of weakness". Epistemic fallibility can then become systemic within financial firms because nobody will have a clear understanding of what other people do not know. Even if an individual is willing to admit such knowledge deficits to themselves, they will not do so to other people.

Epistemic fallibility can all-too-easily spill over into moral fallibility in an industry in which it has become commonplace to expect extremely high rewards for a job done well. As Malcolm Salter (2008: 135) suggests, Enron "crossed the line between limits testing and out-and-out deception". It is not a large step from assuming that it is a personal deficiency to own up to being unsure of what you are doing to deliberately falsifying your account of what just happened. Sure enough, the company collapsed amidst a torrent of accusations that it had defrauded investors out of their money through waging an industrial-scale disinformation campaign about its true balance sheet position (Dembinski & Bonvin 2006: 244–5). "The saying around Enron was, 'If you are not on the edge, you are taking up too much room'" (Smith & Emshwiller 2003: 8). The incentive to try to style out a gap in knowledge is relatively transformed straightforwardly into attempts to lie your way out of even the most perilous situation for fear of the consequences of owning up to prior mistakes. Clearly, this incentive does not play out in a one-size-fits-all manner because it depends on which department of the financial firm you work for. Given their very different dynamics of professional acculturation, for instance, we should expect it to be much less keenly felt among members of the legal compliance team than among members of the trading team who are encouraged to do their own thing so that they might distinguish themselves from all the other traders. But as Sinclair never tired of saying, it is from the trading desk that the big bucks flow, and therefore this is usually the aspect of corporate culture that matters most.

Employees who have backed themselves into a vulnerable position due to their epistemic fallibility may subsequently engage in active dissembling to mask the true fragility of the company's balance sheet. Enron again offers an excellent illustration of the different forms such dissimulation might take. As it headed on what, after the fact, looked to be its inexorable path to bankruptcy, it sent out employees to wine and dine market analysts in the hope of securing positive recommendations on its stock. Yet the stories they were required to tell were inconsistent with what their originators knew to be the firm's true underlying financial position. Prior to its bankruptcy the do-whatever-it-takes mentality was enough to disable potential moral safeguards against lying, but as the true scale of deceit was revealed during the bankruptcy proceedings many Enron executives went to jail (Eichenwald 2005: 576). Then, when federal bankruptcy experts could not work out how to unwind the company's complexly interlocking trading positions to prevent further market contagion, they had to encourage its former Chief Financial Officer, Andrew Fastow, to show them how to liquidate an enormous house of cards built from off-balance sheet special purpose entities. In return, public officials offered Fastow mitigation when his sentencing was due on his original 2002 78-count indictment, which was expanded to 218 counts by a grand jury in 2003 (Fox 2003: vii). The final arraignment included charges of fraud, money laundering, insider trading and conspiracy (Smith 2022: 271).

The response to the twin concerns of epistemic fallibility and moral fallibility has typically been to become increasingly reliant on hypothetical mathematical models. Financial firms now develop abstract mathematical artefacts to guide pretty much everything they do. They use models to simulate what would happen to their trading positions under different market scenarios. They use models to simulate the risk that is embedded in those scenarios. They use models to simulate value flowing onto and off their balance sheets under different degrees of risk aversion. They use models to simulate how their stock price will perform relative to different overall risk profiles. Firms can convince themselves that epistemic fallibility among their personnel is not a problem if their models are capable of telling employees everything they need to know. Models, in other words, are assumed to plug epistemic gaps, even if this merely kicks the can down the road because very few people working for the firm can say, hand on heart, that they know why the models take the form they do and what they are likely to leave unexplained as market conditions change. Having a workforce skilled in these additional facts would obviously be beneficial from a systemic perspective, but they are not considered essential competences for employees whose main concern is to learn how to put the models into use. Likewise, the very possibility of moral fallibility can be set aside if it is assumed that these models act as an automatic pilot to guide the day-to-day activities of everyone at the firm. The only thing that employees are required to do, then, is to internalize the behavioural norms that are written into the systems of equations through which the models are constituted.

Much therefore hinges on how financial models are constructed and how they promise specific visualization techniques for getting an all-important read on the market environment. For a start, there are important conceptual issues at stake here. Just as financial markets do not possess a will to act on their own interests, neither do financial models. It is the most basic point of Sinclair's social foundations of finance approach that it is always necessary to understand the operation of financial markets as a distinctly human system. Exactly the same is true of financial models. Even if it is convenient for firms to think in such a way, a model can never act as a simple automatic pilot. They are thought into existence through human design, and their use on a day-to-day basis always requires further human judgement. Real people exist behind every financial model, and it is these people and not the models themselves who play such an important role in shaping the wider market environment.

There are those who directly commission various models that will subsequently be put to use within the organization. There are those who use them. There are those who encourage that use to be aligned with narratives of corporate success. There are those who sign off on the blurring of lines between uses and misuses within such narratives. There are those who work on pre-emptive rebuttals of accusations that the organization has lost sight of where that line is to be drawn. There are those who test where the outer limits of legality are positioned in any given case. There are those who police potentially damaging news stories related to the models that are currently in use. There are those who create the models in the first place. There are those who choose which particular variants from within the universe of all similarly structured models will become synonymous with the organization's preferred operating procedures. And this is just *within* the organization. Other people from within the wider market environment will also have a hand in determining a model's ultimate success. Their precise content will be treated as proprietary knowledge for as long as possible so that competitors will not have advanced warning of the trading positions a firm will take even before those positions begin to be established. However, enough of the general structure of each model needs to become known within the wider market environment if it is to be credentialled by a coterie of outside observers. Market regulators must be convinced that nothing in a firm's use of models wildly oversteps the mark of prudential activities. Market analysts must also be persuaded to speak positively to investors about the models' performance in securing relatively easy profit flows.

In other words, a whole social ecology exists around the models on which financial firms base so many of their activities. They are epistemic devices used for trying to make sense of the world (Boumans 2005: 27), but this does not happen in what philosophers of science call a direct representational sense (Cartwright 2007: 234). No clear-cut objective exists for firms to model the world as it actually is. It is more important for financial organizations' bottom lines if they model the world as they would like it to be. They have a commercial interest for the models they use to facilitate specific narratives about the market environment: how they might make money from it; how they might protect their trading positions while doing so; how they might persuade investors that they are not being reckless with their savings. None of this requires that the models being used capture the actual essence of the surrounding market environment, complete with the tendency to overreact to news on the basis of exaggerated mood swings. Indeed, it is to financial firms' commercial advantage if the models they use do *not* reflect such features. Their creators are likely to be asked merely what would be expected were firms always to experience smoothly equilibrating price movements. It is only in this way that they can persuade investors to keep making their money available because the impression being left by the models is that firms are always in control of what happens to them, as if the general trajectory of price movements was so predictable that, in effect, it could be known in advance.

Three discrete distinctions thus become apparent: that between epistemic and moral fallibility; that between the uses and misuses of models; and that between the model representing the world as it is thought to be and representing the world that the commissioning firm would like to inhabit. The three interact in ways that become significant when trying to explain price dynamics in contemporary financial markets. The epistemic fallibility of financial firms' employees makes it less likely they will be aware in the moment of whether the models they are using speak directly to the world as it might be in a strict empirical sense. It is just as possible that adherence to those models' predictive capacity reflects a leap of faith that empirical reality lines up perfectly with the firm's commercial interests. The realization that it does not always comes too late to repair the damage already done to the firm's positions by the initial misuse of the models. It is in these moments that the spillover from epistemic fallibility to moral fallibility is most likely to occur, as employees seek to compensate for the sudden lack of the models' representational purchase. Sinclair's social foundations of finance approach does not yet talk explicitly about the development of such fissures within the market environment, but it can be made to do so. His own work on CRAs provides an illuminating case in point.

Credit rating agencies and financial models

Nobody has done more than Sinclair (2005, 2021) to lift the lid on the practices of the biggest American CRAs: S&P, Moody's and Fitch. He set the tone for them to be understood as important market intermediaries. The state has traditionally been viewed by economists as an actor of last resort, the entity to rely upon when there is a missing market for the provision of a good. Sinclair (1994a) spent his whole career inverting this particular optic, revealing instances in which public good provision had failed and a private market had developed in its place (see also Pagliari 2012; Campbell-Verduyn 2017; Kruck 2017). CRAs justify the centrality of their role within the financial system by saying that there is a collective interest in bringing a degree of certainty to pricing dynamics (Abdelal & Blyth 2015: 40). In the absence of a trusted public body to provide classificatory metrics to allow one type of asset to be ranked relative to all others, they argue that it is better for a private firm to fulfil this role than for the task to be left undone. CRAs have developed easy-to-comprehend coding systems that render the intrinsic risk profiles of different investments directly comparable (Kaminsky & Schmukler 2002: 228). This is clearly a regulatory function, even if not in the classical sense of distinguishing between what people are allowed to do and what not. It is more a case of recommending which positions they should be prepared to take and which not, given their underlying attitude towards risk. If all goes well, the mere presence of credible information about relative risk profiles should be a stabilizing factor within the market environment (White 2010: 214).

However, as Sinclair (2010a, 2010d, 2011, 2013b) has also shown, all does not necessarily end well (see also Marandola & Sinclair 2017; Mennillo & Sinclair 2019). CRAs are market *actors* as well as market intermediaries. Their authority comes from appearing to operate at one place removed from other market actors so that they can position financial firms' products on a legibility matrix composed of various scores (anything from AAA to BBB for investment-grade assets, but under BBB for below investment-grade assets). Yet it is more than expert appeal to technical competence that lies behind each individual judgement. If it were the state acting in the place of a missing market, then this might be the overwhelming dynamic in play. Instead, it is private authority rising to a position of prominence in the absence of any obvious source of public authority. This makes a big difference. CRAs still have a good case for asking to be seen as expert actors, but this must also be mixed at all times with maintaining their own ability to be going concerns. They gain legitimacy the more they can persuade others that they enhance market stability, but they can enact no such role if they cannot ensure sufficient flows of fee income to remain in business themselves. Their legitimacy as a market intermediary is therefore inseparable from their self-interested activities as market actors.

Are CRAs thus better conceptualized as "judges" or "consultants", to use Sinclair's (2010b: 8) terms? The answer, of course, is that they are both, but that each role compromises the other; the two certainly do not add up to a coherent whole. CRAs are often the first port of call for financial firms seeking to launch a new investment product because it is unlikely to gain traction in the minds of market analysts unless it first passes a certain rating threshold. The ability to secure a triple-A rating, for instance, has traditionally been a marker of quality that makes it significantly more likely that the new product will ultimately occupy a well-populated market niche. Many funds will have restrictions on the composition of their portfolios, whereby their overall risk profile cannot depart too substantially from that of government bonds backed by the state's guarantee that they will always be redeemable. A triple-A rating is therefore always likely to come complete with a ready-made base of investors. Financial firms seeking to innovate in their product supply will consequently beat a path to the door of the CRAs to seek advice on how best to secure a triple-A rating. The agencies bank an often hefty fee for providing a consultancy service of this nature. They then have a second job in undertaking a formal assessment of the product's creditworthiness and issuing a rating that will be made known to the whole market environment. Further fees follow.

Even a cursory reading of Sinclair's two path-breaking books on CRAs is enough to show that this clear conflict of interest has become particularly influential only relatively recently. If it is pervasive in pretty much everything they were doing in the run-up to the GFC, it was not always so obvious. Perhaps the largest difference in the story being told in 2005's *The New Masters of Capital* and 2021's *To the Brink of Destruction* is that the role of the judge became increasingly subservient to the role of the consultant. The new emphasis became especially evident as firms began to bring ever more exotic financial products to the market (Besedovsky 2018: 75). This was the veritable alphabet soup of obscurely named and equally obscurely priced assets that became well known from inquests of the GFC (Nesvetailova 2008: 108). Earlier ratings practices were dominated by qualitative judgements enacted by a relatively small group of people whose claim to authority rested on "knowing the markets", developing that crucial feel for the way in which tacit knowledge was transmitted within the social ecology of the market environment. This was no longer sufficient, though, when the number of new financial products shot through the roof, with each one standing apart from all the rest through the mathematical skill that was required to understand its structure (see Gotoh, Gaillard & Michalek, this volume).

Two shifts were therefore working in tandem. The CRAs became more reliant on exploiting bankable fees, getting increasingly rich by in effect marking their own homework. Yet this entailed licensing trades in all sorts of exotic financial products that it was unclear if their employees ever really understood but which their ratings nevertheless were designated as safe assets. The agencies moved at speed to rack up significant fees, albeit on an increasingly fragile basis. It is within the presence of such dynamics that the twin perils of epistemic fallibility and moral fallibility rear their heads. The agencies were administering ratings of new securities with much less intensive scrutiny than would have been the case in earlier, more pedestrian phases of their existence. Yet the staff members pushing through these ratings did so unimpeded by whatever gaps in their own knowledge they might have been aware of. They were also faced with precious few good moral options if they did not want their mistakes to be made public, to the detriment of their employers' reputation.

The design of these exotic financial products had one particularly intriguing aspect. They could be said to only have existed at all because of the performative effects of the models which purported to show how they would be profitable. Certainly, they would not have entered the thinking of market analysts as highly tradeable assets with promising risk-to-return ratios were it not for the presence of hypothetical mathematical models that persuaded the agencies to place them on their legibility matrix alongside other assets capable of mimicking the returns on government bonds. It is not only pricing collapses, then, that can run through contemporary financial markets in contagious fashion. Epistemic fallibility can cascade in this way too, due to the intersubjective practices through which financial actors attempt to take a read on the market environment in which they are active.

It has to be the case that someone somewhere will have understood the limits of what the models could say. Presumably these were the people who created the models in the first place, but as they were expected merely to play a technician's role then it is most unlikely that they were positioned in sufficient proximity to the ultimate decision makers to have infected others with their ontological doubts. The limits of hypothetical mathematical models' explanatory purchase are, after all, philosophical limits (see Morgan 2012: 30–37). It is therefore highly likely that line managers within the firm would have given only a perfunctory hearing to any warnings couched in philosophical terms they might have received from the models' creators. They might have been told that no model will work in practice in the same way it does on paper unless the idealized conditions of the model world are perfectly replicated in the real world, but how intently would they have been listening?

The main reassurance that company insiders would have been looking for was that the models worked in their own terms; in other words that they were mathematically tractable. This was very definitely the case, for instance, with David Li's Gaussian copula formula, the method used extensively in the run-up to the GFC by financial institutions that wanted to estimate the default correlation risk on mortgage repayments (on which, see Clarke 2012: 272). It is genuinely a formula, indicating mathematical tractability, rather than just a freestanding mathematical expression that did not permit a solution. Li would surely have known that his formula's predictions were only likely to be worth the paper they were printed on if actual market conditions functioned as neatly as his model required (Muolo & Padilla 2008: 171). After all, he once said that "the most dangerous part [of my model] is when people believe everything coming out of it" (cited in Partnoy 2009: 291). Models of perfect market equilibration clearly become less able to provide insights into the most likely course of events the more that actual market prices are being driven by the exaggerated mood swings that Sinclair (2021: 79) insisted were their most noteworthy feature (see also Rethel & Sinclair 2012). Li's Gaussian copula formula was no less mathematically tractable and therefore no less correct *in itself* in such circumstances (Watson 2014: 31–2). It had merely become entirely unhelpful for financial institutions seeking a safe haven in the face of an unimaginably large haemorrhaging of value.

There are very good reasons to presume that the models' creators would have informed the people commissioning them that mathematical tractability on its own offers no guarantee against market conditions completely invalidating the models' key lessons. Professional self-esteem and personal self-interest would surely have provided a potent combination in persuading the models' creators to have placed a serious health warning on their creations. They would have known that their future in the industry was dependent on avoiding blame if trading solely on the basis of the models' predictions ultimately backfired. This would surely have been enough to have emphasized that the models were only as good as the wider financial environment's ability to track their background assumption of perfectly smooth market equilibration. However, there are equally good reasons to presume that few other people would have heard such warnings for what they were.

Employees on the trading desk would have sought permission from their line managers to work with model builders on the promise that, once embedded into new products, the models would make lots of money for the firm. The line managers would also have had the same financial considerations uppermost in mind when consulting the CRAs about what was required for the product to be rated in similar risk categories to government bonds. The CRAs would have known that what was good for their clients would also show up positively on their own financial bottom lines. The firm's compliance teams would have decided that if the CRAs had expressed no reservations then who were they to begin raising red flags.

In such contexts, all the incentives within the firm would have pointed to a situation that the philosopher Gaile Pohlhaus (2012: 715) describes as "willful hermeneutical ignorance". That is, everyone within this epistemic loop is likely to have convinced themselves that it was better for their established professional sense of self were they to refuse to view the models that promised to bring so many riches through the lens of their creators' ontological doubts. After all, there were bonuses to be earned, promotions to be won and stock options to be redeemed. What price to enter something that seemed to be a purely philosophical debate about the difference between the model world and the real world when there were all these material gains to be made? It would surely have been much easier to turn the other way when confronted with someone saying that the models were not all they were cracked up to be, even if that someone was the model's creator.

We see in such circumstances cascading epistemic fallibility, where the decision to overlook what was surely the most important piece of contextual information flows contagiously from one person to another. An intersubjective loop thus feeds on itself. Viewed from the perspective of Sinclair's final book, the CRAs could have acted as an early circuit breaker in the dynamics through which the GFC arose, but they did not. They had reinvented themselves in the preceding years as an integral element of the securitization process, and this meant that they were actively feeding the contagion rather than counteracting it. Their modus operandi for judging new financial products clearly placed too much confidence in the models' ability to protect value by suppressing risk, creating a shared cognitive perspective of safety that wildly overstated the risk-free nature of untested products. Instead of coming to a carefully considered position on how the firm's cost recovery strategy affected the discounted future value of the security it wanted to bring to the market, they deferred to the models' underlying assumption that a smoothly equilibrating market always delivers higher levels of returns than Treasury bonds but with no extra risk.

The conflation of artefactual and representational models

The changing role of CRAs so ably described in 2021's *To the Brink of Destruction* raises an important issue. Are the agencies now in the business of assessing the risk inherent in holding a particular security or are they passing judgement on the model that describes the idealized price path of that security? As is often the case when a question is posed in either/or terms, the answer is almost certainly neither exclusively one nor exclusively the other. It is harder today than it has ever been to draw strict lines that distinguish between the securitized asset and the model that brings to life its chief characteristics as something to invest in. The stability of the financial environment rests at least to some degree on highly capitalized financial institutions being able to tell the difference between the two. It is only in such circumstances that they can be sure that they have not just bet the bank on an asset that offers no guarantee of stable income flows to cover the initial outlay. However, many of the new exotic financial products have little tangible presence beyond the models in which they are embedded.

CDO-cubeds offer a prime example. Very few people, even those with relatively senior positions at financial institutions, had heard of CDO-cubeds before they became a poster child of the GFC (Leopold 2009: 92). A CDO-cubed is a collateralized debt obligation of a collateralized debt obligation of a collateralized debt obligation (Hayek Kobeissi 2012: 94). A simple collateralized debt obligation is itself sufficiently complex when constructed as a mortgage-backed security arising from the bundling together of various mortgage repayment schedules. Each bundle comprises mortgages sold to people with similar credit histories, and the CRAs gave investment-grade ratings as bubble conditions developed in the 2000s to any bundle where the underlying mortgage holders had tolerably good credit histories (Schwartz 2009: 142). This suggested that the likelihood of correlated mortgage defaults undermining the value of the resulting asset was statistically indistinguishable from the likelihood of a government default undermining the value of US Treasury bonds (Denninger 2011: 39). Imagine, then, the degree of credulousness required to accept the assumptions lying behind the creation of CDO-squareds in this period, which usually involved creating a triple-A rated second-stage CDO out of a tranche of mortgage-backed securities initially rated as triple-B. Another level of credulousness still was required for the development of CDO-cubeds, which usually involved creating a triple-A rated third-stage CDO out of CDO-squareds initially viewed by the agencies as systematically riskier than investment-grade assets. As Duncan Wigan (2010: 116) has argued, the extraordinarily complicated machinations required to transform CDOs into CDO-squareds and CDO-cubeds meant that the end products defied all stress testing. Yet at no stage did any of this innovation place more money in the bank accounts of the original mortgage holders and therefore make them less likely to default on their loans. A clear case of epistemic fallibility ensued when this basic fact was overlooked simply because a model existed which said, under certain idealized conditions, CDO-cubeds could provide risk-free returns. The product and the model describing its idealized price path can thus become increasingly indistinguishable from one another.

Financial firms and CRAs must have been employing people in this period who were able to persuade one another that this new type of securitized asset would continue to offer handsome returns, otherwise they would never have been brought to the market as investment-grade assets in the first place. For this to have happened, though, there must have been general agreement that inferences could be drawn directly to the real world from how the model depicted the dynamic path of cost recovery. Yet epistemic fallibility abounds in such circumstances. It really should not need saying that no economic model ever acts as an empirical description of everyday economic relations because it would be something other than a model if it did (Mäki 2009: 39). This is as true of the Newlyn-Phillips physical model of Keynesian multiplier effects (in which the operator could imitate the impact of pulling policy levers by observing how the machine moved water around the model economy) as it was of the contemporaneous Arrow-Debreu pen-and-paper model of general equilibrium (in which the reader was invited to follow the abstract mathematical proof of why an equilibrium point could be said to exist) (see Phillips 1950; Arrow & Debreu 1954). Models are always conceptual abstractions, but nevertheless different individual constructions can be arrayed along a spectrum of model types depending on the extent to which their creators attempt to bring into them known features of the real world. Where no effort is made to do so, we are looking at purely artefactual constructions, designed around an "if ... then" logic in which the "ifs" are typically extreme renditions of knowingly unrealistic scenarios. By contrast, where the model's parameter values are carefully calculated relative to known real-world trends, we are much more likely to be looking at representational constructions, designed again around an "if ... then" logic, but this time one in which the "ifs" are grounded in something more than mere theoretical possibility.

The models which had such a performative influence in the creation of CDO-cubeds clearly existed right at the furthest reaches of the artefactual end of the spectrum of model types. There was obviously no historical data to show how similarly structured assets had performed in the past when underlying market conditions changed because their whole selling point was that nothing of their nature had been seen before. Despite the fact that we now live in an era of super-computers, the computational capacity still does not exist to work out all possible default risk correlations on the underlying mortgage repayments as riskier tranches of CDOs were transformed within the model world to less risky tranches of CDO-squareds and less risky still tranches of CDO-cubeds. The input values for such multi-layered instruments have to be treated as unobservable for accounting purposes (Valentine 2010: 207). Yet still the impression being given by prime decision makers was that nobody working in relevant financial institutions appeared aware that they were operating within an epistemic bubble when acting as one another's cheerleaders for exotic new securitized products. This was even though the firms innovating in CDO-cubeds often had to purchase some of the less attractive tranches on their own accounts, because in the absence of willing commercial customers, they had to step in to retain the integrity of the whole CDO structure (Kuttner 2010: 6).

The more general problem here is how frequently artefactual models are allowed to masquerade as representational models (on which, see Watson 2024b). Both facilitate new knowledge, but each involves distinct learning practices. When artefactual models are treated as if they are representational models, their true epistemic function can easily be obscured. The models' users can also come to believe that they have learnt something that is beyond the type of model they are working with, such that their epistemic limits become clouded. Artefactual models work best to enable their users to engage in thought experiments about idealized conditions active in purely substitute worlds that it is important not to mistake for our own. However, when they are allowed to masquerade as representational models, all-too-often causal inferences are read off from the substitute to the real world, even though the latter has no palpable presence in the underlying model (Watson 2024a: 96).

The difference is not difficult to explain. The standard position that has developed within the philosophical literature on hypothetical mathematical modelling is to treat the substitute worlds of artefactual economic models as free-floating tools of enquiry (Morrison 1999: 64). This is with good reason, because they are clearly not grounded in any explicit reflection of how real-life market relations are sustained. In the case of CDO-cubeds, the structure of the substitute world in which an investment-grade credit rating looked reasonable has no direct point of anchorage within the actual world in which trillions of dollars were wagered on them being as safe as the underlying models suggested. However, the same models that can become entirely detached from actual market conditions are anything but when it comes instead to economic theory. The free-floating designation is apt in the former instance but misses its target in important ways in the latter. The epistemic fallibility involved in drawing inferences from artefactual models of exotic new financial products to the actual market environment in which they would be bought and sold has no direct counterpart when the lens changes from those markets as they actually exist to how they have been traditionally depicted in economic theory. Artefactual financial models do permit inferences to economic theory, but almost certainly *only* to economic theory.

As is commented on throughout this volume, Sinclair had a more than healthy scepticism of the descriptive capabilities of economic theory. Our conversations over recent years revealed that this was a much more subtle position than an outright rejection of economics as a way of knowing the world. Yet on the specific issue of whether the content of economic theory mirrors what we find when we observe real-world market relations, he was definitely a sceptic. This view formed when he was a public official working in the New Zealand Treasury, and he carried it forward to his second career in academia. It is not without consequence for his social foundations of finance approach, then, that finance theory fell prey to economists' mathematical market models some time between the publication of Harry Markowitz's (1952) first forays into portfolio theory in the early 1950s and Eugene Fama's (1970) formal elaboration of the efficient markets hypothesis less than two decades later. Finance theory borrowed precious little from economics at the start of this period, but by its end had been almost wholly subsumed within it (Bernstein 1992: 47). The most significant element of this change was what it was conventional to assume about the market environment. Prior to the encroachment of economists' mathematical market models into finance theory, attention was placed on the knowledge gaps that ensue when step changes occur in the way that traders read the market environment. In these circumstances, their behaviour departs from the prevailing trend and can temporarily overwhelm smooth reactions in the pricing mechanism. Subsequently, though, all such interest in the intensely human factors governing price movements dissolved. In its place, attention increasingly came to focus on how rational traders are able to arbitrage away irrational jumps in price to create a smoothly equilibrating market environment (Rona-Tas & Hiss 2010: 139). Sinclair (2005: 5; 2021: 80) was something of a throwback in this regard, bemoaning economists' more contemporaneous tendency to treat financial prices as if they reflect fundamental market forces, insisting that they should be viewed instead through the lens of the underlying market mood.

What can be said from this perspective, then, about the array of ever more esoteric securitized assets that did so much to bring about the GFC? It is probably most important to start with the fact that they paid no attention to the possibility that changes in financial prices reflect what individual traders think other traders will be thinking at any particular moment of time. Indeed, it was not merely the case that they did not take such factors into account – they were fundamentally incapable of doing so. Human intuition played no role in how the underlying market environment was conceived, let alone how herd mentalities might develop within those institutions to place pricing mechanisms under sometimes supreme duress. Felix Salmon (2012: 18) has shown that, in model after model, the equilibrating properties of a mysterious correlation parameter, γ, were placed in a realm where they could no longer be challenged. They could be taken as given if the actual market environment behaved as economic theory was able to enforce in its own model worlds, but in any other situation it looks like a very flimsy rationale on which banks' trading desks were allowed to wager the very future of the firm. The models' artefactual nature permitted only inference to economic theory, but in the day-to-day practices of high finance such inferences are all-too-readily mistaken for inferences to the real world. The models promised that fabulous rewards were on offer if the taps of the securitization process could be turned to full volume, and this seems to have been enough for insufficient questions to have been asked about the nature of the inferences that they licenced.

The economist Roger Sugden has developed a well-known philosophical defence of the substitute worlds that arise from his discipline's attachment to artefactual models. He argues that they only need to be credible reflections of "how the world *could be*" under various assumptions that have proved influential in economic theory, not that they have to be accurate reflections of realistic economic conditions (Sugden 2000: 24, emphases in original). There are few reasons to suspect that Sugden is wrong if the target for economic models is *solely* economic theory, and a specialist literature has now developed saying that artefactual models are helpful for initiating abstract thinking (Kuorikoski, Lehtinen & Marchionni 2010: 543). Problems emerge, though, when others go one step further and assume that the axiomatic qualities of economic theory refer to entities that exist outside that theory. This goes against Sinclair's exhortation not to conflate economists' undoubted theoretical prowess with descriptive capabilities. The two must be kept very much separate when considering the epistemic value of economists' hypothetical mathematical modelling. Otherwise, artefactual models can easily be confused for representational models, the wrong implications can be deduced if a person mistakes the type of model they are looking at, human fallibility can ensue, and if it becomes as contagious as it was in the run-up to the GFC, the state can be left with staggeringly large bailout demands from private financial institutions.

Conclusion

I can claim no privileged access to what Sinclair would have most likely set his sights on writing next. I certainly found it fascinating exploring with him over the last 12 months of our time together at Warwick the points at which our evolving research interests might have ended up intersecting. But that very obviously did not translate into an obligation for him to follow me down the same path. I have written this chapter instead to demonstrate the dynamism inherent in the Sinclair agenda. He was intellectually modest, repeatedly playing down his research achievements, but he was also intellectually restless, forever allowing himself to wonder where the outer limits of his programme of research might eventually prove to be. Once he had committed himself to the social foundations of finance approach, he realized that it was always going to be a moving target. It offers rich pickings, but never against the backdrop of research questions that were already set in stone. There is more to the mundane in financial markets than initially meets the eye. The relationship between mundane practices and human fallibility consequently knows no obvious bounds.

So it is with trying to understand the changing role of CRAs within the broader social ecology of finance. Sinclair's intellectual restlessness is captured perhaps most keenly in the difference between 2005's *The New Masters of Capital* and 2021's *To the Brink of Destruction* (see also Germain in this volume). It would be to seriously underestimate the achievements of either book to suggest that they operate on the same conceptual terrain but focus on different events in the life of global finance. There is much more originality in the latter book than this rather restricted reading allows, because the Sinclair agenda was always to seek widening parameters for the social foundations of finance approach. We should not have expected anything other than his sharp eye for detail spotting that day-to-day practices within the CRAs were not as they once were. This was not a one-off big-bang change announced in advance to great fanfare, so much as incremental shifts involving the appointment of a different type of personnel and the incorporation of these people's specific skills into the way in which the agencies interacted with private financial firms. Over time, the ring-fencing of their professional judgement about the likely value investors would experience when buying particular securities was dissolved. In its place, the agencies increasingly tried to face in two directions at once: still ultimately passing judgement on such securities, but only after having pocketed substantial consultancy fees for having advised on the initial securitization process. This led to the demand for new expertise in the modelling practices through which these products were brought to the market.

Identifying this new role for CRAs was a large step forward for the specialist literature. But as Sinclair was well aware, when setting such insights within his own social foundations of finance approach, it raises more questions than it provides answers. Why were some model types considered more relevant than others to the agencies' new business? How did the network operate between the agencies and the firms whose products they were rating so that shared understandings were produced that actual market pricing mechanisms would prove as stable as those in the model world? What contrary voices existed both within the agencies and the firms, and why did they fail to make obvious headway? Who knew where the gaps in network participants' knowledge were and who was sensitive to the effects that epistemic fallibility might have on a firm's cost recovery plans? Did self-silencing occur in these instances and, if so, what form did it take? Did it originate in career progression meetings with line managers about the next bonus, the next promotion, and so on, or was it the result of individuals deciding for themselves that nobody personally had an incentive to kill the goose as it continued to lay golden eggs? Sadly, Sinclair is no longer able to shed light on such issues. It now falls to others to honour his memory by finding answers to these all-important questions.

References

Abdelal, R. & M. Blyth 2015. "Just who put you in charge? We did: credit rating agencies and the politics of ratings". In *Ranking the World: Grading States as a Tool of Global Governance*, A. Cooley & J. Snyder (eds), 39–59. Cambridge: Cambridge University Press.

Arrow, K. & G. Debreu 1954. "Existence of an equilibrium for a competitive economy". *Econometrica* 22 (3): 265–90.

Bernstein, P. 1992. *Capital Ideas: The Improbable Origins of Modern Wall Street.* Hoboken, NJ: Wiley.

Besedovsky, N. 2018. "Financialization as calculative practice: the rise of structured finance and the cultural and calculative transformation of credit rating agencies". *Socio-Economic Review* 16 (1): 61–84.

Bolman, L. & T. Deal 2003. *Reframing Organizations: Artistry, Choice, and Leadership.* Third edn. San Francisco, CA: Jossey-Bass.

Boumans, M. 2005. *How Economists Model the World into Numbers.* Abingdon: Routledge.

Campbell-Verduyn, M. 2017. *Professional Authority after the Global Financial Crisis.* Basingstoke: Palgrave Macmillan.

Cartwright, N. 2007. *Hunting Causes and Using Them: Approaches in Philosophy and Economics.* Cambridge: Cambridge University Press.

Clarke, C. 2012. "Financial engineering, not economic photography: popular discourses of finance and the layered performances of the sub-prime crisis". *Journal of Cultural Economy* 5 (3): 261–78.

Dembinski, P. & J.-M. Bonvin 2006. "Enron: visiting the immersed part of the iceberg". In *Enron and World Finance: A Case Study in Ethics*, P. H. Dembinski, C. Lager, A. Cornford & J-M. Bonvin, 237–51. Basingstoke: Palgrave Macmillan.

Denninger, K. 2011. *Leverage: How Cheap Money Will Destroy the World.* Hoboken, NJ: Wiley.

Dipboye, R. 2018. *The Emerald Review of Industrial and Organizational Psychology.* Bingley: Emerald.

Eichenwald, K. 2005. *Conspiracy of Fools: A True Story.* New York: Crown.

Fama, E. 1970. "Efficient capital markets: a review of theory and empirical work". *Journal of Finance* 25 (2): 383–417.

Fox, L. 2003. *Enron: The Rise and Fall.* Hoboken, NJ: Wiley.

Fusaro, P. & R. Miller 2002. *What Went Wrong at Enron? Everyone's Guide to the Largest Bankruptcy in US History.* New York: Wiley.

Hayek Kobeissi, Y. 2012. *Multifractal Financial Markets: An Alternative Approach to Asset and Risk Management.* London: Springer.

Kaminsky, G. & S. Schmukler 2002. "Rating agencies and financial markets". In *Ratings, Rating Agencies and the Global Financial System*, R. Levich, G. Majnoni & C. Reinhart (eds), 227–50. New York: Springer.

Kanaris Miyashiro, A. 2025. "Models in Use: Financial Modelling, Infrastructures, and Crisis". Unpublished PhD thesis, Department of Politics and International Studies, University of Warwick.

Kruck, A. 2017. "Asymmetry in empowering and disempowering private intermediaries: the case of credit rating agencies". *Annals of the American Academy of Political and Social Science* 670 (1): 133–51.

Kuorikoski, J., A. Lehtinen & C. Marchionni 2010. "Economic modelling as robustness analysis". *British Journal for the Philosophy of Science* 61 (3): 541–67.

Kuttner, R. 2010. *A Presidency in Peril: The Inside Story of Obama's Promise, Wall Street's Power, and the Struggle to Control Our Economic Future.* White River Junction, VT: Chelsea Green.

Leopold, L. 2009. *The Looting of America: How Wall Street's Game of Fantasy Finance Destroyed our Jobs, Pensions, and Prosperity.* White River Junction, VT: Chelsea Green.

MacKenzie, D. 2006. *An Engine, Not a Camera: How Financial Models Shape Markets.* Cambridge, MA: MIT Press.

Mäki, U. 2009. "MISSing the world: models as isolations and credible surrogate systems". *Erkenntnis* 70 (1): 29–43.

Markowitz, H. 1952. "Portfolio selection". *Journal of Finance* 7 (1): 77–91.

Marsh, D. 1999. "Jim Bulpitt (1937–1999)". *British Journal of Politics and International Relations* 1 (3): 269.

Mehrling, P. 2005. *Fischer Black and the Revolutionary Idea of Finance.* New York: Wiley.

Morgan, M. 2012. *The World in the Model: How Economists Work and Think.* Cambridge: Cambridge University Press.

Morrison, M. 1999. "Models as autonomous agents". In *Models as Mediators: Perspectives on Natural and Social Science*, M. Morgan & M. Morrison (eds), 38–65. Cambridge: Cambridge University Press.

Muolo, P. & M. Padilla 2008. *Chain of Blame: How Wall Street Caused the Mortgage and Credit Crisis.* Hoboken, NJ: Wiley.

Nesvetailova, A. 2008. "Three facets of liquidity illusion: financial innovation and the credit crunch". *German Policy Studies* 4 (3): 83–132.

Niehans, J. 1990. *A History of Economic Theory: Classic Contributions, 1720–1980.* Baltimore, MD: Johns Hopkins University Press.

Pagliari, S. 2012. "Who governs finance? The shifting public-private divide in the regulation of derivatives, rating agencies and hedge funds". *European Law Journal* 18 (1): 44–61.

Partnoy, F. 2009. *FIASCO: Blood in the Water on Wall Street.* London: Profile.

Patterson, S. 2010. *The Quants: The Maths Geniuses Who Brought Down Wall Street.* London: Random House.

Phillips, A. W. [Bill]. 1950. "Mechanical models in economic dynamics". *Economica* 17 (67): 282–305.

Pohlhaus, G. 2012. "Relational knowing and epistemic injustice: toward a theory of willful hermeneutical ignorance". *Hypatia* 27 (4): 715–35.

Rona-Tas, A. & S. Hiss 2010. "The role of ratings in the subprime mortgage crisis: the art of corporate and the science of consumer credit rating". In *Markets on Trial: The Economic Sociology of the US Financial Crisis*, M. Lounsbury & P. Hirsch (eds), 113–53. Bingley: Emerald.

Salmon, F. 2012. "The formula that killed Wall Street". *Significance* 9 (1): 16–20.

Salter, M. 2008. *Innovation Corrupted: The Origins and Legacy of Enron's Collapse.* Cambridge, MA: Harvard University Press.

Schwartz, H. 2009. *Subprime Nation: American Power, Global Capital, and the Housing Bubble.* Ithaca, NY: Cornell University Press.

Smith, D. 2022. *Fraud and Corruption: Cases and Materials.* London: Springer.

Smith, R. & J. Emshwiller 2003. *24 Days: How Two Wall Street Journal Reporters Uncovered the Lies that Destroyed Faith in Corporate America.* New York: HarperCollins.

Sugden, R. 2000. "Credible worlds: the status of theoretical models in economics". *Journal of Economic Methodology* 7 (1): 1–31.

Valentine, J. 2010. *Best Practices for Equity Research Analysts: Essentials for Buy-Side and Sell-Side Analysts.* New York: McGraw Hill.

Watson, M. 2007. *The Political Economy of International Capital Mobility.* Basingstoke: Palgrave Macmillan.

Watson, M. 2014. *Uneconomic Economics and the Crisis of the Model World.* Basingstoke: Palgrave Macmillan.

Watson, M. 2024a. *False Prophets of Economics Imperialism: The Limits of Mathematical Market Models.* Newcastle upon Tyne: Agenda Publishing.

Watson, M. 2024b. "'Let me tell you a story': the politics of macroeconomic models". *New Political Economy* 29 (6): 844–56.

White, L. 2010. "The credit rating agencies". *Journal of Economic Perspectives* 24 (2): 211–26.

Wigan, D. 2010. "Credit risk transfer and crunches? Global finance victorious or vanquished?" *New Political Economy* 15 (1): 109–25.

TIMOTHY J. SINCLAIR'S MAIN PUBLISHED WORKS

Sole authored works

Sinclair, T. J. 2021. *To the Brink of Destruction: America's Rating Agencies and Financial Crisis.* Ithaca, NY: Cornell University Press.

Sinclair, T. J. 2019. "Varieties of global governance". In *The Palgrave Handbook of Contemporary International Political Economy,* T. M. Shaw, L. C. Mahrenbach, R. Modi & X. Yi-chong (eds), 75–87. Cham: Palgrave Macmillan.

Sinclair, T. J. 2018. "Credit rating agencies". In *International Organisation and Global Governance.* Second edition, T. Weiss & R. Wilkinson (eds), 379–90. Abingdon: Routledge.

Sinclair, T. J. 2017. "Robert W. Cox's method of historical structures redux". In *From International Relations to World Civilizations: The Contributions of Robert W. Cox,* S. Brincat (ed.), 11–20. Abingdon: Routledge.

Sinclair, T. J. 2016. "Robert W. Cox's method of historic structures redux". *Globalizations* 13 (5): 510–19.

Sinclair, T. J. 2013a. "Credit rating agencies". In T. Weiss & R. Wilkinson (eds), 375–85. Abingdon: Routledge.

Sinclair, T. J. 2013b. "Global financial crisis". In *International Organisation and Global Governance, Issues in 21st-Century World Politics.* Third edn. M. Beeson & N. Bisley (eds), 157–71. Basingstoke: Palgrave Macmillan.

Sinclair, T. J. 2012a. *Global Governance.* Cambridge: Polity.

Sinclair, T. J. 2012b. "Institutional failure and global financial crisis". In *The Consequences of the Global Financial Crisis,* W. Grant & G. Wilson (eds), 139–55. Oxford: Oxford University Press.

Sinclair, T. J. 2012c. "Stay on target! Implications of the global financial crisis for Asian capital markets". In *East Asia and the Global Crisis,* Breslin (ed.), 11–24. Abingdon: Routledge.

Sinclair, T. J. 2011. "Stay on target! Implications of the global financial crisis for Asian capital markets". *Contemporary Politics* 17 (2): 119–31.

Sinclair, T. J. 2010a. "Credit rating agencies and the global financial crisis". *Economic Sociology: The European Electronic Newsletter* 12 (1): 4–9.

Sinclair, T. J. 2010b. "Credit rating agencies". In *The Oxford Handbook of Business and Government,* D. Coen, W. Grant & G. Wilson (eds), 422–39. Oxford: Oxford University Press.

Sinclair, T. J. 2010c. "Global financial crises". In *Issues in 21st-Century World Politics,* M. Beeson & N. Bisley (eds), 214–24. Basingstoke: Palgrave.

Sinclair, T. J. 2010d. "Round up the usual suspects: blame and the subprime crisis". *New Political Economy* 15 (1): 91–107.

Sinclair, T. J. 2010e. "Timothy Sinclair, *The New Masters of Capital* (2005)". In *Beyond Paradigms: Analytic Eclecticism in the Study of World Politics,* R. Sil & P. Katzenstein (eds), 118–24. Basingstoke: Palgrave Macmillan.

Sinclair, T. J. 2009. "Let's get it right this time! Why regulation will not solve or prevent global financial crises". *International Political Sociology* 3 (4): 450–53.

Sinclair, T. J. 2007. "An institutional approach to the politics of global finance". In *Towards a Cognitive Mode in Global Finance: The Governance of a Knowledge-Based Financial System*, T. Strulik & H. Willke (eds), 103–30. Chicago, IL: University of Chicago Press.
Sinclair, T. J. 2006a. "A private authority perspective on global governance". In *Contending Perspectives on Global Governance*, A. Ba & M. Hoffmann (eds), 178–89. Abingdon: Routledge.
Sinclair, T. J. 2006b. "Repoliticizing development studies". *International Studies Review* 8 (1): 125–7.
Sinclair, T. J. 2005. *The New Masters of Capital: American Bond Rating Agencies and the Politics of Creditworthiness.* Ithaca, NY: Cornell University Press.
Sinclair, T. J. (ed.) 2004a. *Global Governance: Critical Concepts in Political Science*, Volumes 1–4. Abingdon: Routledge.
Sinclair, T. J. 2004b. "The making and breaking of reputational governance in global financial markets". In *The State of Europe: Trans-formations of Statehood from a European Perspective*, S. Puntscher Riekmann, M. Mokre & M. Latzer (eds), 237–65. Frankfurt: Campus Verlag.
Sinclair, T. J. 2003. "Global monitor: bond rating agencies". *New Political Economy* 8 (1): 147–61.
Sinclair, T. J. 2002. "Private makers of public policy: bond rating agencies and the new global finance". In *Common Goods: Reinventing European Integration and International Governance*, A. Heritier (ed.), 279–92. Lanham, MD: Rowman & Littlefield.
Sinclair, T. J. 2001a. "The infrastructure of global governance: quasi-regulatory mechanisms and the new global finance". *Global Governance* 7 (4): 441–51.
Sinclair, T. J. 2001b. "International capital mobility: an endogenous approach". In *Structure and Agency in International Capital Mobility*, T. J. Sinclair & K. P. Thomas (eds), 93–110. Basingstoke: Palgrave Macmillan.
Sinclair, T. J. 2000a. "Deficit discourse: the social construction of fiscal rectitude". In *Globalization and its Critics: Perspectives from Political Economy*, R. Germain (ed.), 185–203. Basingstoke: Palgrave Macmillan.
Sinclair, T. J. 2000b. "Reinventing authority: embedded knowledge networks and the new global finance". *Environment and Planning C: Government and Policy* 18 (4): 487–502.
Sinclair, T. J. 1999a. "Bond-rating agencies and coordination in the global political economy". In *Private Authority and International Affairs*, C. Culter (ed.), 153–68. Albany, NY: SUNY Press.
Sinclair, T. J. 1999b. "Synchronic global governance and the International Political Economy of the commonplace". In *Approaches to Global Governance Theory*, M. Hewson & T. J. Sinclair (eds), 157–71. Albany, NY: SUNY Press.
Sinclair, T. J. 1997. "Money talks: budget deficit crises considered as social mechanisms in the global political economy". YCISS Occasional Paper No. 50, July.
Sinclair, T. J. 1996. "Beyond international relations theory: Robert W. Cox and approaches to world order". In *Approaches to World Order*, R. W. Cox with T. J. Sinclair (eds), 3–18. Cambridge: Cambridge University Press.
Sinclair, T. J. 1995. Guarding the Gates of Capital: Credit Rating Processes and the Global Political Economy. PhD thesis, York University, Canada.
Sinclair, T. J. 1994a. "Between state and market: hegemony and institutions of collective action under conditions of international capital mobility". *Policy Sciences* 27 (45): 447–66.
Sinclair, T. J. 1994b. "Passing judgement: credit rating processes as regulatory mechanisms of governance in the emerging world order". *Review of International Political Economy* 1 (1): 133–59.
Sinclair, T. J. 1992a. "Book review of Joyce Kolko, *Restructuring the World Economy*". *Political Science* 44 (1): 68–70.
Sinclair, T. J. 1992b. "Competitiveness strategies and industrial governance in the era of the global political economy". *Problématique: A Journal of Political Studies* 2: 72–94.
Sinclair, T. J. 1989. "Book review of Ellen Meiksins Wood, *The Retreat from Class: A New True Socialism*". *Political Science* 41 (1): 85–7.
Sinclair, T. J. 1988. Relative Autonomy: An Empirical Critique. MA dissertation, University of Canterbury, Wellington, New Zealand. https://ir.canterbury.ac.nz/items/62894c18-454f-4095-bb5a-cd8b26d0622d.

Co-authored works

Chwieroth, J. M. & T. J. Sinclair 2013. "How you stand depends on how we see: international capital mobility as social fact". *Review of International Political Economy* 20 (3): 457–85.

Cox, R. W. (with T. J. Sinclair) 1996. *Approaches to World Order.* Cambridge: Cambridge University Press.

Gotoh, F. & T. J. Sinclair 2017. "Social norms strike back: why American financial practices failed in Japan". *Review of International Political Economy* 24 (6): 1030–51.

Gotoh, F. & T. J. Sinclair 2021. "Varieties of moral hazard in the global automobile industry". In *Moral Hazard: A Financial, Legal, and Economic Perspective,* J. F. Zendejas, N. Gaillard & R. Michalek, 156–75. Abingdon: Routledge.

Hewson, M. & T. J. Sinclair (eds) 1999a. *Approaches to Global Governance Theory.* Albany, NY: SUNY Press.

Hewson, M. & T. J. Sinclair 1999b. "The emergence of global governance theory". In *Approaches to Global Governance Theory,* M. Hewson & T. J. Sinclair (eds), 3–22. Albany, NY: SUNY Press.

King, M. R. & T. J. Sinclair 2001. "Grasping at straws: a ratings downgrade for the emerging international financial architecture". University of Warwick CSGR Working Paper No. 82/0.

King, M. R. & T. J. Sinclair 2003. "Private actors and public policy: a requiem for the new Basel Capital Accord". *International Political Science Review* 24 (3): 345–62.

Marandola, G. & T. J. Sinclair 2014. "Credit rating agencies: a constitutive and diachronic analysis". Sheffield Political Economy Research Institute Papers, University of Sheffield; SPERI Paper No. 16, 1–14.

Marandola, G. & T. J. Sinclair 2017. "Credit rating agencies are poorly understood and the rules developed for them will not work". In *Handbook on the Geographies of Money and Finance,* R. Martin & J. Pollard (eds), 478–98. Cheltenham: Elgar.

Mennillo, G. & T. J. Sinclair 2017. "Global financial crisis". In *Issues in 21st-Century World Politics.* Third edn. M. Beeson & N. Bisley (eds), 157–71. Cham: Palgrave Macmillan.

Mennillo, G. & T. J. Sinclair 2019. "A hard nut to crack: regulatory failure shows how rating really works". *Competition & Change* 23 (3): 266–86.

Rethel, L. & T. J. Sinclair 2012. *The Problem with Banks.* London: Bloomsbury.

Rethel, L. & T. J. Sinclair 2014. "Innovation and the entrepreneurial state in Asia: mechanisms of bond market development". *Asian Studies Review* 38 (4): 564–81.

Sinclair, T. J. & M. Copelovitch. 2022. "Critical dialogue on *Banks on the Brink* and *To the Brink of Destruction*". *Perspectives on Politics* 20 (3): 1081–85.

Sinclair, T. J. & K. Thomas (eds) 2001. *Structure and Agency in International Capital Mobility.* Basingstoke: Palgrave Macmillan.

INDEX